Imagination and the Presence of Shakespeare in *Paradise Lost*

English literary history has long held that Milton renounced Shakespeare, and for some literary critics this meant the renunciation of the creative imagination. This work of criticism by Paul Stevens is the first extensive study to explore the influence of Shakespeare on Milton's poetry and understanding of imagination. With an extraordinary eye and ear, Stevens uncovers Shakespearean echoes in *Paradise Lost* and other works to substantiate his argument that Shakespeare functioned in Milton's intellectual and psychic life as a symbol of the imagination and its potential for creating religious belief. Written in an engaging and clear style, Stevens's book will appeal not only to scholars and students of Milton and seventeenth-century literature but to all those interested in the complex workings of echo and allusion in poetry.

Imagination and the Presence of Shakespeare in *Paradise Lost*

Paul Stevens

The University of Wisconsin Press

Published 1985

The University of Wisconsin Press
114 North Murray Street
Madison, Wisconsin   53715

The University of Wisconsin Press, Ltd.
1 Gower Street
London WC1E 6HA, England

First printing

Printed in the United States of America

For LC CIP information see page 270

ISBN 0-299-10420-6

Chapter Two of this work originally appeared as "Milton
and the Icastic Imagination," in MILTON STUDIES: VOL-
UME XX, James D. Simmonds, editor. Published in 1984 by
the University of Pittsburgh Press. Used by permission.

For
Eileen and Christopher Stevens

Contents

Acknowledgments ix
Introduction: Milton's "Renunciation" of Shakespeare 3
Part One: Faith and Imagination
Chapter One: The Meaning of Magic in the *Mask* 11
  Magic Structures 11
  Rough Magic 19
  Pure-Eyed Faith 27
Chapter Two: The Icastic Imagination 46
  High-Raised Phantasy 46
  The Prophetical Scene or Stage 57
  The Persuasion of Faith 64

Part Two: Imagination and the Reader in *Paradise Lost*
Chapter Three: *Phantastike* Poetry and Our Deception 83
  Behold a Wonder: *A Midsummer Night's Dream* 83
  Satan's Unsettled Fancy 90
  Behold a Wonder: *The Faerie Queene* 103
  Satan's Proud Imaginations 107
Chapter Four: *Eikastike* Poetry and Revelation 122
  The Dissolution of the Satanic Epic 122
  The Emergence of the Divine Epic 145

Part Three: Imagination and Adam and Eve in *Paradise Lost*
Chapter Five: *Phantastike* Imagination and the Fall 181
  The Will-of-the-Wisp 181
  Fancy's Wanton Growth 184
  Eve's Dream and Temptation 188
    The Dream as an Analogy of the Temptation 191
    The Temptation as a Renewal of the Dream 202
  Adam's Narcissism 216
Chapter Six: *Eikastike* Imagination and Regeneration 221
  Escape from Despair 221
  Mountain Vision 233
  Victory over the Dragon 244

Afterword: Transumption and Typology 246
Works Cited 251
Index 263

Acknowledgments

In addition to the debts acknowledged in the body of the work, it is a pleasure to record my more immediate obligations. The study was written at the John P. Robarts Research Library, the Thomas Fisher Rare Book Library, the Centre for Renaissance and Reformation Studies all at the University of Toronto, and the Boatwright Memorial Library at the University of Richmond. The manuscript was revised with the aid of two University of Richmond Summer Research Fellowships, and typed by Rea Wilmshurst and Wendy Thompson. Preliminary versions of the study have appeared as articles in *Milton Quarterly* 17 (October 1983) and *Milton Studies XX* (December 1984).

The study owes much to the influence of Brother Raymond Doyle. It originated in the teaching of Denton Fox, J. R. de J. Jackson, and Northrop Frye, and grew under the guidance of Hugh MacCallum. It benefited from the criticism of Balachandra Rajan, Peter V. Marinelli, William F. Blissett, Joseph A. Wittreich, Jr., and Annabel Patterson. It owes most to Hugh MacCallum for his imagination and to Lynne Magnusson for her skepticism.

Imagination and the Presence of Shakespeare
in *Paradise Lost*

Introduction

Milton's "Renunciation" of Shakespeare

Milton's renunciation of Shakespeare is a popular and recurrent theme in English literary history. One of the most familiar accounts of this renunciation is that of the eighteenth-century scholar Thomas Warton. "Seduced by the gentle eloquence of fanaticism," Milton, according to Warton, "listened no longer to the 'wild and native woodnotes of fancy's sweetest child'."[1] For Warton, although *Paradise Lost* itself remained "the noblest effort of modern poetry,"[2] the renunciation of Shakespeare meant the renunciation of imagination: "those years in which imagination is on the wing, were unworthily and unprofitably wasted on temporary topics, on elaborate but perishable dissertations in defence of innovation and anarchy." The end result was tragic: Milton's "warmest poetical predelictions were at last totally obliterated by civil and religious enthusiasm."[3] In our own century, among those critics who made such a determined attempt "to dethrone Milton,"[4] Milton's renunciation of Shakespeare meant, in Wilson Knight's words, "a denial of the specifically vital with a corresponding emphasis on the mechanical." For "Shakespeare's power seems to derive from trust in a vitality Milton rejects."[5] In the most recent kind of criticism to make literary history its principal concern, the criticism that seeks to amplify the "sophisticated model of literary history, formulated by Harold Bloom," Milton's renunciation of Shakespeare has again come to be seen as a renunciation of imagination.[6] "What does Milton renounce?" asks John Guillory in his *Poetic Authority*. "My argument points to the

1. *Poems upon Several Occasions . . . by John Milton*, ed. Thomas Warton, 2d ed. (London, 1791), p. 425n.
2. *Observations on the Fairy Queen of Spenser*, 2d ed., 2 vols. (London, 1762), II, 33.
3. *Poems*, pp. xiii, 425n.
4. Herbert J. C. Grierson and J. C. Smith, *A Critical History of English Poetry*, rev. ed. (London: Chatto and Windus, 1956), pp. 163–64.
5. *The Burning Oracle* (London: Oxford University Press, 1939), pp. 74, 69.
6. John Guillory, *Poetic Authority* (New York: Columbia University Press, 1983),

imagination itself as the power renounced in exchange for a power gained;" and "Milton's rejection of imagination" is made manifest in "a turn away from Shakespeare" (pp. 18, 21).[7]

What Guillory means by the rejection of imagination is, of course, a little different from what Warton means. Warton means that Milton ceased to use the faculty responsible for poetic creation, whereas Guillory means that Milton ceased to acknowledge that the faculty responsible for poetic creation was the imagination: "Milton succeeds in keeping this faculty wholly distinct from his own idea of creation . . . he never associates his own poetic activity with the fancy, despite (or because of) the precedent of Shakespeare" (p. 20). The power gained in exchange for this power renounced is inspiration. By inspiration Guillory means Warton's "religious enthusiasm" seen from a positive perspective—the direct, unmediated in-breathing of the Spirit. In this, in asserting "Milton's belief in his literal inspiration" (p. 103), he follows the most recent explicators of the prophetic Milton, Angus Fletcher, William Kerrigan, and Joseph A. Wittreich, Jr.,[8] but he goes beyond these critics in emphasizing that for Milton his inspiration was unmediated or literal because it did not involve the activity of the creative imagination—indeed "both Spenser and Milton polemicize against imagination. Neither poet tracks his poetic origins to the door of Phantastes' chamber" (p. ix).

Guillory's emphatic opposition between imagination and inspiration allows me to introduce the argument of the present work. The

p. 131. The mainspring of Bloom's model is of course the "anxiety of influence": "Poetic history . . . is . . . indistinguishable from poetic influence, since strong poets make that history by misreading one another, so as to clear imaginative space for themselves" (*The Anxiety of Influence* [New York: Oxford University Press, 1973], p. 5). See Frank Lentricchia, *After the New Criticism* (Chicago: University of Chicago Press, 1980), pp. 318–46.

7. Cf. Leslie Brisman, *Milton's Poetry of Choice and its Romantic Heirs* (Ithaca: Cornell University Press, 1973), p. 52: "Milton apprehends the Shakespearean imagination in terms that imply the rejection of it."

8. See Angus Fletcher, *The Prophetic Moment* (Chicago: University of Chicago Press, 1971), *The Transcendental Masque* (Ithaca: Cornell University Press, 1971), William Kerrigan, *The Prophetic Milton* (Charlottesville: University Press of Virginia, 1974), and Joseph A. Wittreich, Jr., *Visionary Poetics* (San Marino, Calif.: Huntington Library, 1979). Wittreich, p. 218, provides a convenient account of the development of interest in the prophetic Milton.

Predictably enough, this development has precipitated a reaction. Mary Ann Radzinowicz, *Towards "Samson Agonistes"* (Princeton: Princeton University Press, 1978), for instance, disputes the notion of a literally inspired Milton, but, as Michael Leib points out, *Poetics of the Holy* (Chapel Hill: University of North Carolina Press, 1981), p. 331, she errs in suggesting that Kerrigan represents Milton as "the amanuensis of God" (p. 350), "the *passive* instrument of a holy force" (my emphasis, p. 358).

argument is twofold. First, that the opposition between imagination and inspiration is misleading—that for Milton, certainly the Milton of *Paradise Lost*, the creative imagination is not the antithesis but the instrument of inspiration, and the purpose of inspiration, the in-breathing of the Spirit, is faith. Second, that Shakespeare is not re-nounced but lives in Milton's mind as a constant reminder, a con-tinually stimulating symbol of the magical, liminal possibilities of the imagination—possibilities which when properly understood, understood not necessarily as Shakespeare himself might have un-derstood them, come to be seen not as magical at all but divine. At its highest potential what the imagination conceives is a reflection of what God breathes, and for Milton Shakespearean imagination is a shadowy type of this truth.

It is true that Milton polemicizes against imagination. But what he derogates is imagination divorced from reason, the ungoverned imagination that leads to delusion. What he derogates are those works of fancy which like Circe's narcotic songs and Satan's proud imaginations only lull the sense. It is certainly not true that Milton "never associates his own poetic activity with the fancy." In the same piece of prose that serves as the *locus classicus* for evidence of Milton's desire for prophetic inspiration, the introduction to the sec-ond book of the *Reason of Church-Government*, he implies his de-sire to be considered "a Poet soaring in the high region of his fan-cies."[9] More important, in his poetry, against the false works of fancy, he consistently sets those works of fancy which like the Lady's song in the *Mask* and Adam's dreams in *Paradise Lost* offer such so-ber certainty of waking bliss. For Milton, imagination at its highest potential is not simply a necessary evil—the means by which those of soft and delicious temper may be brought to look upon truth.[10] It is a God-given faculty which trained by reason has a specific purpose in assisting man towards knowledge of his Maker, a knowledge be-yond the power of unaided reason. Adam's reasoning without Eve's fancy will only produce barren leaves. The *educated* imagination is then the peculiar instrument of grace. It provides the psychological

---

9. *Complete Prose Works of John Milton*, gen. ed. Don M. Wolfe, 8 vols. (New Haven: Yale University Press, 1953–82), I, 808. Hereafter cited as Yale. Milton's poetry is quoted from *The Works of John Milton*, gen. ed. Frank Allen Patterson, 18 vols. (New York: Columbia University Press, 1931–38). Hereafter cited as Columbia.

10. Stanley Fish, *Surprised by Sin* (New York: St. Martin's Press, 1967), pp. 69–70. It is this belief that fuels the suspicion that Milton was a poet who ultimately disap-proved of and abjures poetry. See, for instance, Peter Berek, " 'Plain' and 'Ornate' Styles and the Structure of *Paradise Lost*," *PMLA* 85 (1970): esp. 246, or Christopher Grose, *Milton's Epic Process* (New Haven: Yale University Press, 1973), esp. p. 7.

mechanism by which we come to see and believe the evidence of
things not seen; it provides the psychological mechanism by which
we come to faith. Bacon explains it thus:

> For we see that in matters of faith and religion our imagination raises itself
> above our reason; not that divine illumination resides in the imagination;
> its seat being rather in the very citadel of the mind and understanding; but
> that the divine grace uses the motions of the imagination as an instrument
> of illumination, just as it uses the motions of the will as an instrument of
> virtue; which is the reason why religion ever sought access to the mind by
> similitudes, types, parables, visions, dreams.[11]

It is true, as Guillory points out, that in Milton's mind Shakespeare serves almost as a metonym for fancy (p. 71). But since fancy
is as responsible for illumination as illusion it does not follow that
Shakespeare needs to be renounced. Indeed, the opposite is the case:
the presence of Shakespeare almost always in relation to the operation of imagination is apparent even in the heart of *Paradise Lost*.
When, for instance, Raphael strives to make his revelation through
the motions of the imagination, to relate the unspeakable by liken-
ing the war in heaven to the kind of earthly things "that may lift /
Human imagination to such highth / Of Godlike Power" (VI.299–
301), it is not without significance that in a key phrase his words recall those of the Chorus from *Henry V*. The apprehension of the angels at the imminent battle between Michael and Satan recalls the
anticipation of English youth at the imminent war between England
and France, because, as Alistair Fowler notes, the lines

> Now wav'd thir fierie Swords, and in the Aire
> Made horrid Circles; two broad suns thir Shields
> Blaz'd opposite, while expectation stood
> In horror
>
> (VI.304–7)

recall

> For now sits Expectation in the air
> And hides a sword, from hilts unto the point,

---

11. *De Augmentis* (Translation) V.i, quoted from *The Works of Francis Bacon*, ed.
James Spedding et al., 5 vols. (London, 1858–61; rpt. Stuttgart: Fromann-Holzboog,
1963), IV, 406. Hereafter cited as Spedding.

> With crowns imperial, crowns, and coronets,
> Promised to Harry and his followers.
>   (II.Cho.8–11)[12]

As an allusion, that is, a conscious reference to *Henry V*, this recollection suggests a critique of the attitude towards war expressed at the beginning of Shakespeare's national epic. What England looks forward to as an adventure, the angels await only in horror. More important, however, as an echo, that is, a reference that "does not depend on conscious intention,"[13] the recollection acts as a signature revealing the Shakespearean origin of Milton's sense of the power of the imagination. For as an echo the reference suggests that Raphael's need to make the invisible visible brings to Milton's mind the unconscious memory of Shakespeare's Chorus, the Chorus being such a passionate and imperative advocate of the imagination. He would create an epic of classical proportion within this wooden O,[14] he would make his audience see what is not there by exhorting them to work on their "imaginary forces": "Play with your fancies and in them behold" (I.Cho.18, III.Cho.7). Raphael's revelation is an act of grace and the echo from *Henry V* suggests that Milton's understanding of the working of grace is rooted in the Shakespearean origin of his understanding of the imagination.

The presence of Shakespeare in *Paradise Lost* is not limited to what might be dismissed as fragments, and it is the purpose of the present study to substantiate its central proposition, that imagination is the vehicle of faith, by explicating some of the more extensive patterns of Shakespearean echo and allusion—explicating them not in competition but in conjunction with similar patterns from other influences, especially Milton's "original," Spenser[15]—always re-

---

12. See John Carey and Alistair Fowler, eds., *The Poems of John Milton* (London: Longmans, 1968), p. 743n. Shakespeare is quoted from *William Shakespeare: The Complete Works*, gen. ed. Alfred Harbage, rev. ed., The Pelican Shakespeare (London: Penguin, 1969).

13. John Hollander, *The Figure of Echo* (Berkeley: University of California Press, 1981), p. 64, where he offers a "rhetorical hierarchy for the relationship of allusive modes."

14. For Shakespeare's conception of the play in terms of classical epic through the influence of Chapman's *Iliad*, see Gary Taylor, ed., *Henry V*, The Oxford Shakespeare (Oxford: Clarendon Press, 1982), pp. 52–58.

15. Harold Bloom's remark in *A Map of Misreading* (New York: Oxford University Press, 1975), p. 125, that Spenser's "actual influence on *Paradise Lost* is deeper, subtler and more extensive than scholarship so far has recognized," has stimulated

membering of course that for Milton all good words are at best merely an analogy of the Word. The focus of the study is two of *Paradise Lost's* interlocking patterns of loss and recovery, the experience of the reader at the beginning of the poem and the experience of Adam and Eve throughout. Here it will become apparent that the educated imagination is as responsible for recovery as the uninformed imagination is responsible for loss. Before proceeding to *Paradise Lost*, however, it is necessary to unravel the symbolism of magic in the *Mask*.

---

much of the renewed interest in the relationship between the poets. Guillory's book and Maureen Quilligan, *Milton's Spenser* (Ithaca: Cornell University Press, 1983) are representative of this response.

PART ONE

Faith and Imagination

CHAPTER ONE

The Meaning of Magic in the *Mask*

MAGIC STRUCTURES: COMUS AND THE ILLUSIONS OF FANCY

> Some ascribe all vices to a false and corrupt imagination, anger, revenge, lust, ambition, covetousness, which prefers falsehood before that which is right and good, deluding the soul with false shews and suppositions.
>
> Burton, *Anatomy of Melancholy* 1.2.3.2[1]

> Figures are illusory without an explanation.
>
> Calvin, Commentary on Ezekiel 2:3[2]

The baits with which Comus seeks to ensnare the Lady in the *Mask* she describes as "magick structures" (797). The meaning of magic in this context is multiple, but unified by the idea of illusion. Literally, it means the demonic art that transforms appearances and appears to transform substances. What transforms appearances is Comus's "Magick dust" with its ability "to cheat the eye with blear illusion" (165, 155), and what appears to transform substances is "His orient Liquor" (65) with its ability to change men into beasts. Figuratively, the magic dust signifies what Rosemond Tuve calls "delusions the virtuous reason could not counter." They could not be countered because they are delusions created by hypocrisy, the hypocrisy of figures like Spenser's Archimago, and this hypocrisy is, as Tuve explains, "a vice in the creature seen, not in the judgement behind the seeing eye—which is faulty but not guilty."[3] The orient liquor Comus

1. Burton is quoted from Robert Burton, *The Anatomy of Melancholy*, ed. Floyd Dell and Paul Jordan-Smith (London: Routledge, 1931), p. 221.

2. Quoted in Ronald S. Wallace, *Calvin's Doctrine of the Word and the Sacrament* (Edinburgh, 1953; rpt. Grand Rapids, Mich.: Eerdmans, 1957), p. 73.

3. Rosemond Tuve, *Images & Themes in Five Poems by Milton* (Cambridge, Mass.: Harvard University Press, 1957), p. 128.

inherits from his mother, Circe, and the charmed cup of the Renaissance Circe is firmly associated with the pleasures of lust: as Milton explains in his defence of Smectymnuus, those who forsake chastity "are cheated with a thick intoxicating potion which a certain Sorceresse the abuser of loves name carries about."[4]

It is clear from this, the figurative meaning of orient liquor, that Comus has no direct control over substances: the real ability to transform substances lies not with the magician, but with his victims. The orient liquor, unlike the magic dust, cannot have its effect imposed—it must be chosen. As the Lady points out, no matter how much Comus waves his wand, "Thou canst not touch the freedom of my minde" (662). That he can unthread the joints and crumble the sinews of the brothers is simply the measure of their moral vulnerability. Comus's magic is as strong as the flesh is weak. Indeed, the only way in which he can be said to control substances is indirectly through his control of appearances. He does have the ability "To inveigle and invite th' unwary sense" (537), to project the illusion that sensual pleasure is so desirable that there is either no need or no possibility of resisting it. Now the mental faculty through which these illusions are projected is the fancy or imagination.[5]

The Lady's phrase, "magick structures," refers to at least three kinds of structure: first, a physical structure, Comus's "*stately Palace, set out with all manner of deliciousness*" (stage direction following 1. 657); second, a conceptual structure, the picture of things

4. Yale, I, 891–92. For a detailed account of the relationship between Circe and lust, see George Sandys, *Ovid's Metamorphosis*, ed. Karl K. Hulley and Stanley V. Vandersall (Lincoln: University of Nebraska Press, 1970), pp. 652–54.

5. As implied by the use of the terms in the introduction, Milton, like most of his contemporaries, uses "fancy" and "imagination" interchangeably. Cf. Pierre de la Primaudaye, *Suite de l'Académie Françoise* (Paris, 1580; rpt. Genève: Slatkine Reprints, 1972), p. 61: "il n'y aura point de danger, si nous usons de ces noms [l'imagination et la fantasie] indifféremment"; or Sir Thomas Browne, *Religio Medici* i.47, in *Religio Medici and Other Works*, ed. L. C. Martin (Oxford: Clarendon Press, 1964), p. 45: "in my retired and solitary imaginations, to detaine me from the foulenesse of vice, [I] have fancyed to my selfe the presence of my deare and worthiest friends."

For the skeptical tradition that explained magic in terms of the power of the imagination, see, for instance, Michel de Montaigne, *The Essays*, trans. John Florio (London, 1603; rpt. Menston, Yorks.: Scolar Press, 1969), I.xx (pp. 40–45); Reginald Scot, *The Discoverie of Witchcraft*, introd. Hugh Ross Williamson (Carbondale: Southern Illinois University Press, 1964), esp. III.ix (pp. 64–66) and XI.xx (p. 183); Burton, *Anatomy* 1.2.3.2 (pp. 220–24); Thomas Hobbes, *Leviathan*, ed. C. B. Macpherson (Harmondsworth: Penguin, 1968), I.ii (p. 92). See also Keith Thomas, *Religion and the Decline of Magic* (London: Weidenfeld and Nicolson, 1971), pp. 205, 210, 224, 242–43, 438, 625.

② conceptual structural
③ verbal

presented by Comus and symbolized by the palace; and third, a verbal structure, Comus's language which is both the vehicle and the verbal manifestation of his world-picture. The first two structures have their foundation in the third and it is this, Comus's language, that reveals the actual operation of fancy.

Comus' language.

It is no accident that Comus's language should appear Shakespearean: "It shows," says F. R. Leavis, ". . . the momentary predominance in Milton of Shakespeare." What Leavis means by Shakespearean is the vitality of the "line of wit": "the Shakespearian life of this [11. 714–15] is to be explained largely by the swift diversity of associations that are run together." So powerful is the simultaneous description and imitation of life in the verse that the "total effect is as if words withdrew themselves from the focus of our attention and we were directly aware of a tissue of feelings and perceptions." Unfortunately, according to Leavis, this Shakespearean use of English is confined to lines 709–35 of Comus's seduction speech: "the Shakespearian passage in *Comus*," says Leavis, "is exceptional."[6] Although Shakespeare's presence in the masque is obviously not so narrowly confined,[7] what Leavis means by Shakespearean, it is true, is peculiarly apparent in Comus's language. This does not indicate, however, some momentary flicker of talent before final decline into the Grand Style, but much more simply a sense of decorum, the need to suit style to speaker or situation. What is at issue then is not the presence but the significance of this Shakespearean vitality of wit. Leavis's insistence on the verbal imitation of life, "the emotional and sensory texture of actual living,"[8] as a criterion for poetry suggests that for him there is something ideal about our sense experience of the actual world. This is hardly the case for Milton's Lady. She recognizes in Comus's language the same wit, the same swift diversity of associations, but interprets them differently. For her the imitation of sense-experience has no value in itself and Comus's vitality only signifies the "dazling fence" of "dear Wit, and gay Rheto-

Shakespearean
Swift diversity of associations.
decorum
style + speaker suited.

6. *Revaluation* (London, 1936; rpt. New York: Norton, 1963), pp. 48–49, 57.
7. For some indication of the pervasiveness of Shakespeare's presence in the *Mask*, see Ethel Seaton, "*Comus* and Shakespeare," *E&S* 31 (1946): 68–80; Alwin Thaler, *Shakespeare and Our World* (Knoxville: University of Tennessee Press, 1966), pp. 139–227; Carey and Fowler, pp. 171, 175–229n; J. B. Leishman, *Milton's Minor Poems* (Pittsburgh: University of Pittsburgh Press, 1969), pp. 173–246; Angus Fletcher, *The Transcendental Masque*, esp. pp. 202–9; *A Variorum Commentary on the Poems of John Milton*, gen. ed. Merritt Y. Hughes, 6 vols. (New York: Columbia University Press, 1970–), III, 765–66; Rachel Trickett, "Shakespeare and Milton," *E&S*, n.s. 31 (1978): 23–35; Guillory, pp. 68–93, and Quilligan, pp. 212–18.
8. Leavis, p. 51.

rick" (790, 789). By rhetoric she means the suasive organization and articulation of wit and by wit she means what, in Locke's terms, is the antithesis of judgment:

For *Wit* lying most in the assemblage of *Ideas*, and putting those together with quickness and variety, wherein can be found any resemblance or congruity, thereby to make up pleasant Pictures, and agreeable Visions in the Fancy: Judgement, on the contrary, lies quite on the other side, in separating carefully, one from another, *Ideas*, wherein can be found the least difference, thereby to avoid being misled by similitude, and by affinity to take one thing for another.[9]

The functions that Locke attributes to wit and judgment, Milton's Adam attributes to fancy and reason:

> But know that in the Soule
> Are many lesser Faculties that serve
> Reason as chief; among these Fansie next
> Her office holds; of all external things,
> Which the five watchful senses represent,
> She forms Imaginations, Aerie shapes,
> Which Reason joyning or disjoyning, frames
> All what we affirm or what deny, and call
> Our knowledge or opinion; then retires
> Into her private Cell where Nature rests.
> Oft in her absence mimic Fansie wakes
> To imitate her; but misjoyning shapes,
> Wilde work produces oft, and most in dreams,
> Ill matching words and deeds long past or late.
> (*PL* V.100–13)[10]

9. John Locke, *An Essay Concerning Human Understanding*, ed. Peter H. Nidditch (Oxford: Clarendon Press, 1979), p. 156.

10. What Adam offers here is a distillation of the Aristotelian psychology of the Renaissance, a psychology common to both Milton and Shakespeare and out of which Locke's psychology developed. See, for instance, Gianfrancesco Pico della Mirandola, *On the Imagination* [1501], trans. Harry Caplan (1930; rpt. Westport, Ct.: Greenwood Press, 1971); La Primaudaye, *Suite de l'Académie Françoise* [1580]; Thomas Wright, *The Passions of the Minde* (London, 1601; rpt. Hildesheim: Georg Olms, 1973); Peter Charron, *Of Wisdome*, trans. Samson Lennard (London, n.d. [before 1612]; rpt. Amsterdam: Da Capo Press, 1971); Burton, *Anatomy* [1620]; or Edward Reynolds, *A Treatise of the Passions and Faculties of the Soule of Man* (London, 1640; rpt. Gainesville, Fla.: Scholars' Facsimiles & Reprints, 1971).

For modern treatments of the subject, see Murray W. Bundy, *The Theory of Imagination in Classical and Medieval Thought* (Urbana: University of Illinois Press, 1927); Lawrence Babb, *The Elizabethan Malady* (East Lansing: Michigan State Col-

When the pleasant pictures created in the fancy by Locke's wit are subjected to the light of reason or judgment, they appear no less misjoined and ill-matching than the wild work of Milton's mimic fancy. Thus, it becomes increasingly clear that what the Lady recognizes in Comus's wit is the illusions of fancy uninformed by reason. In other words, the foundation of Comus's magic structures is the emptiness of fancy uninformed by reason.

The particular example of "Shakespearian life" that Leavis dwells on—"And set to work millions of spinning Worms, / That in their green shops weave the smooth-hair'd silk" (714–15)—seems to confirm the case. The style this most resembles is Shakespeare when he is specifically concerned with operation of fancy. As Queen Mab's dream transforms gnats into coachmen—"Her wagoner, a small grey-coated gnat" (*Rom.* I.iv.64)—and "Bottom's dream" transforms mustardseed into an aristocratic household—"That same cowardly, giantlike ox-beef hath devoured many a gentleman of your house" (*MND* III.i.178–79)—so Comus transforms silkworms into industrious weavers. This is the kind of imaginative animism or fancifulness that critics like Blackmore condemned in Shakespeare as "irregular Poetick phrenzy," filling "the world with endless Absurdities,"[11] and that Shakespeare himself condemned through Theseus as the work of "a fine frenzy" (V.i.12) and through Mercutio as being "Begot of nothing but vain fantasy" (I.iv.98). Fancy here is felt to be vain, empty or illusory, because, innocent as its creations are, they have no substance, only appearance: things are linked through nothing more substantial than superficial or visual resemblance, and the finished creation corresponds to no reality visible or intelligible. Shakespeare's awareness of the dangers of misshaping fancy is epitomized in the irresponsibility of fancy's personification, Puck, and Puck's "mimic" (III.ii.19)—the nocturnal misjoining of Bottom's body to an ass's head—is remembered in Adam's account of fancy: "Oft in her [Reason's] absence mimic Fansie wakes / To imitate her; but misjoyning shapes" (*PL* V.110–11). Indeed, so firmly is Shakespeare associated in Milton's mind with fancy that he often appears to use Shakespeare consciously as a means of calling attention to the presence of fancy's work—not always in a negative sense, as we shall see. Thus, references, whether conscious or unconscious, to Shake-

---

lege Press, 1951); J. B. Bamborough, *The Little World of Man* (London: Longmans, 1952); Kester Svendsen, *Milton and Science* (Cambridge, Mass.: Harvard University Press, 1956); and E. Ruth Harvey, *The Inward Wits* (London: Warburg Institute, 1975).

11. Quoted in Arthur Johnston, *Enchanted Ground* (London: Athlone Press, 1964), p. 8.

speare in the *Mask*, especially to *A Midsummer Night's Dream* and
The Tempest, take on a signal importance.[12]

There is more to Comus's language than fancy out of control—just
as Adam recognizes that there is more to Eve's dream than mimic
fancy's wild work—"But with addition strange" (*PL* V.116). That addition strange here is rhetoric or the suasive organization of fancy's
images. What in dreams is accidental is deliberate in Comus's promise of "delight / Beyond the bliss of dreams" (811–12). Like Plato's
sophist, Comus is a juggler and a magician[13] who

> under fair pretence of friendly ends,
> And well plac't words of glozing courtesie
> Baited with reasons not unplausible
> Wind me into the easie-hearted man,
> And hug him into snares.
>
> (160–64)

Comus's deliberateness suggests not the absence of reason, but its
subversion by desire. Subverted reason, which manifests itself as
rhetoric, has the effect of transforming the creations of unrestrained
fancy into something deeply perverse. The silkworm image, which
in itself is innocuous enough, by its context in an argument whose
sole purpose is the satisfaction of desire becomes one of the means
by which Comus would "charm my judgement, as mine eyes" (757).
What Comus's language reveals then is not simply unrestrained
fancy, but fancy perverted by desire. It is in this sense that imagination is "false and corrupt," verminous—in Burton's words, "the common carrier of passions" (*Anatomy* 1.2.3.2 [p. 224]).

As Comus's language is largely the verbal manifestation of perverted fancy, so its success, the success of his magic, depends upon
the reciprocal operation of uninformed fancy in the minds of his victims. The potency of Comus's magic liquor lies in the vividness of
his victims' own fancy. Just as his language creates pleasant pictures
of the visible world without the distinctions perceived in that world
by judgment or reason, so the effectiveness of his language, its ability to provoke desire, depends upon his victims' concentration on
words as pictures at the expense of their consciousness of words as

12. See Frank Kermode, ed., *The Tempest*, 6th ed., The Arden Shakespeare (London: Methuen, 1962), p. xlviiin; John M. Major, "*Comus* and *The Tempest*," *SQ* 10
(1959): 177–83; J. Blondel, "From *The Tempest* to *Comus*," *RLC* 49 (1975): 204–16;
and Guillory, pp. 68–93.

13. Cf. *Sophist*, 235–235b.

words—visualization or sensation at the expense of analysis. For just as fancy is illusory when uninformed by reason, so are images when uninformed by words, or as Calvin puts it, "Figures are illusory without an explanation." With this concentration on sensation at the expense of analysis, not only is the effect of Comus's language illusory—it is narcotic. It has the same effect as his mother's songs which "in pleasing slumber lull'd the sense" (259).

Comus's creation of illusion and the Lady's penetration of it externalize not only the psychological functions of fancy moved by desire and reason seeking to control it, but also the reading habits of visualization and analysis. Their conflict is reenacted in the minds of the masque's audience in the actual process of understanding what Comus is saying. As Comus begins describing the seeming pleasures of the world, echoing Mercutio, he unconsciously refers to his own language as the offspring of fancy: "See here be all the pleasures / That fancy can beget on youthfull thoughts" (667–68). Predictably enough, the ambiguity is concentrated in the imperative "See." When the magic structure of his language goes unnoticed, when it appears transparent, when words are apprehended as though they were nothing but pictures, then "See" refers to "pleasures" as the beauty of the visible world, "the *April* buds in Primrose-season" (670), and fancy suggests a faculty that "begets" merely in the sense of reproducing or recording what is seen. If we relax our critical sense, as Comus encourages the Lady to do, "Why are you vext Lady? why do you frown? / Here dwell no frowns" (665–66), then the final effect is as Leavis describes it—direct awareness of "a tissue of feelings and perceptions." But the first part of what he considers the effect—"as if words as words withdrew themselves"—is really the method. For when we become conscious and focus on the language, we comprehend, as opposed to apprehend, something entirely different. "See" refers to "pleasures" as the verbal felicities of the speech and fancy suggests a faculty that begets in the sense of actually creating or inventing what is seen.

Thus, Milton appears to emphasize the need for reason to modify fancy by creating a tension between visualizing what is heard and analyzing it. For most of Comus's speech this tension reveals itself in the contradiction between denotation and connotation: the significance of what the word pictures is reversed by the significance of those words, those texts it echoes. When Comus talks of the primrose season, the beauty of physical primroses is immediately overshadowed by the memory of the primroses of Ophelia or Macbeth's night porter—primroses that line the path of dalliance to the ever-lasting bonfire.[14] When Comus points out to the Lady that

> If you let slip time, like a neglected rose
> It [beauty] withers on the stalk with languish't head
> (742–43),

the picture of beauty withering is overshadowed by our knowledge that this is the language of an Ovidian lover like Shakespeare's Venus, a lover for whom there is little or no difference between nature and human nature:

> Make use of time, let not advantage slip;
> Beauty within itself should not be wasted.
> Fair flowers that are not gath'red in their prime
> Rot and consume themselves in little time.
> (*Venus and Adonis* 129–32)

Venus's seductive rhetoric is formally reproved by Adonis in such a way that our memory of it makes a similar reproval by the Lady of Comus redundant:

> 'What have you urged that I cannot reprove?
> The path is smooth that leadeth on to danger.
> I hate not love, but your device in love,
> That lends embracements unto every stranger.
> You do it for increase. O strange excuse,
> When reason is the bawd to lust's abuse!

> 'Call it not love, for Love to heaven is fled
> Since sweating Lust on earth usurped his name;
> Under whose simple semblance he hath fed
> Upon fresh beauty, blotting it with blame;
> Which the hot tyrant stains and soon bereaves,
> As caterpillers do the tender leaves.'
> (787–98)

Thus, Milton's language—for those whose ears be true—imitates the operation of reason checking fancy by counterpointing Comus's appeal to visualization with a simultaneous appeal to analysis. It is this attentiveness to language that the Lady exhibits by her refer-ences to wit and rhetoric and that enables both her and us to pene-

14. See *Hamlet* I.iii.50 and *Macbeth* II.iii.18.

trate the illusions of fancy. Here in the *Mask* these illusions, it is
true, are easy enough to dissolve, but what is important is not the act
but the method of dissolving illusion. For when we come to confront
the illusions of Satan, things are not quite so straightforward.

ROUGH MAGIC:
PROSPERO AND THE INVENTIONS OF FANCY

> As some are so molested by phantasy, so some again
> by fancy alone, and a good conceit, are as easily
> recovered. . . . So diversely doth this phantasy of
> ours affect, turn and wind, so imperiously command
> our bodies, which, as another *Proteus, or a Chame-*
> *leon, can* take all shapes; *and is of such force* (as
> Ficinus adds) *that it can work upon others as well as*
> *ourselves.* . . . [Witches and wizards] can cause and
> cure not only diseases, maladies, and several infir-
> mities, by this means [the forcible imagination] . . .
> in parties remote, but move bodies from their places,
> cause thunder, lightning, tempest.
>   Burton, *Anatomy* 1.2.3.2. (pp. 223–24)

There is another kind of magic in the *Mask* besides that of Comus.
The work of Comus's demonic art is undone by the magic of the Attendant Spirit, the magic that surrounds the Lady's chastity. While
the effect of Comus's magic is characterized by delusion and symbolized by the weakness of the physical eye, the effect of the Attendant
Spirit's magic is characterized by perception and symbolized by the
acuteness of the ear. While Comus urges the Lady to *see* the pleasures of fancy, she regrets his inability to *hear* the angelic voices that
tell "of things that no gross ear can hear" (457):

> Thou hast nor Ear, nor Soul to apprehend
> The sublime notion, and high mystery
> That must be utter'd to unfold the sage
> And serious doctrine of Virginity.
>   (783–86)

Through the weakness of the noblest of the senses, the eye, Comus's
magic symbolizes the frailty of all the outward senses and the most
outward of the inward senses, the fancy. Through the acuteness
of the ear, the sense most associated with words, the Attendant

Spirit's magic symbolizes the harmony of reason, the rational control of all the senses, inward and outward, and the perception available to the soul when in that state of harmony. In this state, a new kind of seeing becomes possible. The idea of harmony raises the analogy of music and reason, and throughout Milton's poetry the sensible effect of music is identified with the cognitive impact of reasoning:

> How charming is divine Philosophy!
> Not harsh, and crabbed as dull fools suppose,
> But musical as is *Apollo*'s lute.
>
> (475–77)

And when visions are made available "to our high-rais'd phantasie" ("At a Solemn Musick" 5) through music—

> There let the pealing Organ blow,
> To the full voic'd Quire below,
> In service high, and Anthems cleer,
> As may with sweetness, through mine ear,
> Dissolve me into extasies,
> And bring all Heav'n before mine eyes
>
> ("Il Penseroso" 161–66)

—they serve as an analogy for the revelation available to the mind through fancy when in harmony with reason. In this state, the fancy reflects the intelligible world in visible terms. In the *Mask*, the revelation to the harmonious soul is presented very deliberately in Platonic terms. Guided by conscience, the Lady sees things invisible to mortal eyes—she perceives the ideal form of her own virtue: "thou umblemish't form of Chastity, / I see ye visibly" (214–15). Thus, the Attendant Spirit's magic symbolizes not only the control of unrestrained or perverted fancy but its redirection towards the imagination of the good.

In this, the Attendant Spirit's magic is clearly related to that of Prospero, and before continuing with the Attendant Spirit's magic it is important to clarify the significance of Prospero's "Art."

Just as the illusions of Comus's magic recall the unrestrained fancy of *A Midsummer Night's Dream*, so the illumination of the Attendant Spirit's magic recalls the creative operation of fancy in *The Tempest*. Apart from Comus's language, the presence of Shakespeare in the *Mask* is most powerfully felt in the Ariel-like conception of the Attendant Spirit and the Miranda-like conception of the Lady. While Ariel reveals the process of Prospero's art, Miranda reveals its purpose. Miranda's innocence exemplifies the harmony of mind where reason controls the senses and frees the soul from the burden of self-regarding desire. In her, fancy is firmly under the control of reason and directed towards the imagination of the good, the "brave" and the "noble." In Antonio, for instance, things seen become objects that provoke desire and out of which desire creates fantasies: the shipwreck, a drowned prince and sleeping king, provokes the desire for advancement through Sebastian and "My strong imagination sees a crown / Dropping upon thy head" (II.i.202–3). In Miranda, however, the shipwreck provokes the opposite response: as Prospero perceives, "The direful spectacle of the wrack . . . touched / The very virtue of compassion in thee" (I.ii.26–27). And her compassion is intensified by the fancy that the wrecked ship was "a brave vessel / (Who had no doubt some noble creature in her)" (I.ii.6–7). In Antonio, fancy forms imaginations that reflect his selfish desires; in Miranda, they reflect her desire for the good. The purpose of Prospero's art is to exorcise the former, the illusions of self-regarding desire, and to fulfil the latter, the hopes of selfless desire. The first part of his purpose is concentrated in his treatment of the courtiers, and Caliban and his confederates; the second part, in his treatment of Ferdinand and Miranda.

The public manifestation of private virtue, the social face of rational harmony, is civility, and civility is precisely the achievement of fancy in the service of reason: "whatsoever distinguisheth the civility of *Europe* from the Barbarity of the *American* savages, is," according to Hobbes, "the workmanship of Fancy but guided by the Precepts of true Philosophy,"[15] and, according to Milton, civility is central to the purpose of poetry—"to inbreed and cherish in a great people the seeds of vertu, and publick civility, to allay the perturbations of the mind, and set the affections in right tune."[16] Thus, in as much as Prospero's purpose is civility, the role of Ariel, the chief of those spirits that "enact / My present fancies" (IV.i.121–22) is critical. Just as fancy is firmly under the control of reason in Miranda, so Ariel, unlike Puck, is firmly under the control of Prospero in the execution of his art. And just as fancy looking to the good acts as the eye of compassion in Miranda, so Ariel performs the same act for Prospero:

15. "Answer to Davenant's Preface to *Gondibert* (1650)," in *Critical Essays of the Seventeenth Century*, ed. J. E. Spingarn, 3 vols. (Oxford: Clarendon Press, 1908), II, 60.
16. *Reason of Church-Government* II, Introduction (Yale, I, 816–17).

Ariel: Your charm so strongly works 'em,
That if you now beheld them, your affections
Would become tender.
Prospero: Dost thou think so, spirit?
Ariel: Mine would, sir, were I human.
Prospero: And mine shall.
                                            (V.i.17–20)

The precision of Ariel's obedience is emphasized throughout the play: "Ariel, thy charge / Exactly is performed" (I.ii.237–38), "Of my instruction hast thou nothing bated" (III.iii.85). It is this obedience that finally earns him the sobriquet of diligence: "Bravely, my diligence" (V.i.241). Whereas Ariel's freedom suggests the unrestrained but innocent fancy of the fairies of *A Midsummer Night's Dream*—"Where the bee sucks, there suck I; / In a cowslip's bell I lie" (V.i.88–89)—and his imprisonment suggests his inability to enact the perverted fancies of Sycorax, a magician like Comus, his obedience to Prospero suggests the application of intelligent imagination to exorcise illusion and realize hope.

The first aim of Prospero's magic is to reverse the process of fancy subverted by desire. Illusions are created that they may be penetrated. Reason is infected that it may be cleared. First, what control reason has is completely unhinged. Reason is infected by the symbolic illusion of a tempest:

Prospero:
Who was so firm, so constant, that this coil
Would not infect his reason?
Ariel: Not a soul
But felt a fever of the mad.
                                            (I.ii.207–9)

In their "madness," Prospero's "enemies" are confronted by the external shows of their own internal fantasies. Prompted by Caliban and his dreams—"in dreaming, / The clouds methought would open and show riches / Ready to drop on me" (III.ii.137–39)—he, Stephano, and Trinculo discover the trumpery of Prospero's cave. The "three men of sin" (III.iii.53), Antonio together with Alonso and Sebastian, both of whom have been at some time prompted by Antonio's imagination, his "sleepy language" (II.i.205)—"My strong imagination sees a crown / Dropping upon thy head"—discover the vanishing banquet. Dreams are emphasized here because it is in dreams as in passion that reason is ruled by fancy. The spiritual state of the two groups is registered by their perception of Ariel.

For Caliban and his confederates, Ariel is the malignant Puck of their own unrestrained fancy. Just as Puck separates Demetrius and Lysander by mimicking their voices (*MND* III.ii.401–30), so Ariel reduces Stephano and Trinculo to slapstick by mimicking Trinculo's voice (III.ii.41–84). Just as Puck misleads "night-wanderers, laughing at their harm" (*MND* II.i.39), so Ariel's spirits lead Caliban "like a fire-brand, in the dark / Out of my way" (II.ii.6–7). According to Stephano, "Monster, your fairy, which you say is a harmless fairy, has done little better than played the Jack with us" (IV.i.196–98). Besides knave, "Jack" means jack-o'-lantern or will-o'-the-wisp, and the will-o'-the-wisp as an image of beguiling fancy is explained in Swan's *Speculum Mundi*:

These kindes of lights are often seen in Fennes and Moores. . . . Wherefore the much terrified, ignorant, and superstitious people may see their own errours in that they have deemed these lights to be walking spirits. . . . They are no spirits, and yet leade out of the way, because those that see them are amazed, and look so earnestly after them that they forget their way.[17]

Caliban and his confederates are susceptible to malignant fancy precisely because they are ignorant and superstitious: "Servant-monster? the folly of this island! They say there's but five upon this isle: we are three of them. If th'other two be brain'd like us, the state totters" (III.ii.4–7). Unlike the courtiers, these characters do not have the intelligence to be truly "perfidious" (I.ii.68). For the men of sin, Ariel appears as the image of their own corrupt fancy. The delicious banquet that vanishes at the command of a harpy suggests the beautiful images of fancy controlled by a reason perverted by desire. The harpy itself is a traditional figure for the wild work of fancy—Tasso, for instance, refers to "Centaurs, Harpies, and Cyclopes . . . flying horses and the other monsters that fill the fables of romance" as being typical of "phantastic imitation."[18] And here it signifies the same monstrous union of fair seeming and foul substance as Satan's

17. John Swan, *Speculum Mundi* (Cambridge, 1635), pp. 94–95. Cf. Montaigne, *Essays* I.xx (p. 41): "It is very likely that the principall credit of visions, of enchauntments, and such extraordinary effects, proceedeth from the power of imaginations, working especially in the mindes of the vulgare sort, as the weakest and seeliest, whose conceit and beliefe is so seized vpon, that they imagine to see what they see not."

18. *Discourses on the Heroic Poem*, ed. Mariella Cavalchini and Irene Samuel (Oxford: Clarendon Press, 1973), p. 30.

Sin: the physical appearance of the harpies that steal the Trojans' food and then confront them with their guilt is described by Virgil as "uirginei uolucrum uultus, foedissima uentris" (*Aeneid* III.216; "birds with girls' countenances, and a disgusting outflow from their bellies").[19] This is the meaning exploited by Milton in his use of the vanishing banquet as a temptation of Christ: Christ recognizes in Satan's "diligence" (*PR* II.387) nothing but guile and

> with that
> Both Table and Provision vanish'd quite
> With sound of Harpies wings, and Talons heard.
> (*PR* II.401–3)

It is appropriate that the fancies of Caliban and his confederates, the dream of riches and their "bloody thoughts," should be shattered by the barking of unintelligent dogs, while the illusions of the courtiers should be dissolved by the rational discourse of Ariel as a harpy. Prospero's magic enables the desires of the two groups to speak to their respective masters in their own language. The dogs speak with inarticulate fury and the harpy speaks with the same articulate authority as Virgil's Fury (*Aeneid* III.247–57). Prospero refers to the dogs as "Fury, Fury! there tyrant, there! hark, hark" (IV.i.256–57), and the harpy of Shakespeare's Virgilian source refers to herself as "Furiarum ego maxima" (*Aeneid* III.252; "I, chief among all the Furies").[20] Both groups are then disabused by a view of the fury of their own passionate desires, for fury is the word used by both Ferdinand and Prospero to characterize upstart passion: Ferdinand associates the fury of the sea with his passion (I.ii.393), and Prospero takes part "with my nobler reason, 'gainst my fury" (V.i.26).

With Caliban's group, the efficacy of Prospero's art is concentrated in Caliban himself. The fruitless pursuit of fantasy breeds in Caliban at least the promise of some progress in civility: "and I'll be wise hereafter, / And seek for grace" (V.i.295–96). With the courtiers, the efficacy of Prospero's art is concentrated in Alonso. The conscience that is dead in Antonio (II.i.269–84) is brought back to life in Alonso. Ariel's words give the experience of Ferdinand's "death" a moral context—a rational context far more profound than Sebastian's explanation of mistaken policy (II.i.119–31):

19. The *Aeneid* is quoted from *P. Vergili Maronis Opera*, ed. R. A. B. Mynors (Oxford: Clarendon Press, 1969), and the translations of it from Vergil, *The Aeneid*, trans. W. F. Jackson Knight (Harmondsworth: Penguin, 1964).

20. For the traditional association of Harpies with Furies, see Carey and Fowler, p. 535n.

> But remember
> (For that's my business to you) that you three
> From Milan did supplant good Prospero;
> Expos'd unto the sea, which hath requit it,
> Him and his innocent child; for which foul deed
> The pow'rs, delaying, not forgetting, have
> Incensed the seas and shores, yea, all the creatures,
> Against your peace. Thee of thy son, Alonso,
> They have bereft.
> (III.iii.68–76)

The effect of this account on Alonso is similar to that of the Elder Brother's discourse on chastity on the Second Brother in the *Mask*: it is apprehended as music. Ariel the harpy's most unmusical language, his "foul and muddy" syntax, is heard as harmony and simultaneously recreated through Alonso's "clearer" syntax, alliteration, and assonance, as harmony:

> The winds did sing it to me; and the thunder,
> That deep and dreadful organ-pipe, pronounced
> The name of Prosper; it did base my trespass.
> (III.iii.97–99)

The harmony of his response belies Alonso's apparent despair: the translation of the harpy's words into music reflects the healing of Alonso's mind.[21] With the resurrection of conscience, the coming to consciousness, the awakening from the dream world where fancy rules reason, Ariel's solemn music now becomes the aural image of the mind returning to harmony: "A solemn air, and the best comforter / To an unsettled fancy" (V.i.58–59). Thus, as desire is checked fantasies dissolve in the clear light of reason:

> The charm dissolves apace;
> And as the morning steals upon the night,
> Melting the darkness, so their rising senses
> Begin to chase the ignorant fumes that mantle
> Their clearer reason.
> (V.i.64–68)

The second aim of Prospero's magic is to fulfil the hopeful imagina-

21. Significantly, Milton echoes Alonso's words to evoke the harmony of the spheres—"And let the base of Heav'ns deep Organ blow, / And with your ninefold

tions of selfless desire. In this, the focus is on Ferdinand and Miranda. In his perception of Ariel, in his response to Ariel's music, Ferdinand reveals an innocence similar to Miranda's. The harmony of reason apparent in Alonso at the end of the play is apparent in Ferdinand from the point at which we first see him. Just as the solemn air comforts Alonso's fancy and morning steals on night clearing his reason, so the harmony and morning sounds of the song of Ariel as a water-nymph clears Ferdinand's infected reason: the wild waves are hushed, watchdogs bark, and a cock crows (I.ii.375–87). Whereas the music Caliban hears only excites desires that rise to consciousness as "riches," the music Ferdinand hears allays the perturbations of his mind and sets his affections in right tune:

> This music crept by me upon the waters,
> Allaying both their fury and my passion,
> With its sweet air.
>   (I.ii.392–94)

Whereas the music the courtiers hear goes uncomprehended—at best Gonzalo recognizes Ariel's warning as a humming—the music Ferdinand hears is a song, whose words promise the transformation of Alonso's "death" into "something rich and strange" (I.ii.402).

In Ferdinand, as in Miranda, fancy is directed towards the imagination of the good. Besides Miranda's compassion and Ferdinand's ability to hear, if not fully understand, the promise of transformation, this is evident in their willingness—in the actual world their too ready willingness—to see each other in ideal terms. From a realistic perspective their innocence appears as naïveté and their Platonic language as hyperbole. For her, he is "A thing divine" (I.ii.419)—appearance and substance coincide in his "brave form" (I.ii.412): "There's nothing ill can dwell in such a temple" (I.ii.458).[22] For him, she is a goddess: the ideal form—"So perfect and so peerless . . . created / Of every creature's best" (III.i.47–48)—of what others only imitate—"Many a time / Th'harmony of their tongues hath into bondage / Brought my too diligent ear" (III.i.40–42). However, their

---

harmony / Make up full consort to th'Angelike symphony" ("On the Morning of Christ's Nativity" 130–32).

22. As Kermode (p. 39n) points out, this sentiment is a commonplace of Renaissance Neoplatonism: as witness, Castiglione: "And therefore, as there can be no circle without a centre, no more can beawty be without goodnesse. Wherupon doeth verie sildome an ill soule dwell in a beawtifull bodye" (*The Book of the Courtier*, trans. Sir Thomas Hoby [London, 1900; rpt. New York: AMS Press, 1967], p. 348). In Miranda's version, this commonplace is buttressed by the Pauline allusion to the body as a temple: "What? know ye not that your body is the temple of the Holy Ghost?" (I Cor. 6:19). The Bible is quoted from the Authorized Version unless otherwise indicated.

idealism is substantiated and their perceptions saved from complete inaccuracy by the art that has made them the objects of each other's desire for the good. This "Fair encounter / Of two most rare affections!" (III.i.74–75) is manipulated by Prospero. Ferdinand is drawn to Miranda by Ariel's music, and Miranda's response to Ferdinand's image is shaped by Prospero's word—"thou mightst call him / A goodly person" (I.ii.416–17). In each other, desire for the good is fulfilled and imagination satisfied: "Nor can imagination form a shape, /Besides yourself, to like of" (III.i.56–57).

Thus, Ferdinand's ordeal is not an exorcism so much as a fulfilment. For him, Ariel is perceived in the image of his own idealism.[23] Ariel appears first as the unseen image of the water-nymph, an image that is realized in the actual shape of Miranda: "Most sure, the goddess / On whom these airs attend!" (I.ii.422–23). Ariel next appears to Ferdinand as the moving spirit of the betrothal masque, an image that is realized in the actual betrothal of the lovers: "Look down, you gods, / And on this couple drop a blessèd crown!" (V.i.201–2). Both the water-nymph and the masque reflect the innocence of the lovers in terms of their chastity: the water-nymph appears to be related to those invoked by Iris, "Come, temperate nymphs, and help to celebrate / A contract of true love" (IV.i.132–33), and the dramatic point of the masque is the defeat of Venus and her son (IV.i.86–101). While the dreams of the courtiers, and Caliban and his confederates, dreams in which fancy rules reason, dissolve with the waking clearance of reason, the dreams of Ferdinand and Miranda, dreams in which fancy serves reason in picturing the good, are translated into the certainty of waking reality. It is this translation that establishes the potency of Prospero's rough magic. The airy fabric of *The Tempest* will dissolve just as surely as that of the betrothal masque, but because the masque leaves an actual betrothal, the play leaves an actual model of hope substantiated through the creative operation of fancy. Because Prospero fulfils hope, the play becomes something of an assurance of things hoped for.

PURE-EYED FAITH:
THE LADY AND THE PERCEPTIONS OF FANCY

> For as the euill and vicious disposition of the braine
> hinders the sounde iudgement and discourse of man
> with busie & disordered phantasies . . . so is that

23. In this relativity of perception, if we adapt John Smith's dictum to read, "Such as Men themselves are, such will the good seem to be," it is possible to see the influ-

> part, being well affected, not onely nothing disor-
> derly or confused with any monstrous imaginations
> or conceits, but very formall, and in his much multi-
> formitie *uniforme*, that is well proportioned, and so
> passing cleare, that by it, as by a glasse or mirrour,
> are represented vnto the soule all maner of bewtifull
> visions.
>
>   George Puttenham
>
> a sanctified *fancie* will make every creature a *ladder*
> *to heaven*.
>
>   Richard Sibbes[24]

There is nothing overtly religious about *The Tempest*, but the play is
full of noises, biblical words and phrases, that echo the sounds of
man's fall and redemption. Captive Israel's grief—"By the rivers of
Babylon, there we sat down, yea, we wept, when we remembered
Zion. . . . How shall we sing the Lord's song in a strange land?" (Ps.
137 : 1, 4)—is echoed and transformed in Ferdinand's lament:

> Sitting on a bank,
> Weeping again the King my father's wrack,
> This music crept by me upon the waters,
> Allaying both their fury and my passion
> With its sweet air.
>   (I.ii.390–94)

Jonah's redemption—"And the Lord spake unto the fish, and it
vomited out Jonah upon dry land" (Jonah 2 : 10)—is remembered in
the punishment of the men of sin—"the never-surfeited sea" has
been made "to belch up you" on the island (III.iii.55–56)—the implication being that the redemption of the courtiers is prefigured in
their fall. Most striking, fragments of Isaiah's prophecy that Ariel
"shalt be brought down" by a great tempest, but finally even those of
erroneous spirit "shall come to understanding" (Isa. 29) are echoed
throughout the play.[25] These echoes are not in themselves essential

---

ence of what Cassirer calls "the core of English Neoplatonism" (Ernst Cassirer, *The
Platonic Renaissance in England*, trans. James P. Pettegrove [London: Nelson, 1953],
p. 28).

24. Puttenham is quoted from *The Art of English Poesie* (1589), I.viii (pp. 19–20),
in *Elizabethan Critical Essays*, ed. G. Gregory Smith, 2 vols. (Oxford: Clarendon
Press, 1904), pp. 1–193. Sibbes is quoted from *The Soules Conflict with It Selfe* (London, 1635), p. 258.

25. For full treatment of the Isaiah echoes, see Ann Pasternak Slater, "Variations
within a Source: From Isaiah XXIX to *The Tempest*," *ShS* 25 (1972): 125–35.

to the meaning of the play, but they do encourage the view of the process and purpose of Prospero's art as a secular analogy of the process and purpose of faith. Since the play provides an assurance of things hoped for, it is only too tempting to reconstruct it as a vision of faith—faith being of course "the substance of things hoped for, the evidence of things not seen" (Hebrews 11 : 1). The process of faith is persuasion: "Here *substance* means," Milton says, "that we are persuaded that the *things hoped for* will be ours, just as firmly as if they not only already existed but were actually in our possession."[26] Now, this process of persuasion when described by William Perkins sounds remarkably like the imagination of the good in the creative process of fancy:

this saving faith hath this power and property, to take that thing in it selfe invisible, and never yet seene, and so lively to represent it to the heart of the beleever, and to the eie of the minde, as that after a sort he presently seeth and enjoyeth that invisible thing, and rejoyceth in that sight, and enjoying of it: and so judgement is not onely convinced, that such a thing shal come to passe, though it be yet to come; but the mind (as farre as Gods word hath reuealed, and as it is able) conceiues of that thing, as beeing really present to the view of it.[27]

The purpose of faith is then to see "things invisible to mortal sight" (*PL* III.55). This kind of seeing means the conviction of hope's truth, and the conviction of good coming out of evil that is the triumph of Adam's faith, the conviction that providence "all this good of evil shall produce, / And evil turn to good" (*PL* XII.470–71), recalls the same conviction in Gonzalo:

> Was Milan thrust from Milan that his issue
> Should become kings of Naples? O, rejoice
> Beyond a common joy.
> (V.i.205–7)[28]

The characteristic response to both fancy and faith is wonder, and the "joy and wonder" (*PL* XII.468) of Adam's faith is not unrelated to the "wonder and astonishment" ("On *Shakespear* 1630" 7) that Shakespeare's fancy precipitates.

If *The Tempest* is an analogy, then the *Mask* is an allegory of

26. *Christian Doctrine* I.xx (Yale, VI, 472).
27. *A Clowd of Faithfull Witnesses*, in *The Workes of . . . Mr. W. Perkins*, 3 vols. (Cambridge, 1608–37), III, 2.
28. Cf. Kermode, p. 1.

faith.[29] The difference between analogy and allegory is revealed in the way that what appears as the creative process of fancy in *The Tempest* appears explicitly as a process of faith in the *Mask*. The Lady's first speech is a verbal imitation of the experience of this process. In the Lady, as in Miranda, fancy is firmly under the control of reason and directed towards the imagination of the good. Though it seems likely that the Lady initially loses her way through a failure of fancy—"gray-hooded Eev'n" (187) beguiles her fancy, making reason unmindful that evening will become "theevish Night" (194)[30]—she is able, as we have seen above, to resist Comus precisely because her fancy is governed by reason, and when reason is challenged by fancy in her first speech, it is overcome with a thought. The "thousand fantasies" that "Begin to throng into my memory" (204–5) are ineffectual because they are immediately recognized as fantasies and then banished with the reflection—"These thoughts may startle well, but not astound / The vertuous mind" (209–10). What enables this control is conscience, the conscience that is dead in Antonio and reborn in Alonso, and conscience means consciousness or reason—"an intellectual judgement of one's own deeds."[31]

Up to this point, the two processes appear much the same. With the imagination of the good, however, things change. In Miranda, the emphasis falls on imagination as the creation of images in the fancy, images that correspond to external realities only through the human agency of Prospero's art. In the Lady, the Platonism is more serious and the emphasis falls on imagination as the perception of ideas through their reflection as images created in the fancy, images that are shown to correspond to external realities through the divine agency of heaven's "aereal" spirit. The reality of the images that materialize before the Lady's inner eye—"pure ey'd Faith," "white-

29. Cf. Georgia B. Christopher, *Milton and the Science of the Saints* (Princeton: Princeton University Press, 1982), p. 53: the *Mask* "yields a surprisingly firm and coherent structure if one approaches it with the Reformation assumptions about faith." My phrase "analogy of faith" should not be confused with the technical, theological use of the phrase; see Yale, VI, 582n.

30. See pp. 92–93.

31. *Christian Doctrine* II.ii (Yale, VI, 652). Milton goes on to explain that what conscience decides may be directed either by the light of nature or of grace. It is clear that the Lady's decisions are made by the light of grace—what appears to her as the "holy dictate of spare Temperance" (766), "the sage / And serious doctrine of Virginity" (785–86). The point is that grace is prevenient: the process of faith, as we shall see, is initiated by nature responding to grace. The Lady's virtue is thus both her own and heaven's—"a hidden strength / Which if Heav'n gave it, may be term'd her own" (417–18).

handed Hope," and the "unblemish't form of Chastity" (212, 214)—
is substantiated by a Spirit that is both her own and heaven-sent. In
The Tempest, there is nothing to suggest that the good is not simply
the invention, the autonomous creation of the human mind; in the
Mask, however, there is everything to suggest that the good is a perception of the mind in a state of rational harmony—a state of harmony that ultimately depends on reason informed by revelation. The
action of the masque is essentially the fulfilment of the Lady's perception of pure-eyed faith—faith is pure-eyed because it sees the
good for what it is: the ideal reality that exists outside the human
mind:

> I see ye visibly, and now believe
> That he, the Supreme good, t'whom all things ill
> Are but as slavish officers of vengeance,
> Would send a glistring Guardian if need were
> To keep my life and honour unassail'd.
>
> (215–19)

Whereas the ambiguity of the analogy of faith is crystallized in Prospero's response to Miranda's "brave new world"—"'Tis new to thee"
(V.i.184)—the certainty of the allegory is crystallized in the Attendant Spirit's triumphant echo of the Lady's "if need were":

> if Vertue feeble were,
> Heav'n it self would stoop to her.
> (1021–22)

Now imagination as perception suggests the "second kind of phantasy" that Murray W. Bundy distinguishes in Plato's thought—a process of fancy that produces images of the ideal objects contemplated
by the soul.[32] According to the *Timaeus*, "some gentle inspiration of
the understanding" (71c) is "reflected as in a mirror which receives
likenesses of objects and gives back images of them to the sight"
(71b).[33] This kind of fancy, according to Bundy, has the effect of mak-

32. Bundy, p. 51. As Guillory, p. 180, points out, Bundy's distinction is an overstatement. What is important, however, is not that Bundy misreads Plato, but that he misreads Plato in the same way as "most Platonists who love art," especially the Italian
critics of the 16th century. Cf. William B. Hunter, Jr., "Prophetic Dreams and Visions
in *Paradise Lost*," *MLQ* 9 (1948): 277–85, and Isabel G. MacCaffrey, *Spenser's Allegory* (Princeton: Princeton University Press, 1975), pp. 13–32.

33. Plato is quoted from *The Dialogues of Plato*, trans. B. Jowett, 4th ed., 4 vols.
(Oxford: Clarendon Press, 1953).

ing an idea "intelligible through its perfect embodiment, its expression in sensible terms."[34] William B. Hunter, Jr., has suggested that it is this operation of fancy that Adam is referring to in his two dreams (*PL* VIII.287–309, 452–78).[35] In the first dream, for instance, a shape divine is perceived through its reflection in the fancy:

> When suddenly stood at my Head a dream,
> Whose inward apparition gently mov'd
> My fancy to believe I yet had being,
> And livd: One came, methought, of shape Divine,
> And said, thy Mansion wants thee, *Adam*, rise,
> First Man, of Men innumerable ordain'd
> First Father, call'd by thee I come thy Guide
> To the Garden of bliss, thy seat prepar'd.
>
> (VIII.292–99)

It is clear, however, that this is not exactly the same as the operation described by Plato. Whereas here revelation is immediately comprehensible to the intellect or intuitive reason, in the *Timaeus* revelation is only comprehensible to reason once the dream is over:

And he who would understand what he remembers to have been said, whether in a dream or when he was awake, by the prophetic and inspired nature, or would determine by reason the meaning of the apparitions which he has seen, and what indications they afford to this man or that, of past, present or future good and evil, must first recover his wits. (71e–72)

In the *Timaeus*, revelation bypasses reason altogether—it is a gift given "not to the wisdom, but to the foolishness of man" (71e). With the unfallen Adam, however, revelation only bypasses discursive reason—it is a gift given to the intuitive reason through fancy. So in the *Mask*, the Lady's visions are intuitive—immediately comprehensible to the intuitive reason: "in cleer dream, and solemn vision" angels "Tell her of things that no gross ear can hear" (456–57). The virtues practiced and contemplated by her are reflected in her fancy in the visible forms of angels:

> O welcom pure-ey'd Faith, white-handed Hope,
> Thou hovering Angel girt with golden wings,
> And thou unblemish't form of Chastity,
> I see ye visibly.
>
> (212–15)

---

34. Bundy, p. 53.
35. "Prophetic Dreams."

Imagination as the perception of ideas makes it increasingly apparent why the ear is so important. The ideas or virtues that the Lady
visualizes first enter her mind as words—as the "holy *dictate* of
spare Temperance," or "the sage / And serious *doctrine* of Virginity"
(766, 785–86; my emphasis)—just as Christian revelation, the revelation that informs conscience, first enters the mind as the Word:
"So then faith cometh by hearing," says St. Paul, "and hearing by the
word of God" (Rom. 10:17).[36] It is for this reason that the imagination of the good in the process of faith depends upon the ear as its
symbol of apprehension. Just as Comus's rhetoric with its emphasis
on seeing is the verbal manifestation of fancy subverted by desire, so
sacred song with its emphasis on hearing is the verbal manifestation
of fancy harmoniously ordered and directed towards the imagination
of the good.

Sacred song is the echo or re-creation of the word of God and as
such it symbolizes the operation of prevenient grace. This operation,
that grace precedes virtue and virtue means learning how to hear and
respond to the sublime notions and high mysteries apprehended by
the ear, is accurately expressed in the disability of the mythological
Echo—she cannot initiate anything, she can only respond:

> How oft would shee have woo'd him with sweete words!
> But, Nature no such liberty affords:
> Begin she could not, yet full readily
> To his expected speech she would reply.
> *(Met.* III.378–81)[37]

The Lady's sacred song to Echo is the effect of grace, the forms that
appear in her imagination persuading her to believe:

> I see ye visibly, and now believe
>
> . . . .
> I cannot hallow to my Brothers, but
> Such noise as I can make to be heard farthest

---

36. For a convenient explanation of the symbolic relationship between the ear and
faith, see William G. Madsen, *From Shadowy Types to Truth* (New Haven: Yale University Press, 1968), pp. 145–80. See also Barbara K. Lewalski, "Structure and the
Symbolism of Vision in Michael's Prophecy, *Paradise Lost*, Books XI–XII," *PQ* 42
(1963): 25–35.

37. Ovid is quoted from Sandys because the frequency of verbal resemblances suggest that Sandys' translation was as much in Milton's mind as the Latin. Compare, for
instance, the ambitious rebel, Typhon, "That durst affect the Empire of the skyes: /
Oft he attempteth, but in vaine, to rise" (*Met.* V.346–70), with the ambitious rebel,
Satan, "With vain attempt . . . / Who durst defie th'Omnipotent to Arms" (*PL* I.44, 49).

> Ile venter, for my new enliv'nd spirits
> Prompt me.
>
> (215, 225–28)

In particular, her song is a response to fantasies transmuted by conscience into echoes that remind her of Echo:[38] "airy tongues" are transmuted into the breath of God. The fantasies that tempt the Lady are primarily aural:

> Of calling shapes, and beckning shadows dire,
> And airy tongues, that syllable mens names
> On Sands, and Shoars, and desert Wildernesses.
>
> (204–6)

It is as if the night sounds of the forest were animated by the residual noises of Comus's tumult: for instance, Comus's parody of Ariel's "Come unto these yellow sands, / And then take hands" (*Tmp.* I.ii.375–76)—

> And on the Tawny Sands and Shelves,
> Trip the pert Fairies and the dapper Elves;
> . . . .
> Com, knit hands
>
> (117–18, 143)

—re-sounds here as "On Sands, and Shoars, and desert Wildernesses." But because Comus's parody, an imitation intended to deceive, is echoed "perfet in my list'ning ear" (202), it is immediately recognizable as a fantasy and so disarmed of its power to deceive. The phrase, "airy tongues, that syllable mens names," once disarmed by conscience of its transparent value, its value as a picture of actual things, appears to work subconsciously in the Lady's mind as an echoic allusion, that is, grace manifesting itself in an echo intended to recall Juliet's voice reaching out through the darkness to Romeo:

> Bondage is hoarse and may not speak aloud,
> Else would I tear the cave where Echo lies
> And make her airy tongue more hoarse than mine
> With repetition of "My Romeo!"
>
> (*Rom.* II.ii.161–64)

38. Cf. Fletcher, *The Transcendental Masque*, p. 199: "an echo is the phonic recollection of a sign, 'air' echoing 'impair,' in such a way that the structural implications of that sign, as well as its immediate meaning are present to the mind." See also, Hollander, pp. 55–60.

After the Lady's own words echo a question with a confirmation—

> Was I deceiv'd, or did a sable cloud
> Turn forth her silver lining on the night?
> I did not err, there does a sable cloud
> Turn forth her silver lining on the night
> (220–23)

—the thought of a Juliet-like appeal to Echo reaches consciousness.[39] In singing her song the Lady provides a reflection of the divine breath—"a soft and solemn breathing sound" that "might create a soul / Under the ribs of Death" (554, 560–61). For her brothers, "*That likest thy* Narcissus *are*" (236), she now provides the sounds that signify the descent of grace, sounds that are intended to do for the brothers what the "airy tongues" did for her: as the "airy tongues" lead her to invoke heaven's aid, so her song to Echo is intended to lead them back to her. She herself for a moment becomes Echo, the "*Daughter of the Sphear*" who gives "*resounding grace to all Heav'ns Harmonies*" (240–42). Echo, according to Henry Reynolds, is

the Reflection of this diuine breath, or Spirit vpon vs; or . . . *the daughter of the diuine voice;* which the beatifying splendor it shedds & diffuses through the Soule, is justly worthy to be reuerenced and adored by Vs. This *Ecco* descending vpon a *Narcissus,* or such a Soule as (impurely and vitiously affected) slights, and stops his eares to the Diuine voice, or shuts his harte from diuine Inspirations, through his being enamour'd of not himselfe, but his owne shadow meerely.[40]

The Lady's song resounding grace suggests a conception of poetry in which, says Reynolds, "Poems are not the inuentions of men, but gifts and graces of heauen. . . . [They] *are all full of most high Mysteries; and haue in them that splendor that is shed into the fancy and intellect, rauisht, and inflamed with diuine fury.*"[41] Poetry as the shedding or resounding of grace through the fancy is ultimately what the magic of the Attendant Spirit symbolizes. Thus, the Lady's song as an invocation *for* resounding grace is answered and the divine voice reflected in the magical action of the Attendant Spirit, a pattern of action precipitated by the song and completed by an answer-

---

39. This process is obviously related to the way Adam and Eve come to interpret the curse on the serpent and seek forgiveness in *Paradise Lost*, Book X.

40. *Mythomystes* [1632] (London, n.d.; rpt. Menston, Yorks.: Scolar Press, 1972), pp. 110–11. Cf. Hollander, pp. 15–16.

41. Ibid., pp. 22–23.

ing echo of the song: "Com Lady while Heaven lends us grace" (937).
What is specifically invoked and given is grace, and grace is of course
"the heavenly grace of faith."[42] The Attendant Spirit's action is then
the gracious echo of faith—the fulfilment and symbolic reenactment
of the process of faith.

Grace in the form of Echo operates in a number of ways—we have
already seen how Comus's illusions may be penetrated by attention
to echoic allusions, and how the Lady is led to song by airy tongues.
As far as the reader or audience is concerned, the prompting of grace
can be heard in the way the process of faith experienced in the Lady's
first speech keeps on being echoed throughout the masque. Like a
musical theme the process is repeated in different keys. What the
Lady receives intuitively, her brothers discover discursively and the
Attendant Spirit reenacts symbolically.

In the brothers' discourse, the rational control of fancy is both acted
out and described. It is acted out when the Second Brother begins
to imagine his sister's perils (349–57) and is checked by the Elder
Brother's common sense. The Lady's aural fantasies are paralleled by
the Second Brother's fantasies, fantasies that reflect his own increasingly alarmed state of mind. The rising degree of emotion is registered by the accelerating pattern of surmises—"Where . . . whether
. . . Perhaps . . . Or . . . what if . . ."—which climax in the imme-
diacy of "Or while we speak. . . ." The quality of the emotion is registered in the emotions attributed to the Lady: "lost . . . fraught with
sad fears . . . wild amazement, and affright. . . ." Fancy subverted by
fear is checked by the Elder Brother's abrupt—

> Peace Brother, be not over-exquisite
> To cast the fashion of uncertain evils
> (358–59)

—and finally returned to harmony by his account of chastity. The
Second Brother's response to this account echoes Ferdinand's response to Miranda:

> How charming is divine Philosophy.
> Not harsh, and crabbed as dull fools suppose,
> But musical as is *Apollo's* lute
> (475–77)

---

42. *Of Education* (Yale, II, 367).

echoes

> O, she is
> Ten times more gentle than her father's crabbèd;
> And he's composed of harshness!
>
> (III.i.7–9)

The control of fancy is described when the Elder Brother, in the same speech on chastity, explains the invulnerability of the Lady's virtue to will-o'-the-wisps and the other creations characteristic of unrestrained fancy:

> Som say no evil thing that walks by night
> In fog, or fire, by lake, or moorish fen,
> Blew meager Hag, or stubborn unlaid ghost,
> That breaks his magick chains at *curfeu* time,
> No Goblin, or swart Faëry of the mine,
> Hath hurtfull power o're true Virginity.
>
> (431–36)

With the imagination of the good the pattern of enactment and description is reversed. The imagination of the good is described when the Elder Brother, continuing his speech on chastity, explains how the harmonious soul comes to exemplify faith, that is, to see the evidence of things not seen:

> So dear to Heav'n is Saintly chastity,
> That when a soul is found sincerely so,
> A thousand liveried Angels lacky her,
> Driving far off each thing of sin and guilt,
> And in cleer dream, and solemn vision   Inspiration.
> Tell her of things that no gross ear can hear.
>
> (452–57)

As for the enactment, the Elder Brother's imagination of the good becomes an act of faith when his belief in the invulnerability of chastity is questioned. What he has learnt from others, what "Som say" and to which antiquity testifies, he has to substantiate by his own action. The Attendant Spirit's warning speech (512–79) precipitates a renewal of the Second Brother's alarm: "is this the confidence / You gave me Brother?" (582–83). The Elder Brother holds firm and though he sees no angelic forms—it is significant that neither of the brothers recognizes the Attendant Spirit—he does assert the embryonic idea of *felix culpa*—"Yea even that which mischief meant

most harm, / Shall in the happy trial prove most glory" (590–91)—
and he does see the final consolidation of evil:

> But evil on itself shall back recoyl,
> And mix no more with goodness, when at last
> Gather'd like scum, and setl'd to it self
> It shall be in eternal restless change
> Self-fed, and self-consum'd, if this fail,
> The pillar'd firmament is rott'nness,
> And earths base built on stubble.
>
> (592–98)

[margin handwritten: Setl'd]

The "pillar'd firmament," one of the few overt biblical allusions in
the masque,[43] echoes Job's "pillars of heaven" and his affirmation of
God's glory—"The pillars of heaven tremble and are astonished at
his reproof" (Job 26:11)—an affirmation which anticipates God's
own affirmation of his glory in the vision he grants Job (38–41). The
echo is thus very carefully placed: for the reader it is an allusion that
answers the Elder Brother's residual doubt and suggests that his
"righteousness" will be rewarded with vision.

In the activities of the Attendant Spirit, the process of faith swells to
fill the structure of the masque and fulfil the Lady's initial act of
faith. In this the Attendant Spirit operates like Ovid's Echo or the
traditional echo song—reflecting the sound and answering the sense.
In Herbert's poem, "Heaven," for instance, which identifies Echo
with the gracious promptings of the Word, echo is used to substantiate the promise of eternal bliss:

> Are holy leaves the Echo then of blisse?
>   *Echo.*   Yes.
> .   .   .   .
> Light, joy, and leisure; but shall they persever?
>   *Echo.*   Ever.
>   (11–12, 19–20)[44]

The Attendant Spirit both reflects and answers the Lady because he

43. For other biblical references in the liturgical context of St. Michael's day, see
James G. Taffe, "Michaelmas, the 'Lawless Hour,' and the Occasion of Milton's
Comus," *ELN* 6 (1968–69): 257–62, and William B. Hunter, Jr., "The Liturgical Con-
text of *Comus,*" *ELN* 10 (1972–73): 11–15.

44. Herbert is quoted from *The Works of George Herbert,* ed. F. E. Hutchinson (Oxford: Clarendon Press, 1941). Cf. Hollander, pp. 28–29.

is the true reflection, the outward show, of her faith. Just as Ariel reflects the spiritual states of those he treats, so the Attendant Spirit does that of the Lady. And just as Puck personifies unrestrained fancy, and Ariel creative fancy, so the Attendant Spirit personifies the spirit of God that both animates and fulfils the Lady's belief. Thus, his magic realizes the process of faith, the control of unrestrained fancy and the imagination of the good. Haemony, a symbol of the Lady's harmony,[45] is used to protect the brothers against the illusions of fancy, and the waters from Sabrina's "fountain pure" (911), a symbol that unites the waters of grace with those of the muses because grace sheds its light through the fancy, is used to realize the Lady's imagination of the good.

The Attendant Spirit's first magical act is to arm the Brothers with haemony. If haemony is defined by its purpose in the masque then it soon becomes apparent what it is. The Elder Brother, rather like Spenser's Redcross, is prepared to use force against the spirits of the "damn'd Magician":

> all the greisly legions that troop
> Under the sooty flag of *Acheron,*
> *Harpyes* and *Hydra's,* or all the monstrous forms
> 'Twixt *Africa* and *Inde.*
>
> (601–5)

These monstrous forms are the grotesque misjoinings of perverted fancy made manifest. As we have seen, this is what the harpy signifies in both *The Tempest* and *Paradise Regained,* and here, as the Spirit points out the Elder Brother's vulnerability, his words recall those of Ariel in harpy's form to the courtiers:

> But here thy sword can do thee little stead,
> . . . .
> He with his bare wand can unthred thy joynts,
> And crumble all thy sinews
>
> (610, 613–14)

45. Cf. Sharon Cumberland and Lynn Veach Sadler, "Phantasia: A Pattern in Milton's Early Poems," *MiltonQ* 8 (1974): 50–55: "'haemony', the mysterious herb so close to 'harmony'" (p. 54). Haemony is a symbol so comprehensive that it more than adequately encompasses everything from Charlotte F. Otten's "existing plant . . . *andros-haemon(y)*" ("Milton's Haemony," *ELR* 5 [1975]: 95) to Cedric C. Brown's much more fruitful "sword of the word of God" ("The Shepherd, the Musician, and the Word in Milton's Masque," *JEGP* 78 [1979]: 534).

recalls

> Your swords are now too massy for your strengths
> And will not be uplifted.
>   (III.iii.67–68)

The Elder Brother's weakness is the measure of his vulnerability to
the allurements of fancy. The haemony is intended to make him and
his younger brother invulnerable: it is

> of sov'ran use
> 'Gainst all inchantments, mildew blast, or damp
> Or gastly furies apparition.
>   (638–40)

The "gastly furies apparition" suggests the perverted fancy of Antonio because furies appear as harpies—"harpy-footed Furies" (*PL*
II.596). The "mildew blast, or damp" suggests the uncontrolled
fancy of Caliban because "mildew blast" is the same kind of withering disease as the "urchin blasts" that Puck, the "shrewd medling
Elfe" (845–46), inflicts on sheep, and these in turn are related to
the "urchin-shows" (II.ii.5) that Ariel's spirits inflict on Caliban.
Haemony is thus the harmony of the senses, the temperance, and
the control of fancy that is figured in the Lady's chastity—the quality
that enables her to resist Comus's attempted seduction. The Lady's
chastity depends of course on grace, reason informed by revelation, a
revelation that normally comes to man through the Word of God.[46]
Here in the pastoral fiction of the *Mask* the Word is symbolized by
sacred song and its echoes, songs full of "*high Mysteries*" and the
"*splendor that is shed into the fancy and intellect, rauisht, and inflamed with diuine fury.*" It is for this reason that the final antidote
to Comus's magic is the Lady's Orphic, that is, prophetic song:

> Yet should I try, the uncontrouled worth
> Of this pure cause would kindle my rap't spirits
> To such a flame of sacred vehemence,
> That dumb things would be mov'd to sympathize,
> And the brute Earth would lend nerves, and shake,
> Till all thy magick structures rear'd so high,
> Were shatter'd into heaps o're thy false head.
>   (792–98)[47]

46. It is in this sense that haemony is related to the Word. Cf. Brown: "Behind it all
[the description of haemony] is the controlling image in Peter of the word as flowering
plant, together with imagery drawn from the different versions of the parable of the
sower" (p. 534).
47. In Platonic terms, the "superior power" (800) that sets off these words, the sa-

The brothers' destruction of the orient liquor reenacts the Lady's success in controlling fancy and their failure to reverse the rod reemphasizes the dependence of the Lady's virtue, and the good that that virtue realizes, on the revelations of faith. To be exact, the Lady's paralysis dramatizes the inability of the human mind unaided by heaven to sing the Orphic song, that is, to imagine the good that will release it from the bondage of the flesh—because the good is a perception, not an invention of the imagination. Thus, whereas in Shakespeare Ferdinand is paralyzed and cannot win Miranda without the rough magic, the human magic of Prospero—

> Come, from thy ward!
> For I can here disarm thee with this stick
> . . . .
> Thy nerves are in their infancy again
> And have no vigor in them
> (I.ii.472–73, 485–86)

—in Milton the Lady is paralyzed and cannot realize the good without the divine magic of heaven:

> Nay Lady sit; if I but wave this wand
> Your nerves are all chain'd up in Alabaster,
> And you a statue.
> (678–80)

The Attendant Spirit's second magical act is to invoke Sabrina. It *Sabrina* is in Sabrina that the processes of fancy and faith most clearly come together, for her assistance symbolizes the imagination of the good in the process of faith, the imagination that is the fruit but also the seed of virtue. Her appearance parallels the imagined appearance of Chastity in the process as first experienced by the Lady (214) and the "liveried Angels" in the process as described by the Elder Brother (454). The good that is only imagined by them, the redemptive or transforming power of grace, is now realized by Sabrina, and their faith thus confirmed. And as their faith is confirmed so the reader or audience is offered an assurance of things hoped for through the response of our imagination to that of the poet's.

Sabrina, like the form of Chastity, appears in response to an act

---

cred vehemence that would move her Orphic song, is what, according to Reynolds, is called "among the Greeks . . . force, potency, or vehemence"; it is the "Celestiall or Intellectuall" love that animates songs like Solomon "his Canticle" (*Mythomystes*, p. 15). In Christian terms, it is the Holy Spirit.

of imagination. She appears in response to the Attendant Spirit's "warbled Song," an act of fancy that sheds the splendor of grace into our fancy. Sabrina personifies that splendor. The Attendant Spirit's song is an act of fancy which recalls the songs of those spirits that enact Prospero's fancies, especially Iris's invocation to the Naiades: "Come, temperate nymphs" (IV.i.132). And when Sabrina responds, she identifies herself with these same spirits of fancy: as they "on the sands with printless foot / Do chase the ebbing Neptune" (V.i.34– 35), so she—"from off the waters fleet / Thus I set my printless feet" (895–96). The effect of her song and the following ritual is similar to the effect of the song of Ariel in water-nymph's form on Ferdinand. Just as the water-nymph's song allays the fancies of his passion and leads him to Miranda, for him the realization of the good in the secular analogy of faith, so Sabrina's song and her "viold li-quors" allay the fancies of Comus's rhetoric and his orient liquor, and lead to the Lady's elevation, the realization of the good in the allegory of faith. As the water-nymph disappears leaving Miranda, so Sabrina descends leaving the Lady rising. As the water-nymph's song is consummated in Miranda, so Sabrina's rising is consummated in the Lady's rising. However, whereas the water-nymph is simply a creation of fancy and Miranda simply a chaste human being, Sabrina is a perception of fancy, a visible reflection in the fancy of the ideal form of Chastity, and the Lady's elevation is her own idealization. Being saved by her own faith means that she becomes the good she contemplates in her imagination.

The healing of the Lady, the fulfilment of her faith, is then the symbolic reenactment of her own idealization—a process described by Raphael when he refers to the way that all things return to God "Till body up to spirit work" (PL V.478). Besides dramatizing the need for divine aid, the Lady's paralysis emphasizes the permanent susceptibility of body to the sensual allurements of subverted fancy. First, the Lady remains bound "Through the force, and through the wile / Of unblest inchanter vile" (905–6). As we have seen, the strength of Comus's magical power, his force and wile, is the weak-ness of the fancy when not governed by reason. Second, Sabrina's "viold liquors" release the Lady from a "marble venom'd seat / Smear'd with gumms of glutenous heat" (915–16): "marble venom'd" suggests the antithesis between fair seeming and foul substance and the "gumms of glutenous heat" suggest the lechery of Circe and Comus. And third, the "viold liquors" are generally used to heal the contamination of malignant fancy, the "urchin blasts, and ill luck signes / That the shrewd medling Elfe delights to make" (844–45). All of this conforms closely to Sandys' interpretation of the story of

Ulysses and Circe—that Circe's rod "presents those false and sinister perswasions of pleasure" and that souls so enchanted can never "returne into their Country (from whence the soule deriveth her caelestiall originall) unlesse disinchanted, and cleansed from their impurity."[48] Through the heavenly grace of faith, the reflection of the good in the fancy, the healing of the body's susceptibility to the allurements of ungoverned fancy coincides with the body's working up to spirit—a process of idealization anticipated in Sabrina's divinization. The Lady is anointed with "Drops . . . from my fountain pure" (911), just as Sabrina has ambrosial oils "Dropt in" through "the porch and inlet of each sense" (839, 838). And most important, Sabrina's "quick immortal change" (840) recalls the divinization of the chaste soul as described by the Elder Brother. As a result of the clear dreams and solemn visions that no gross ear can hear, the chaste soul becomes immortal:

> Till oft convers with heav'nly habitants
> Begin to cast a beam on th'outward shape,
> The unpolluted temple of the mind,
> And turns it by degrees to the souls essence,
> Till all be made immortal.
> (458–62)[49]

The structural parallels between *The Tempest* and the *Mask* emphasize both the similarity and dissimilarity between the processes of autonomously creative fancy and faith. It is a relationship already suggested in "Il Penseroso." Shakespeare appears to be consigned to the world of "L'Allegro" as "fancies childe," but in the last allusion to secular imagination in "Il Penseroso," the last allusion before the series of references to religious imagination that climaxes in the prospect of "something like Prophetic strain" (174), Milton invokes the creative fancy of *The Tempest*:

> And as I wake, [let] sweet musick breath
> Above, about, or underneath,
> Sent by som spirit to mortals good,
> Or th'unseen Genius of the Wood.
> (151–54)

48. Sandys, p. 654.
49. The relationship of this process to that of imagination is emphasized by Wordsworth's memory of it in the poet's words to his sister in "Tintern Abbey," 137–42 (*The*

Almost immediately, however, the following antithesis stresses the inadequacy of secular fancy by comparison with fancy in a religious context:

> But let my due feet never fail,
> To walk the studious Cloysters pale.
>   (155–56)

The reference to *The Tempest* is both a memory of Ariel, "som spirit to mortals good," and an anticipation of the Attendant Spirit, "th' unseen Genius of the Wood," and it is in their relationship that the similarity and dissimilarity between the processes of autonomously creative fancy and faith is concentrated. When the Spirit associates himself with Ariel, he also carefully distinguishes himself. The Spirit's closing words recall the opening words of Ariel:

> But now my task is smoothly don
> I can fly, or I can run
> Quickly to the green earths end,
> Where the bow'd welkin slow doth bend,
> And from thence can soar as soon
> To the corners of the Moon
>   (1011–16)

recalls

> All hail, great master. Grave sir, hail. I come
> To answer thy best pleasure, be't to fly,
> To swim, to dive into the fire, to ride
> On the curled clouds. To thy strong bidding task
> Ariel and all his quality.
>   (I.ii.189–93)

Whereas Ariel's task is to fly, the Attendant Spirit can only fly once his task is done. Whereas Ariel's task is the application of autono-

---

Poetical Works of William Wordsworth, ed. E. de Selincourt, 2d ed., [Oxford: Clarendon Press, 1952], II, 263):

> and, in after years,
> When these wild ecstasies shall be matured
> Into a sober pleasure; when thy mind
> Shall be a mansion for all lovely forms,
> Thy memory be as a dwelling-place
> For all sweet sounds and harmonies.

mously creative fancy or invention as figured in "flight," the Attendant Spirit's task is something more than "flight." Once Ariel completes his task he returns to the fairy world of uncontrolled but innocent fancy, a world where imagination has free play. Once the Attendant Spirit has completed his task he also returns to a world where imagination can have free play, but from his perspective that world is the world of Ariel's task, the world of autonomously creative fancy. For in the final analysis, the fancy of the Attendant Spirit's task is not simply creative, but procreative, reflective or echoic: whereas the activity of fancy in *The Tempest* is essentially the re-creation of the visible world, the activity of fancy in the *Mask* is a reflection of the intelligible world in visible terms. When Milton refers to the "Poet soaring in the high region of his fancies," he is referring to poetry as the operation of fancy at its highest potential and as such it is the instrument of the heavenly grace of faith.

CHAPTER TWO

The Icastic Imagination

In the previous chapter, we distinguished between three modes of fancy: first, fancy ungoverned by reason as the source of delusion; second, fancy governed by reason as the autonomous creator or inventor of the good; and third, fancy governed by reason as the procreator, the reflector, or mirror of the good. It became apparent from the evidence of the *Mask* that this third mode of fancy coincided in some way with the process of faith. My purpose in this chapter is to clarify the relationship between fancy and faith, and to do so by suggesting through what theories of poetry and prophecy Milton's formative experience of Shakespearean imagination is likely to have been distilled.

HIGH-RAISED PHANTASY:
THE ICASTIC IMAGINATION IN POETRY

> For I will not deny but that man's wit may make Poesy, which should be *eikastike*, which some learned have defined, 'figuring forth good things', to be *phantastike*, which doth contrariwise infect the fancy with unworthy objects; as the painter, that should give the eye either some excellent perspective, or some fine picture, fit for building or fortification, or containing in it some notable example, as Abraham sacrificing his son Isaac, Judith killing Holofernes, David fighting with Goliath, may leave those, and please an ill-pleased eye with wanton shows of better hidden matters.
>
> Sidney, *An Apology for Poetry*[1]

In his *Apology for Poetry* Sidney distinguishes between two kinds of poetry—*phantastike* and *eikastike*. What he calls *phantastike*—

1. Sidney is quoted from Sir Philip Sidney, *An Apology for Poetry*, ed. Geoffrey Shepherd (London: Nelson, 1965), p. 125.

"the nurse of abuse, infecting us with many pestilent desires, with a siren's sweetness drawing the mind to the serpent's tale of sinful fancy" (p. 123)—clearly corresponds to fancy ungoverned by reason. What he calls *eikastike*, though it might appear to correspond to the fancy of *The Tempest*, fancy as the creator of the good, actually refers much more closely to the fancy of the *Mask*, fancy as the mirror of the good.

Shakespeare's intensely empirical representation of fancy as the creator of the good, the inventor of new realities, brave new worlds, appears to receive a sanction in Sidney's theory of the poet as maker of a second nature:

> Only the poet, disdaining to be tied to any such subjection, lifted up with the vigour of his own invention, doth grow in effect into another nature, in making things either better than Nature bringeth forth, or, quite anew, forms such as never were in Nature. . . .
> [Nature's] world is brazen, the poets only deliver a golden. (p. 100)

There is, however, a difference. Prospero claims that poetic invention, the creations of fancy, are images of nothing but themselves, insubstantial and baseless:

> These our actors,
> As I foretold you, were all spirits and
> Are melted into air, into thin air;
> And, like the baseless fabric of this vision,
> The cloud-capped tow'rs, the gorgeous palaces,
> The solemn temples, the great globe itself,
> Yea, all which it inherit, shall disolve,
> And, like this insubstantial pageant faded,
> Leave not a rack behind.
>   (IV.i.148–56)

Sidney, on the other hand, indicates two ways in which poetic invention is anything but baseless—that poetic invention is both a cause and a consequence of something substantial. The first way, poetic invention as a cause, is already implicit in *The Tempest* itself. As we have seen, the play stands as an assurance of things hoped for. The substance of the play's vision, the rack it does leave behind, is the very idea of fancy's creativity and the model of a new nature, the brave new world that fancy can create. Sidney explains it in these terms: the golden world that the poet delivers is not wholly imaginative [that is, imaginary], as we are wont to say by them that build castles in the air; but so far substantially it worketh, not only to make a Cyrus, which had been but a particular excellency as Nature might have done, but to bestow a Cyrus upon the world to make many Cyruses, if they will learn aright why and how that maker made him. (p. 101)

The second way, poetic invention as a consequence, makes it clear that Sidney's understanding of *eikastike* is not fancy autonomously creative or innovative, but fancy procreative or reflective. It is here that Sidney and Shakespeare part company. For the nature that fancy creates, according to Sidney, is not really new, but the re-creation of an original nature, now lost: the images that fancy creates are in fact reflections of Ideas. When fancy is *eikastike*, when it figures forth good things, its inventions are the consequence or imprint of Ideas. Fancy's new actuality is an imitation, not of the sensible world, but of the ideal: consider, says Sidney, whether or not nature has brought forth

so true a lover as Theagenes, so constant a friend as Pylades, so valiant a man as Orlando, so right a prince as Xenophon's Cyrus, so excellent a man in every way as Virgil's Aeneas. Neither let this be jestingly conceived, because the works of the one be essential, the other in imitation or fiction; for any understanding knoweth the skill of the artificer standeth in that *Idea* or fore-conceit of the work, and not in the work itself. And that the poet hath that *Idea* is manifest. (pp. 100–101)[2]

Frequently, Sidney suggests a purely innovative fancy—the most excellent poets, those who "most properly do imitate to teach and delight, and to imitate borrow nothing of what is, hath been, or shall be"—but he then so qualifies it as to render it reflective—these poets "range, only reined with learned discretion, into the divine consideration of what may be and should be" (p. 102). Thus, whereas Bacon's reason bows and buckles the mind to the actual nature of things,[3] Sidney's fancy bows and buckles the mind to the ideal nature of things. For Sidney purely creative fancy is in fact reflective, and it is for this reason, not because they lose themselves in a divine madness, that poets are prophets: "These be they that, as the first and most noble sort may justly be termed *vates*" (p. 102). For Shake-

2. Cf. S. K. Heninger, Jr., "Sidney and Milton: The Poet as Maker," in *Milton and the Line of Vision*, ed. Joseph Anthony Wittreich, Jr. (Madison: University of Wisconsin Press, 1975), esp. pp. 66–69.

3. See *Advancement of Learning* II (Spedding, III, 343–44).

speare the substance of fancy's inventions is in their effect; for Sidney, the substance is also in their effect, but much more in their cause, in the ideas they shadow or reflect.

The origin of Sidney's term for the reflective process of fancy, *eikastike*, is not difficult to find. The immediate source is Italy and the literary criticism to which Milton refers as the *"Italian* commentaries of *Castelvetro, Tasso, Mazzoni* and others."[4] There, in Tasso in particular,[5] imagination as the sensible reflection of ideas is identified with the icastic imagination or likeness making that Plato in the *Sophist* opposes to phantastic imagination or semblance making. Using analogies drawn from the visual arts to explain image making in speech, Plato says that likeness making means producing an exact copy, "a copy which is executed according to the proportions of the original, similar in length and breadth and depth, each thing receiving also its appropriate colour" (235d–e), while semblance making means producing an image that as a result of deliberate illusion, such as perspective, only seems to resemble the original. For Plato, as Panofsky puts it, the distinction is "between objectively correct and *trompe l'oeil* imitation."[6] But for the Renaissance, in a writer such as Comanini, the distinction has come to mean "the contrast between the representation of actually existing objects and the representation of actually nonexisting objects."[7] In Tasso's *Discourses on the Heroic Poem* (1594),[8] the distinction is developed a stage further. Since the only truly existing things are intelligible not visible, icastic imagination comes to mean the faithful copy not of the actual but of the ideal:

But if [the poet's] images are of existing things, this imitation belongs to the icastic imitator. But what shall we say exists, the intelligible or the visible?

4. *Of Education* (Yale, II, 404).

5. See Baxter Hathaway, *The Age of Criticism* (Ithaca: Cornell University Press, 1962), esp. pp. 394–96, and Bernard Weinberg, *A History of Literary Criticism in the Italian Renaissance,* 2 vols. (Chicago: University of Chicago Press, 1962), esp. I, 339–41. See also Erwin Panofsky, *Idea,* trans. Joseph J. S. Peake (Columbia: University of South Carolina Press, 1968), pp. 165, 212–15n, 242n; Shepherd, in Sidney, *Apology,* pp. 202–3n; Cavalchini and Samuel, in Tasso, *Discourses on the Heroic Poem,* p. xxvii; James Nohrnberg, *The Analogy of* The Faerie Queene (Princeton: Princeton University Press, 1976), pp. 102–10; MacCaffrey, *Spenser's Allegory,* pp. 3–10.

6. *Idea,* p. 215n.

7. Ibid.

8. "The *Discorsi del poema heroica* was not published until 1594, but it was probably written between 1575 and 1580" (Weinberg, I, 340). See also Cavalchini and Samuel, in Tasso, *Discourses on the Heroic Poem,* pp. xi–xii.

Surely the intelligible, in the opinion of Plato too, who put visible things in the genus of non-being and only the intelligible in the genus of being. (p. 32)

In the light of this, William Kerrigan's dismissal of icastic in Sidney as "historical and quotidien" seems a little hasty.[9] As examples of what he means by icastic images, Tasso offers "the images of the angels that Dionysius describes . . . the winged lion, the eagle, ox, and angel, which are the images of the evangelists" (p. 32). Though these images may appear to be fantastic, they are in fact icastic. Mazzoni, commenting on the "beautiful poetic phantasies" of the Song of Solomon, explains how

the purely phantastic poem, which by its nature looks on the false in the way that has been explained, was not known to the Hebrews, and the poem of the Song of Solomon is not of that kind, but is one of those which under the husk of the literal sense conceals pure and complete truth. Hence it can be called phantastic with respect to the literal sense, but icastic with respect to the allegorical sense.[10]

Because icastic images are reflections of the intelligible, Tasso speculates on the existence of two kinds of fancy. Besides the fancy that resides in the sensible part of the soul, there may be another, higher kind of fancy in the intellectual part: icastic images

do not belong principally to phantasy and are not its proper object, since phantasy is [a faculty] in the divisible part of the mind, not the indivisible, which is the intellect pure and simple, unless besides the phantasy which is a faculty of the sensitive soul there were another which is a faculty of the intellective. (p. 32)

He goes on to identify this "intellectual imagination" with Dante's *alta fantasia*, the imaginative power that allows the poet access to a vision of God: of intellectual fantasy he writes:

although both our theologians and the Platonic philosophers postulate this faculty, Aristotle neither knew of nor admitted it. Nor did Plato in the *Sophist*; otherwise he would not have distinguished icastic from phantastic imitation, since the icastic too would belong to the intellectual imagination. Perhaps this is what Dante was referring to when he said:

9. *The Prophetic Milton*, p. 56.
10. *On the Defense of the Comedy of Dante* III.vi, quoted from *Literary Criticism: Plato to Dryden*, ed. Allan H. Gilbert (New York: American Book, 1940), p. 390. Hereafter cited as Gilbert.

Here power failed the high phantasy
[*Par.* xxxiii.142]

and elsewhere:

Then rained down within the high fantasy
One crucified, scornful and fierce.
[*Purg.* xvii.25–26] (p. 33)

Whether, however, *alta fantasia* implies two different faculties or one faculty operating in two different ways, it seems fairly clear that Tasso's icastic fancy and Dante's *alta fantasia* both refer to the same reflective operation of the imagination[11]—as the lines preceding Tasso's quotation from the *Purgatorio* confirm:

O imaginativa che ne rube
   talvolta sì di fuor, ch'om non s'accorge
   perché dintorno suonin mille tube,
chi move te, se 'l senso non ti porge?
   Moveti lume che nel ciel s'informa,
   per sé o per voler che giù lo scorge.
De l'empiezza di lei che mutò forma
   ne l'uccel ch'a cantar più si diletta,
   ne l'imagine mia apparve l'orma;
e qui fu la mia mente sì ristretta
   dentro da sé, che di fuor non venìa
   cosa che fosse allor da lei ricetta.
Poi piovve dentro a l'alta fantasia
   un crucifisso, dispettoso e fero
   ne la sua vista, e cotal si moria.

O imagination, that do sometimes so snatch us from outward things that we give no heed, though a thousand trumpets sound around us, who moves you if the sense affords you naught? A light moves you which takes form in heaven, of itself, or by a will that downward guides it. Of her impious deed who changed her form into the bird that most delights to sing, the impress appeared in my imagination, and at this my mind was so restrained within itself, that from outside came naught that was then received by it. Then rained down within the high fantasy one crucified, scornful and fierce in his mien, and so was he dying.[12]

Although the impress that forms in the imagination has a sensible appearance, its substance is intelligible, that is, it originates in

11. See Bundy, pp. 225–56, and Hathaway, p. 379n.
12. *Purg.* xvii.13–27. The text and translation of *The Divine Comedy* is quoted from Dante Alighieri, *The Divine Comedy*, trans. Charles S. Singleton, 3 vols. (Princeton: Princeton University Press, 1970–75).

heaven, in the mind of God. *Alta fantasia* is the imagination when it is moved by God, when he imprints the sensible images of ideas in it, and it seems likely that *alta fantasia* is what Milton means by "our high-rais'd phantasie" and the "Poet soaring in the high region of his fancies."

Underlying the conception of the reflective operation of the imagination is the conviction that for man in "the dark lanthorn of the body"[13] knowledge, especially knowledge of God, is impossible without images. This conviction is apparent in the fundamental association of knowledge with seeing: "How does knowing differ from opining and believing? . . . The true answer to this question can be given in three words, 'By being vision.'"[14] When knowledge is of things not in the visible world, it remains vision through its dependence on sensible symbols formed in the imagination. In the *Convivio*, when Dante explains the failure of *alta fantasia* to apprehend the divine fully, he indicates the dependence of understanding on fancy:

Our intellect, by defect of that power whence it draws whatsoever it contemplates (which is an organic power, to wit the fantasy), may not rise to certain things, because the fantasy may not aid it, for it hath not wherewithal. Such are the substances sejunct from matter, which, even though a certain consideration of them be possible, we may not understand nor comprehend perfectly.[15]

The same sense of the impossibility of knowing without picturing is apparent in Aristotle:

Now for the thinking soul images take the place of direct perceptions. . . . Hence the soul never thinks without a mental image;[16]

in Aquinas:

It is impossible for our intellect, in its present state of being joined to a body capable of receiving impressions, actually to understand anything without turning to sense images. . . .

13. Nathanael Culverwell, *Spiritual Opticks* (London, 1652), p. 178.
14. A. E. Taylor, quoted in John Hick, *Faith and Knowledge*, 2d ed. (Ithaca: Cornell University Press, 1966), p. 200.
15. *Convivio* III.iv.9, quoted in Singleton, III, pt. 2, 586.
16. *De Anima* III.vii, quoted from Aristotle, *On the Soul, Parva Naturalia, On Breath*, trans. W. S. Hett, rev. ed. Loeb Classical Library (London: Heinemann, 1957), p. 177.

. . . The proper object of the human intellect, on the other hand, since it is joined to a body, is a nature or 'whatness' found in corporeal matter—the intellect, in fact, rises to the limited knowledge it has of invisible things by way of the nature of visible things;[17]

and in Milton:

our understanding cannot in this body found it selfe but on sensible things, nor arrive so cleerly to the knowledge of God and things invisible, as by orderly conning over the visible and inferior creature.[18]

As Raphael points out, even for unfallen man, it is from "Fansie and understanding" that "the Soule / Reason receives, and reason is her being" (*PL* V.486–87). Reason here may mean both the absolute and the faculty that allows us to apprehend it, but the process of apprehension still depends upon fancy and its sensible images.

Because knowledge of God is not available through imageless reasoning, when Milton looks to heaven, the icastic imagination is very much in evidence.

In the early poetry, the desire that his fancy might "figure forth good things," reflect images of the ideal or the divine, is especially intense. Just as the vision of God is presented to Dante's *alta fantasia*, so Milton prays that the vision of divine poetry, "That undisturbed Song of pure concent, / Ay sung before the saphire-color'd throne" may be presented "to our high-rais'd phantasie" ("At a Solemn Musick" 6–7, 5).[19] The image of the poet "soaring in the high region of his fancies with his garland and his singing robes about him" also leads us back to the aspirations of the early poetry.[20] In "At a Vacation Exercise," the poet appears searching for the appropriate language, the "richest Robes, and gay'st attire" with which to clothe "some naked thoughts" (21–23). Chief among these thoughts is the desire itself for such a language, such robes "as may make thee search thy coffers round" (31), that he might use in the service of "some graver subject" (30)—to "cloath my fancy in fit sound" (32).

17. *Summa Theologiae* I.84.7, quoted from St. Thomas Aquinas, *Summa Theologiae*, gen. ed. Thomas Gilby, O.P., 60 vols. (New York: Blackfriars, 1964–81), XII, 41. Hereafter cited as Gilby.

18. *Of Education* (Yale, II, 368–69).

19. Cf. Tuve, *Images & Themes*, p. 59, on *phantasia*, the "sole faculty by which man can be rapt beyond man's mortal limits to see the perfection he can no longer see plain." Cf. also Cumberland and Sadler, "Phantasia," esp. p. 55.

20. *Reason of Church-Government* II, Introduction (Yale, I, 808).

When he gives an example of what that graver subject might be, we know he is referring to the sensible reflection of Ideas:

> Such where the deep transported mind may soare
> Above the wheeling poles, and at Heav'ns dore
> Look in, and see each blissful Deitie
> How he before the thunderous throne doth lie.
>
> (33–36)

As Irene Samuel points out, this image is an allusion to the festival of the gods which "in *Phaedrus* is the grand occasion for sight of the Ideas."[21] There Plato appears as both philosopher and what Milton calls "fabulator maximus" ("De Idea Platonica" 38). He uses both figure and abstraction, lively images and bare words. The figure is the festival to which Milton alludes:

> Zeus, the mighty lord, holding the reins of a winged chariot, leads the way in heaven, ordering all and taking care of all; and there follows him the array of gods and demi-gods. . . . They see many blessed sights in the inner heaven, and there are many ways to and fro, along which the blessed gods are passing, every one doing his own work. . . . But when they go to the banquet and festival, then they move up the steep vault of heaven. (246e–47b)

At the outset Plato explains that the gods themselves are figurative, only sensible images of the divine: "fancy, not having seen nor surely known the nature of God, may imagine a mortal creature having both a body and also a soul which are united throughout all time" (246c–d). And when the figure approaches its climax, the sight of the Ideas, Plato abandons his singing robes and adopts the language of a philosopher:

> But of the heaven which is above the heavens, what earthly poet ever did or ever will sing worthily? It is such as I will describe; for I must dare to speak the truth, when truth is my theme. There abides the very being with which true knowledge is concerned; the colourless, formless, intangible essence, visible only to mind, the pilot of the soul . . . justice, and temperance, and knowledge absolute, not that to which becoming belongs, nor that which is found, in varying forms, in one or other of those regions which we men call *real*, but real knowledge really present where being is. (247c–e)

Plato's careful distinction between figure and abstraction is not apparent in Milton. First, in the "Vacation Exercise" when Milton ar-

21. *Plato and Milton* (Ithaca: Cornell University Press, 1947), p. 137.

rives at the time climactic point, he turns away from the abstract description of the Ideas and descends through a series of sensational images that are meant to represent practical knowledge of the sensible world:

> Then passing through the Spherse of watchful fire,
> And mistie Regions of wide air next under,
> And hills of Snow and lofts of piled Thunder,
> May tell at length how green-ey'd *Neptune* raves.
>   (40–43)[22]

Second, when he does deal with the Ideas in a poem of the same period, they appear almost as personifications, fully integrated into the figure:

> And Joy shall overtake us in a flood,
> When every thing that is sincerely good
> And perfectly divine,
> With Truth, and Peace, and Love shall ever shine
> About the supreme Throne
> Of him, t'whose happy-making sight alone,
> When once our heav'nly-guided soul shall clime,
> Then all this Earthy grosness quit,
> Attir'd with Stars, we shall for ever sit,
>   Triumphing over Death, and Chance, and thee O Time.
>   ("On Time" 13–22)

The ultimate source of this integration is perhaps St. Augustine's assimilation of the abstract Ideas of Plato into the mind of the personal God of Christianity.[23] It is in Milton's turning away from pure abstraction that he and Plato part. Despite the concessions made to imagination in the later dialogues, truth for Plato, if not mathematical, is a matter of dialectic, reasoning or logic, that owes nothing to imagination, and the good is apprehended through a state of mind called *"intelligence or rational intuition* (noesis) *and knowledge* (episteme . . .) *in the full sense."*[24] By rational intuition or intuitive reason, Plato means discursive reason writ large:

22. Cf. *Prolusion* III (Yale, I, 246–47).
23. See *City of God* XI.10, in *The Works of . . . Augustine*, ed. Marcus Dods, 15 vols. (Edinburgh, 1871–76), I, 447–50. Hereafter cited as Dods.
24. F. M. Cornford, ed., *The Republic of Plato* (1941; rpt. Oxford: Clarendon Press, 1966), pp. 218–19.

Then by the second section of the intelligible world you may understand me to mean all that unaided reasoning apprehends by the power of dialectic . . . never making use of any sensible object, but only of Forms, moving through Forms from one to another, and ending with Forms. (*Republic* 511)[25]

By intuitive reason, Milton means something different. Raphael certainly agrees with Plato that, for unfallen man at least, the difference between intuitive and discursive reason is only a matter of degree. But then, as we have seen, reason at any level, according to Raphael, does not discard fancy but depends upon it, and cognition without imagination, according to the *Reason of Church-Government*, is not possible in this life:

For Truth, I know not how, hath this unhappinesse fatall to her, ere she can come to the triall and inspection of the Understanding, being to passe through many little wards and limits of the severall Affections and Desires, she cannot shift it, but must put on such colours and attire, as those Pathetick handmaids of the soul please to lead her in to their Queen.[26]

It is precisely appropriate colors and attire that Milton is searching for in the "Vacation Exercise"—to "cloath my fancy"—and it is precisely the possibility of this coloring of truth that Plato rejects in the *Phaedrus*:

For sight is the most piercing of our bodily senses; though not by that is wisdom seen; her loveliness would have been transporting if there had been a visible image of her, and the other ideas, if they had visible counterparts, would be equally lovely. (250d)

But Sidney reverses Plato's point, emphasizing that visible images of the ideal constitute the peculiar glory of poetry:

if the saying of Plato and Tully be true, that who could see virtue would be wonderfully ravished with love of her beauty—this man [the poet] sets her out to make her more lovely in her holiday apparel, to the eye of any that will deign not to disdain until they understand. (p. 119)

As the closing phrase suggests, underlying Sidney's reversal of Plato is Christianity's reversal of Platonic rationalism: "Unless you believe, you shall not understand" (Cf. Isa. 7:9; Isa. 6:9 and Mark

25. Quoted from Cornford, p. 221.
26. Yale, I, 830.

4:12). The precedence of belief over comprehension sanctions the poet's desire to elevate imagination over ratiocination. Implicit in "At a Solemn Musick" is the same elevation of high-raised fancy as an integral part of intuitive reason over discourse. For there the vital operation of poetry, Orpheus's art—"Dead things with inbreath'd sense able to pierce" (4)—coincides with the life-giving operation of Scripture in that both bypass discourse and appeal directly to the eye of the soul:

> But let them chaunt while they will of prerogatives, we shall tell them of Scripture; of custom, we of Scripture; of Acts and Statutes, stil of Scripture, til the quick and pearcing word enter to the dividing of their soules, & the mighty weaknes of the Gospel throw down the weak mightines of mans reasoning.[27]

The belief in icastic imagination evident in the early poetry leads to a yearning for the "Prophetic strain" and, as we shall see, the icastic imagination that moves poetry at its highest potential also moves prophecy.

THE PROPHETICAL SCENE OR STAGE:
THE ICASTIC IMAGINATION IN PROPHECY

> [Prophecy] is the highest degree of man and the ultimate term of perfection that can exist for his species; and this state is the ultimate term of perfection for the imaginative faculty. This is something that cannot by any means exist in every man. And it is not something that may be attained solely through perfection in the speculative sciences and through improvement of moral habits, even if all of them have become as fine and good as can be. There still is needed in addition the highest possible degree of perfection of the imaginative faculty in respect of its original natural disposition.
>
> Maimonides, *Guide of the Perplexed* II.36[28]

John Smith's discourse *Of Prophecy* (1660) provides the most comprehensive contemporary account of the function of imagination

27. *Reason of Church-Government* II.ii (Yale, I, 827).
28. Maimonides is quoted from Moses Maimonides, *The Guide of the Perplexed*,

in prophecy. By prophecy Smith does not mean just the prophetic books, but the whole of Scripture—for prophecy is *"the way where-by revealed truth is dispensed and conveyed to us"* (p. 171).[29] Following the rabbinical tradition of Maimonides and his commentator, Joseph Albo, Smith distinguishes four degrees of prophecy "according to the relative proportion of rational understanding to imaginative sensation."[30] The highest degree, the *gradus mosaicus,* occurs when there is a direct illumination of the understanding without the aid of imagination. The second degree, the prophetic grade proper, occurs in dreams and visions, usually mediated by an angel, when there is an indirect illumination of the understanding through imagination controlled by reason—"when the rational power is most predominant; in which case . . . the mind of the prophet is able to strip those things, that are represented to it in the glass of fancy, of all their materiality and sensible nature, and apprehend them more distinctly in their own naked essence" (p. 183). The third grade, the hagiographical, says Smith quoting Albo, occurs in "words of wisdom, or song, or divine praise, in pure and elegant language" (p. 238) when there is an indirect illumination of the understanding through the joint operation of imagination and reason—"when the strength of the imaginative and rational powers equally balance each other" (p. 183). The lowest degree occurs "when the imaginative power is most predominant, so that the impressions made upon it are too busy, and the scene becomes too turbulent for the rational faculty to discern the true mystical and anagogical sense of them clearly" (p. 181). With this kind of prophecy, illumination is only possible on rational analysis after the event and then "with much obscurity still attending it" (p. 182). There is another degree which Smith rather confusingly refers to as the lowest degree, the *filia vocis.* This was a

trans. Shlomo Pines, introd. Leo Strauss (Chicago: University of Chicago Press, 1963), p. 369. Cf. Morton W. Bloomfield, Piers Plowman *as Fourteenth-Century Apocalypse* (New Brunswick, N.J.: Rutgers University Press, 1961), pp. 170–74, and Wittreich, *Visionary Poetics,* p. 29.

29. Smith is quoted from John Smith, *Select Discourses,* ed. H. G. Williams, 4th ed. (Cambridge, 1859). Smith's treatise is discussed in relation to Milton by Basil Willey, *The Seventeenth-Century Background* (1934; rpt. Harmondsworth: Penguin, 1964), pp. 134–41; Hunter, "Prophetic Dreams"; Kerrigan, pp. 108–12; Guillory, pp. 13–14, 17; and Barbara K. Lewalski, "The Genres of *Paradise Lost:* Literary Genre as a means of Accommodation," *MiltonS* 17 (1983): 79–80, 92. See also John Spencer Hill, *John Milton: Poet, Priest, and Prophet* (Totowa, N.J.: Rowman and Littlefield, 1979), esp. pp. 77–113.

30. Kerrigan, p. 111.

voice heard descending from heaven directing affairs, but not a part of true prophecy.

Basil Willey used Smith's discourse as evidence for the "dissociation of sensibility" in his scholarly substantiation of T. S. Eliot's theory, *The Seventeenth-Century Background.*[31] Willey used the discourse to show among other things the growing intellectual aversion to imagination in the seventeenth century. This aversion, he feels, is epitomized in the juxtaposition of the lowest and highest degrees of prophecy:

The inferiority of mere 'imagination' to 'Reason' could not be more emphatically stated: 'The Pseudo-Prophetical Spirit is seated onely in the Imaginative Powers and Faculties inferior to Reason'; whereas in the *gradus mosaicus* 'all imagination ceaseth, and the Representation of Truth descends not so low as the Imaginative part; but is made in the highest stage of Reason and Understanding.' (p. 136)

Willey's emphasis here, however, and his "impression" that Smith when handling imagination is "dealing with comparatively uncongenial material" (p. 137) amounts to a considerable distortion of the text.

First, the inferiority of mere "imagination" to "Reason" is hardly a notion that arose in the seventeenth century. Indeed, it is difficult to imagine anyone before the Romantic period defending imagination against reason when imagination separate from or in opposition to reason was by definition considered delusory—"begot of nothing but vain fantasy." Second, the identification of the lowest degree of prophecy with false prophecy or the pseudo-prophetical spirit— "This last group, then, includes all the pseudo-prophets" (p. 136)— is a misrepresentation. Smith carefully distinguishes between the pseudo-prophetical spirit which "is seated only in the imaginative powers" (p. 193) and the lowest degree of prophecy where the imaginative power is not alone but only "most predominant" (p. 181). If Willey's identification were true, then the prophecies of this lowest degree—Zachariah, Ezekiel, and Daniel—would be false. Third, the juxtaposition of highest and lowest degrees obscures the fact that most of the discourse is devoted to those degrees, especially the second, the prophetic grade proper, where the role of imagination is essential. Though it is certainly true that Smith's transcendental

31. The influence of Eliot's theory, which is implicit throughout Willey's book, becomes explicit at pp. 44–45, 83–84.

temper draws him to the prospect of a mode of cognition that is imageless,[32] it is equally true that when he is thinking of prophecy in general, he is thinking primarily of those degrees that most fruitfully involve imagination. This is especially clear, for instance, when Smith announces that his prime interest is in the psychology of prophecy:

> But the main thing that we shall observe in this description is, that faculty or power of the soul upon which these extraordinary impressions of divine light or influence are made; which, in all proper prophecy, is both the rational and imaginative power. (p. 180)

Or when he turns aside to deal with false prophecy and touches on the familiar Janus-faced nature of imagination: fancy ungoverned by reason leads to illusion, while fancy governed by reason leads to illumination: false prophecy is "seated only in the imaginative power, from whence the first occasion of this delusion ariseth," but "that power is also the seat of all [true] prophetical vision" (p. 194).

When Smith actually describes how the imagination works in prophecy, his description corresponds exactly to the reflective operation of fancy that the literary critics refer to as icastic. Although he refers to the *locus classicus* of reflective imagination in the *Timaeus* (70d–72b)[33] only in terms of disapproval (pp. 192, 197), as he proceeds through the various degrees of prophecy the basic idea of fancy as a mirror reflecting sensible images of the intelligible back to the mind remains constant. Analyzing the dreams and visions of prophecy proper, he describes the reflective operation thus:

> Now to these ecstatical impressions, whereby the imagination and the mind of the prophet was thus ravished from itself, and was made subject wholly to some agent intellectual informing it and shining upon it, I suppose St. Paul had respect. 'Now we see . . . by a glass, in riddles or parables;' for so he seems to compare the highest illuminations which we have here, with that constant irradiation of the Divinity upon the souls of men in the life to come: and this glassing of divine things by hieroglyphics and emblems in the fancy which he speaks of, was the proper way of prophetical inspiration. (p. 185)

32. Cf., for instance, his attitude to mathematics: "*mathemata*, or mathematical contemplations, whereby the souls of men might farther shake off their dependence upon sense, and learn to go as it were alone, without the crutch of any sensible or material thing to support them" (*The True Way or Method of Attaining Divine Knowledge*, in *Select Discourses*, p. 11).

33. See pp. 31–32.

In conflating the mirror images of the *Timaeus* and I Corinthians 13 : 12, Smith makes imagination the glass, not as he says earlier (in the discourse on *Divine Knowledge*) a blemish on the glass, "a gross dew on the pure glass of our understandings" (p. 22). Here imagination is operating as an integral part of a cognitive process. Plato's suspicion of reflective imagination is reversed: revelation is not made as in the *Timaeus* to the foolishness of men but to their wisdom, to understanding through imagination, to those whose faculties are rationally ordered:

A troubled fancy could no more receive these ideas of divine truth to be impressed upon it, and clearly reflect them to the understanding, than a cracked glass, or troubled water, can reflect sincerely any image to be made upon them. (p. 253)

The fact that imagination is operating reflectively, however, does not mean that the cognitive process is passive, but like Drayton's account of the poet's mind, it "by inspiration conceaveth / What heaven to her by divination breatheth": [34]

It may be considered that God made not use of idiots or fools by whom to reveal His will, but such whose intellects were entire and perfect; and that He imprinted such a clear copy of His truth upon them; as that it became their own sense, being digested fully into their understandings; so as they were able to deliver and represent it to others, as truly as any can paint forth his own thoughts. (p. 284)

Thus, for Smith prophecy, apart from the mosaic grade, was largely the creation of the icastic imagination. Despite his reliance on rabbinical sources, Smith's discourse is, as Kerrigan has pointed out, well within the mainstream of traditional Christian thought on the psychology of prophecy: "Smith rarely cited Thomas Aquinas, although he arrived at a theory of degrees of inspiration which recapitulates Aquinas almost perfectly."[35] Aquinas describes the process of prophetic revelation using the same key metaphor of the mirror:

It is these similitudes [the figurative language of prophecy], made light by the divine light, which deserve the name of mirror for [sic] more than the

34. *Endimion and Phoebe* 521–22, quoted from *The Works of Michael Drayton*, ed. J. W. Hebel et al., 5 vols. (1941; rpt. Oxford: Blackwell, 1961). Cf. MacCaffrey, *Spenser's Allegory*, p. 13.
35. Kerrigan, p. 108.

divine essence. For in a mirror images are formed from other realities, and this cannot be said of God. Yet the enlightening of the mind in a prophetical mode can be called a mirroring, in so far as is reflected in it an image of the truth of the divine foreknowledge.[36]

However, by identifying the mirror of prophetic imagination with the glass of St. Paul, Smith not only emphasizes the function of imagination in knowing God, but, most important, he identifies this psychology of prophetic revelation as it appears in the Old Testament with every Christian's way of knowing God in the New. Although the ultimate goal, a goal not attainable in this life, is, as it was for St. Augustine and Aquinas, intellectual vision, a knowledge of God that transcends the sensible, the way to that goal is through the sensible—through imagination. As Donne puts it, the Christian comes to know God "by reflexion" in a glass of "darke similitude and comparison."[37]

Although Smith never uses the term "icastic," other contemporary commentators on prophecy do. Henry More, for instance, in his *Synopsis Prophetica* refers to his catalogue of figurative devices used in prophecy as "the chief *Icastick* terms that occur in the Prophetick style," and these icastic figures that occur in visions and dreams are "divinatory Impresses."[38] Literary critics, like Mazzoni, of course, saw prophecy as the model of icastic imagination: "the ancient Hebrews did not know the kind of poetry that deals with the false, but only that which deals with the true, and by Plato is called icastic."[39]

It becomes increasingly apparent that poetry at its highest potential and prophecy, "the way whereby revealed truth is dispensed and conveyed to us," coincide in the psychological process that produces them.[40] As the poet is an icastic imitator so he is a prophet and as the prophet is an icastic imitator so he is a poet. Both parts of the equation, poet as prophet and vice versa, are apparent in Sidney:

36. *Summa Theologiae* II–II.173.1 (Gilby, XLV, 53).
37. *The Sermons of John Donne*, ed. Evelyn M. Simpson and George R. Potter, 10 vols. (Berkeley: University of California Press, 1962), VIII, 220, 225.
38. *Synopsis Prophetica; The Second Part of the Enquiry into the Mystery of Iniquity*, quoted from *The Theological Works of . . . Henry More* (London, 1708), p. 557.
39. *Defense of the Comedy of Dante* III.vi (Gilbert, p. 390).
40. Cf. Wittreich, *Visionary Poetics*, p. 218: "it is clear that for both Spenser and Milton the poet and prophet are one."

And may not I presume a little further, to show the reasonableness of this word *vates*, and say that the holy David's psalms are a divine poem? . . . For what else is the awakening his musical instruments, the often and free changing of persons, his notable *prosopopeias*, when he maketh you, as it were, see God coming in his majesty, his telling of beasts' joyfulness, and hills leaping, but a heavenly poesy, wherein almost he showeth himself a passionate lover of that unspeakable and everlasting beauty to be seen by the eyes of the mind, only cleared by faith. (p. 99)

And though he denies the first part of the equation, poets as prophets, Smith implicitly accepts the second part, prophets as poets, when he transforms the mirror metaphor into that of a stage:

the prophetical scene or stage upon which all apparitions were made to the prophet, was his imagination; and that there all those things which God would have revealed unto him were acted over *symbolically, as in a masque.* (p. 229)

The equation is also implicit in the introduction to the second book of the *Reason of Church-Government*.[41] There in the context of his role as the Jeremiah-like prophet denouncing error in "the cool element of prose," Milton refers to his preferred role as the poet teaching truth "soaring in the high region of his fancies": the context makes it clear that the articulation of "high-raised fancy," *alta fantasia*, or the icastic imagination, is not an activity inferior to the prophecy that manifests itself as the denunciation of error. In fact, Milton's conception of poetry appears to embrace both the second and third degrees of Smith's hierarchy of prophetic revelation. At first, he seems to be thinking of the third or hagiographical degree. The prophetic works that Milton sees as poetic models are almost exactly the same as those composed by Smith's hagiographi: Milton mentions Job, the Song of Solomon, the Apocalypse, and "those frequent songs throughout the law and prophets" (Yale, I, 816), while Smith mentions "the Book of Psalms, Job, the works of Solomon and others" (p. 237). Both Milton's poetry and hagiographical prophecy involve an element of accommodation not only to the author, but by the author. For Milton, the poet should teach over "the whole book of sanctity and virtu through all the instances of example with such

41. Cf. John F. Huntley, "The Images of Poet & Poetry in Milton's *The Reason of Church-Government*," in *Achievements of the Left Hand*, ed. Michael Leib and John T. Shawcross (Amherst: University of Massachusetts Press, 1974), pp. 83–120. For a slightly different view, see Hill, pp. 105–6.

delight to those especially of soft and delicious temper who will not so much look upon Truth herselfe, unlesse they see her elegantly drest" (Yale, I, 817–18). While, according to Smith, "these Hagiographi, or holy writers, ordinarily expressed themselves in parables and similitudes, which is the proper work of fancy; yet they seem only to have made use of such dress of language to set off their own sense of divine things, which in itself was more naked and simple, the more advantageously, as we commonly see in all other kind of writings" (p. 239). However, when it comes to the source of poetic creation, it is clear that Milton's conception of poetry corresponds to the second or prophetic grade proper. The inspiration of "that eternall Spirit who can enrich with all utterance and knowledge, and sends out his Seraphim with hallow'd fire of his Altar to touch and purify the lips of whom he pleases" (Yale, I, 820–21) has little to do with the inspiration of the hagiographi. It is quite literally the inspiration of Isaiah, the archetype of the visionary prophet:

In the year that King Uzziah died, I saw also the Lord sitting upon a throne, high and lifted up, and his train filled the temple. . . .
Then said I, Woe is me! For I am undone, because I am a man of unclean lips, and I dwell in the midst of a people of unclean lips; for mine eyes have seen the King, the Lord of hosts.
Then flew one of the seraphim unto me, having a live coal in his hand, which he had taken with the tongs from off the altar.
And he laid it upon my mouth and said, lo, this hath touched thy lips; and thine iniquity is taken away, and thy sin purged.
Also I heard the voice of the Lord, saying, Whom shall I send, and who will go for us? Then said I, Here am I; send me. (Isa. 6:1, 5–8)

THE PERSUASION OF FAITH:
THE ICASTIC IMAGINATION AS THE
GROUND OR EVIDENCE OF FAITH

What were Milton's grounds for legitimizing vicarious, imaginary experience and the attractive powers of poetry?
Huntley, "Images of Poet & Poetry," p. 115

But the Grace of song, that maketh for man all things that soothe him, by adding her spell, full often causeth even what is past belief to be indeed believed.
Pindar, quoted in Tasso, *Discourses on the Heroic Poem*, p. 35

The most convincing evidence of Milton's familiarity with the icastic imagination is in *Paradise Lost* itself. Adam's dreams in Book VIII are prophetic.[42] The book is to a large extent concerned with the limits of man's knowledge. The opening of the book deals with the kind of knowledge that it is not proper for man to know—that is, the knowledge of "things remote / From use, obscure and suttle" (VIII.191–92). This knowledge is forbidden chiefly because its possession depends on the operation of speculative reason, reason suborned by wayward fancy. As Adam acknowledges, anxiety over things "too high / To know what passes there" (VIII.172–73) will not molest us

> unless we our selves
> Seek them with wandring thoughts, and notions vain.
> But apt the Mind or Fancie is to roave
> Uncheckt.
>
> (VIII.186–89)

The only knowledge that speculative reason yields is the empty wisdom, the vanity of Ecclesiastes: "fume, / Or emptiness, or fond impertinence" (VIII.194–95). It only leads to Babel-like mental constructs:

> Hereafter, when they come to model Heav'n
> And calculate the Starrs, how they will weild
> The mightie frame, how build, unbuild, contrive
> To save appeerances, how gird the Sphear
> With Centric and Eccentric scribl'd o're,
> Cycle and Epicycle, Orb in Orb.
>
> (VIII.79–84)

In dramatic opposition to this is the kind of knowledge that is available to man. Adam's account of his first awakening is a parable of the true direction of consciousness—not to reduce heaven to the measure of man's comprehension, but to raise comprehension to heaven, not to scan but to admire: "Straight toward Heav'n my wondring Eyes I turnd" (VIII.257). He then enacts the ascent *per viam eminentiae*, a process whose principle he later learns from Raphael: "In contemplation of created things / By steps we may ascend to God" (V.511–12). He reads the book of God's works, coming to the climax with himself—"My self I then perus'd" (VIII.267). This reading leads to a critical response: "But who I was, or where, or from what

---

42. Cf. Hunter, "Prophetic Dreams."

cause, / Knew not" (VIII.270–71). He soon arrives at the limit of unaided reasoning with the deist conception of a maker:

> how came I thus, how here?
> Not of my self; by some great maker then,
> In goodness and in power praeeminent.
> (VIII.277–79)

The weak mightiness of unaided reason, its fallibility, is answered
by the mighty weakness of revelation. The tone of revelation is
poetic:[43] "On a green shadie Bank profuse of flours / Pensive I sate
me down" (VIII.286–87) recalls the poetic activities of the Attendant
Spirit, the agent of revelation in the *Mask*:

> I sate me down to watch upon a bank
> With Ivy canopied, and interwove
> With flaunting Hony-suckle, and began
> Wrapt in a pleasing fit of melancholy
> To meditate upon my rural minstrelsie,
> Till fancy had her fill.
> (VIII.542–47)

These lines are themselves a reversal of the negative operation of
fancy perpetrated by Oberon in *A Midsummer Night's Dream*:

> I know a bank whereon the wild thyme blows,
> Where oxlips and the nodding violet grows,
> Quite over-canopied with luscious woodbine,
> With sweet musk-roses, and with eglantine;
> There sleeps Titania sometime of the night,
> Lulled in these flowers with dances and delight;
> . . . .
> And with the juice of this I'll streak her eyes,
> And make her full of hateful fantasies.
> (II.i.249–54, 257–58)

The actual process of revelation corresponds to the second, Isaiah-
like degree of prophecy as described by Smith. Adam's invocation to

43. The tone is so poetic that, for Keats, Adam's dream became a symbol of the poetic imagination: "The Imagination may be compared to Adam's dream—he awoke
and found it truth. . . . Adam's dream will do here, and seems to be a conviction that
Imagination and its empyreal reflexion is the same as human life and its spiritual
repetition" (letter to Benjamin Bailey, 1817, quoted from *The Letters of John Keats,
1814–21*, ed. Hyder Edward Rollins, 2 vols. (Cambridge, Mass.: Harvard University
Press, 1958), I, 185.

the sensible world, "Tell me, how I may know him, how adore" (VIII.280), is answered by the sensible world only in as much as divine knowledge is reflected to the understanding as sensible images in the fancy:

> When suddenly stood at my Head a dream,
> Whose inward apparition gently mov'd
> My fancy to believe I yet had being,
> And livd: One came, methought, of shape Divine.
> (VIII.292–95)

Revelation is not, as Hunter maintains, to the imagination alone,[44] but through imagination to intuitive reason. The harmony of imagination and reason is manifest in the harmony between what is seen and what is heard: the visual sensations of the dream are informed by the verbal explanation of the shape divine:

> . . . thy mansion wants thee, *Adam*, rise,
> First Man, of Men innumerable ordain'd
> First Father, call'd by thee I come thy Guide
> To the Garden of bliss, thy seat prepar'd.
> (VIII.296–99)

Adam has a complete and accurate understanding of what is happening as it is happening, and the accuracy of what his imagination perceives is confirmed when the dream turns out to be literally true:

> . . . whereat I wak'd, and found
> Before mine Eyes all real, as the dream
> Had lively shadowd.
> (VIII.309–11)

The lively reflection of Eden turns out to be real and what is more important so does that of the shape divine:

> hee who was my Guide
> Up hither, from among the Trees appeer'd
> Presence Divine. Rejoycing, but with aw
> In adoration at his feet I fell
> Submiss: he rear'd me, and Whom thou soughtst I am,
> Said mildely.
> (VIII.312–17)

44. "Prophetic Dreams," p. 283.

The significance of this realization of the dream is complex. As far as prophetic revelation is concerned, the awakening imitates the progression from the second to the mosaic grade. Instead of lively shadows, or sensible images, Adam sees the divine face to face. But what he sees is no different from the simulacrum of the dream: the image turns out to have been icastic in the most prosaic Platonic sense of an exact copy. This may be meant to emphasize both the unfallen state of Adam and the fallen state of the reader: that before the fall Adam never has to see through a glass darkly—he always sees *in speculo lucido*, whereas after the fall the reader can only see what Adam saw through the dark glass of sensible images. Of course, Milton is only representing God as he represents himself in Genesis—but by prefixing a prophetic dream of that representation he underlines a favorite theme of his monism—that invisible and visible realities may be more alike than we suppose. As he points out in the *Christian Doctrine*, "After all, if *God is said to have created man in his own image, after his own likeness,* Gen. i.26, and not only his mind but also his external appearance . . . and if God attributes to himself again and again a human shape and form why should we be afraid of assigning to him something he assigns to himself."[45] This same sentiment is apparent in Raphael's references to Adam—"Inward and outward both, his image faire" (VIII.221)—and to Eve—"In outward also her resembling less / His image who made both" (VIII.543–44). It is also related to the angel's famous conjecture—"though what if Earth / Be but the shaddow of Heav'n, and things therein / Each to other like, more than on earth is thought?" (V.574–76). It all indicates a turning away from the prospect of the imageless reality "imagined" by Smith and the Platonic tradition.

More important than this, however, the realization of the dream is the substantiation of faith. For Adam's dreams not only imitate the process of icastic imagination in both poetry and prophecy but they imitate the process of faith. Like the Lady's song—an act of fancy that effects "Such sober certainty of waking bliss" (*Mask* 262)—the imagination of the good in Adam's dream is a persuasion to believe— "a dream, / Whose inward apparition gently mov'd / My fancy to believe." The garden of bliss created in his imagination is the idealization of nature—compard to Eden "what I saw / Of Earth before scarce pleasant seemd" (VIII.305–6)—common to both poetry and faith. "Only the poet," says Sidney, ". . . doth grow in effect into another nature, in making things either better than Nature bringeth

45. *Christian Doctrine* I.ii (Yale, VI, 135–36).

forth, or, quite anew, forms such as never were in Nature."[46] While "the wonderful power of saving faith," says William Perkins, is that it "makes things which are not in nature, to have in some sort a being and subsistence."[47] On awakening, Adam's belief in things not seen gives way to sight: for just as faith, according to St. Augustine, "is to believe that which you do not yet see, the reward of that faith is to see that which you believe."[48] It is certainly true that imagination raises and erects the mind by submitting the shows of things to the desires of the mind, but when those desires are for the good and are inspired by heaven, then imagination is the instrument of faith.[49] In Adam's dreams, through the operation of icastic or reflective imagination, poetry, prophecy, and faith all come together.

Adam's experience on coming to consciousness, his account of "how human Life began" (VIII.250), reveals a pattern of cognition that recurs throughout Milton's poetry. The pattern describes how the frustrated striving of the "eye" is arrested and superseded by revelation to the "ear." The symbolic antithesis between eye and ear, which we encountered in the *Mask*, is ultimately explained by the traditional Christian antithesis between sight and faith: Milton's reference in the *Reason of Church-Government* to those that live "by sight and visibility, rather then by faith"[50] is an allusion to the *locus classicus* of the tradition in St. Paul: "We walk by faith not by sight" (II. Cor. 5 : 7). By "sight" is meant discursive knowledge of the actual world—as R. G. Collingwood puts it, "the perception by which we apprehend the particular finite things in the world of sense." By faith is meant the intuitive knowledge of the ideal world, and, since St. Augustine placed the Platonic Ideas in the divine mind, it means intuitive knowledge of the divine: the perception "by which we apprehend the infinite and wholly spiritual nature of God."[51] Both "sight" and faith are then perceptions or kinds of seeing: whereas

46. *Apology*, p. 100.
47. *A Clowd of Faithfull Witnesses* (*Workes*, III, 9).
48. Sermon 43, quoted from *Introduction to the Philosophy of Saint Augustine*, ed. John A. Mourant (University Park: Pennsylvania State University Press, 1964), p. 39.
49. Cf. Gianfrancesco Pico, p. 89: "The Light of Faith, . . . making perspicuous the verities of Holy Writ that are impervious to the light of nature, is of greatest service to either type of imagination [that is, the imagination moved by either simple physical desires or more complex mental ones]. It supports and conducts each by the hand, sweeping each up, so to speak, and elevating it above its own nature."
50. Yale, I, 778.
51. *Faith & Reason*, ed. Lionel Rubinoff (Chicago: Quadrangle Books, 1968), p. 110.

"sight" means seeing in the sense of understanding the visible world, faith means seeing in the sense of understanding the invisible; whereas the object or medium of "sight" is nature, the book of God's works, the medium of faith is Scripture, the book of God's words. Because the medium of "sight" is visible, God's works, the physical sense that symbolizes its mode of apprehension is the eye. Thus, in the process of Adam's apprehension of the actual world the activity of the eye is stressed: "my wondring Eyes I turnd, / And gaz'd . . . about me round I saw . . . / My self I then perus'd, and Limb by Limb / Survey'd" (VIII.257–68). Because the medium of faith is invisible, God's words, the physical sense that symbolizes its mode of apprehension is the ear—"Is it the Eye alone that wee live by?" asks Vaughan, "We live also by the eare and by that Inlet wee receive the glad tydings of Salvation."[52] Thus, the kind of knowledge not available to the eye or the "weak mightines of mans reasoning" is revealed, not indirectly through Scripture, but in Adam's case immediately to his mind in God's words. The power of "sight" so evident in Adam's ability to name "What e're I saw" (VIII.273) cannot provide knowledge of the ideal or divine—that is a matter for faith.

Now, the process of faith, as we mentioned above, is persuasion:[53] it is, according to Milton, a "FIRM PERSUASION IMPLANTED IN US BY THE GIFT OF GOD, BY VIRTUE OF WHICH WE BELIEVE, ON THE AUTHORITY OF GOD'S PROMISE, THAT ALL THOSE THINGS WHICH GOD HAS PROMISED US IN CHRIST ARE OURS, AND ESPECIALLY THE GRACE OF ETERNAL LIFE."[54] Just as Adam's dream, a prophetic revelation to his fancy, persuades him to believe, so the realization of that dream, a poetic revelation to the reader's fancy, is meant to persuade us to believe. Like the realization of the desires of Ferdinand and Miranda in The Tempest, it is an assurance of things hoped for. In The Certainty of Faith, Henry More emphasizes the naturalness of this process of persuasion: "Faith and Belief, though they be usually appropriated to Matters of Religion, yet those Words in themselves signifie nothing else but, A Perswasion touching the Truth of a thing arising from some ground or other."[55] The point is, however, precisely this—

52. The World Contemned, quoted from The Works of Henry Vaughan, ed. L. C. Martin, 2d ed. (Oxford: Clarendon Press, 1957), p. 326. Vaughan's poetry is also quoted from this edition. Obviously the symbolism is not now literally valid—we read Scripture with our eyes.
53. See p. 29.
54. Christian Doctrine I.xx (Yale, VI, 471).
55. A Brief Discourse of the True Grounds of the Certainty of Faith in Points of Religion (Works, p. 765).

what ground? The radical difference between natural and supernatural knowledge is the different ground or evidence for persuasion: "sight" or natural knowledge is the evidence of things seen, faith is the evidence of things not seen; the object which "sight" contemplates is the visible world, the object which faith contemplates is the invisible world of Scripture—"For God's mysteries," says Calvin, "pertaining to our salvation are of the sort that cannot in themselves and by their own nature (as is said) be discerned; but we gaze upon them only in his Word."[56] The Word is made available to the understanding through the imagination of the biblical writers to the imagination of the reader.[57] The only way that the gap between visible and invisible realities may be leapt is through imagination, not imagination as pure invention (*phantastike*), but imagination as the visible reflection of the invisible (*eikastike*), the kind of seeing that comes by means of the ear. In this sense imagination provides the ground or evidence of faith. It is because of the incompetence of discursive reason, a form of reason whose proper object is the visible world, to deal with the invisible world that Bacon admits that "in matters of Faith and Religion, we raise our Imagination above our Reason; which is the cause why Religion sought ever access to the mind by similitudes, types, parables, visions, dreams."[58] Bacon's point is acceptable if by "imagination" we understand fancy educated by conscience, and by "reason" we understand discursive knowledge of the sensible world. In the translation of his *De Augmentis* Bacon goes on to provide a classic account of the function of the imagination in the process of faith:

For we see that in matters of faith and religion our imagination raises itself above our reason; not that divine illumination resides in the imagination; its seat being rather in the very citadel of the mind and understanding; but that the divine grace uses the motions of the imagination as an instrument of illumination, just as it uses the motions of the will as an instrument of virtue; which is the reason why religion ever sought access to the mind by similitudes, types, parables, visions, dreams.[59]

56. *Institution of the Christian Religion* [*Basel, 1536*], trans. Ford Lewis Battles (Atlanta: John Knox Press, 1975), p. 59.

57. The writers of the New Testament are inspired in the same way as the prophets of the Old. As Peter explains after the descent of the Holy Spirit at Pentecost, Christian witness means the restoration of the prophetical spirit: "For these are not drunken, as ye suppose. . . . But this is that which was spoken by the prophet Joel. . . . I will pour out in those days of my Spirit; and they shall prophesy" (Acts 2 : 15–18). Cf. Smith, *Of Prophecy* (*Select Discourses*, pp. 278–83).

58. *Advancement of Learning* II (Spedding, III, 382).

59. *De Augmentis* (Translation) V.i. (Spedding, IV, 406).

We have already suggested that the persuasion of faith as expressed
by Perkins is implicitly grounded in an act of imagination: the theory outlined by Bacon explains the experience described by Perkins:

> this saving faith hath this power and property, to take that thing in it selfe
> invisible, and never yet seene, and so lively to represent it to the heart of the
> beleever, and to the eie of the minde, as that after a sort he presently seeth
> and enjoyeth that invisible thing, and rejoyceth in that sight, and enjoying of
> it: and so judgement is not onely convinced, that such a thing shall come to
> passe, though it be yet to come; but the mind (as farre as Gods word hath
> reuealed, and as it is able) conceiues of that thing, as beeing really present to
> the view of it.[60]

Just as Comus's fancy is magical in as much as it precipitates the
transformation of men into beasts, so imagination in the persuasion
of faith is magical in as much as it transforms sinners into Christ-
like men:

> the sight of Christ makes an universal change of us. The camelion takes to it
> the colours of the things which it seeth, and are neere unto it: and the
> beleeving heart takes to it the disposition and minde that was in Christ cru-
> cified, by viewing and beholding of Christ.[61]

Though Perkins never mentions the word "imagination," in Bishop
Reynolds' *Treatise of the Passions and Faculties of the Soule of
Man*, the importance of imagination in the process of persuasion becomes explicit. Dealing with the office of imagination to the will he
points out:

> And therefore, in that great worke of mens *conversion* unto God, he is said
> to *allure* them, and to speak *comfortably* to them, to *beseech*, and to *per-
> swade* them; to set forth Christ to the Soule, as *altogether lovely*, as the
> *fairest of ten thousand*, as the *desire of the Nations*, as the *Riches of
> the World*, that men might be inflamed to love the beauty of Holinesse.
> (pp.19–20)

Reynolds then goes on to make the connection between poetry and
prophecy in the reformation of the will, the persuasion of faith:

> And this was done by those Musicall, Poeticall, and Mythologicall perswa-
> sions; whereby men in their discourses, did as it were paint Vertues and
> Vices; giving unto spirituall things Bodies and Beauties, such as might best

60. *A Clowd of Faithfull Witnesses* (*Workes*, III, 2).
61. *A Commentrie upon the Epistle to the Galatians* (*Workes*, II, 223).

affect the Imagination: Yea, God himselfe hath been pleased to honour this way of setting out higher Notions, in that wee finde some roome in the holy Scripture for Mythologies . . . for Parables, Similitudes and Poeticall numbers and Raptures, whereby heavenly Doctrines are shadowed forth, and doe condiscend unto humane frailties. (p. 21)[62]

Thus, just as God revealed himself through the imagination of the prophets, so the success of that revelation depends upon the reciprocal operation of the imagination in the reader: "There must be a double light. So there must be a Spirit in me, as there is a Spirit in Scripture before I can see any thing."[63] This is the true operation of which Comus's use and appeal to fancy is merely a parody. When the reader's imagination operates icastically, as a glass faithfully reflecting sensible images of the divine, he too becomes a kind of prophet: Scripture, says Milton, "must not be interpreted by the intellect of a particular individual, that is to say, not by his merely human intellect, but with the help of the Holy Spirit, promised to each individual believer. Hence the gift of prophecy, I Cor. xiv."[64] The revelation of Scripture, if it is to effect the persuasion of faith, needs to be answered by the imaginative re-creation of the Word in the mind of the reader: "Having prophecy," says Perkins, "let us prophecy [sic] according to the proportion of faith."[65] In order to know Christ you must picture him—you must

behold him often, not in the wooden crucifex after the Popish manner, but in the preaching of the word, and in the Sacraments, in which thou shalt see *him crucified* before thine eies, Gal. 3.1. Desire not here upon earth to behold him with the bodily eie but looke upon him with the eie of truth and lively faith.[66]

It is the answering operation of "lively faith" or the icastic imagination, the spirit of prophecy in the reader re-creating the revelation of

62. Cf. Sibbes, *The Soules Conflict*, pp. 258–59: "Whilest the soule is joyned with the body, it hath not only a necessary but a *holy* use of *imagination*, and of *sensible* things whereupon our imagination worketh; what is the use of the *Sacraments* but to help our *soules* by our *senses*, and our *faith* by *imagination*; as the soule receives much *hurt* from imagination, so it may have much good thereby." Sibbes, however, goes on to make it clear that imagination only helps confirm an existing faith; it is not instrumental in the creation of faith.

63. Sibbes, quoted in Geoffrey F. Nuttall, *The Holy Spirit in Puritan Faith and Experience*, 2d ed. (Oxford: Blackwell, 1947), p. 23.

64. *Christian Doctrine* I.xxx (Yale, VI, 579–80).

65. *The Art of Prophecying* (*Workes*, II, 649).

66. *A Declaration of the True Manner of Knowing Christ Crucified* (*Workes*, I, 625).

prophecy in Scripture, that is the mark of the indwelling Christ, the interior teacher. The internal manner of Christ's teaching is paralleled by the external: "our Saviour Christ's manner of teaching," says Richard Sibbes, "was by a lively representation to men's fancies, to teach them heavenly truths in an earthly, sensible manner."[67] Now when this re-creation of revelation is directed towards other men, we have the "prophecy" of preaching and, more important, what Milton calls "another persuasive method,"[68] the "prophecy" of poetry. *Paradise Lost* is the response in Milton of the spirit of prophecy to Scripture, but directed towards eliciting a similar response in others—fit though few. It is in this way that Milton hopes by justifying the ways of God to men to justify himself.

The clearest evidence for the icastic imagination as the ground of faith is in the invocations to *Paradise Lost.* The invocation to Book III, for instance, has certain obvious similarities to the apostrophe to *alta fantasia* in *Purgatorio* xvii.13–27. In Dante the images formed in the fancy originate not in the sensible world but in heavenly light:

> O imaginativa . . .
> chi move te, se 'l senso non ti porge?
>   Moveti lume che nel ciel s'informa,
>   per sé o per voler che giù lo scorge.
> De l'empiezza di lei che mutò forma
>   ne l'uccel ch'a cantar più si diletta,
>   ne l'imagine mia apparve l'orma;
> e qui fu la mia mente sì ristretta
>   dentro da sé, che di fuor non venia
>   cosa che fosse allor da lei recetta.

O imagination . . . who moves you if the sense affords you naught? A light moves you which takes form in heaven, of itself, or by a will that downward guides it.
    Of her impious deed who changed her form into the bird that most delights to sing, the impress appeared in my imagination, and at this my mind was so restrained within itself, that from outside came naught that was then received by it.

In Milton the sensible images of poetry cannot originate in the sensible world because for him in his blindness the "Book of knowledg fair" is "expung'd and ras'd" (III.47, 49). At first poetry appears to

67. *The Soules Conflict,* p. 256.
68. *Reason of Church-Government* II, Introduction (Yale, I, 819).

originate in other poetry (III.26–40). Despite his blindness, Milton continues to read poetry; despite the universal blank that is now nature's works, he continues to wander through imagined landscapes: "Yet not the more / Cease I to wander where the Muses haunt" (III.26–27). Reading over the creations of imagination precipitates a reciprocal imaginative response. This is evident implicitly from the metaphoric quality of the description of his reading, and explicitly from:

> Then feed on thoughts, that voluntarie move
> Harmonious numbers; as the wakeful Bird
> Sings darkling, and in shadiest Covert hid
> Tunes her nocturnal Note.
>
>   (III.37–40)

The "as" is both temporal and modal: Milton writes both at the same time and in the same manner as the nightingale sings. As the final lines of the invocation suggest, however, the response of icastic imagination to the Bible and the classics depends upon the operation of the spirit within, the spirit which itself originates in heavenly light. Before Milton can see the sensible images of the divine council, images which owe so much to Sion and blind Maeonides, before he can re-create them, "thou Celestial light" must "Shine inward":

> So much the rather thou Celestial light
> Shine inward, and the mind through all her powers
> Irradiate, there plant eyes, all mist from thence
> Purge and disperse, that I may see and tell
> Of things invisible to mortal sight.
> Now had the Almighty Father from above.
>
>   (III.51–56)

These lines, of course, not only refer to the sensible reflection of the divine, the icastic operation of imagination, but to the heavenly grace of faith: in Scripture "the grace of Holy Spirit is compared to light."[69] Milton is consistent in his use of his own blindness as a metaphor for the transition from "sight" to faith. A good example is Sonnet XIX which turns on the familiar pattern of the frustrated striving of the "eye" being arrested and superseded by revelation

69. *The Enchiridion of Erasmus*, trans. and ed. Raymond Himelick (Bloomington: Indiana University Press, 1963), p. 102. For the association of "Celestial light" with Wisdom and the Son, see pp. 152, 154.

through the "ear." The poem falls into two parts—question and answer.

> When I consider how my light is spent,
> Ere half my days, in this dark world and wide,
> And that one Talent which is death to hide,
> Lodg'd with me useless, though my soul more bent
> To serve therewith my Maker, and present
> My true account, least he returning chide,
> Doth God exact day-labour, light deny'd,
> I fondly ask.
>
> (1–8)

The question simulates the working of "sight," the attempt of discursive reason to unravel unaided the moral consequences of a physical problem. The irony consists in the nature of the problem—the loss of sight itself. Thus, the loss of physical sight is imitated by the failure of figurative "sight"—discursive reasoning. The growing anxiety of the labyrinth of conditional clauses—"When I consider . . . though my soul more bent / To serve . . . least he returning chide"—only yields a foolish question: "Doth God exact day-labour, light deny'd." Consolation, however, is implicit in such failure, for "sight" must give way to faith. And so, the answer is a moment of faith:

> But patience to prevent
> That murmur, soon replies, God doth not need
> Either man's work or his own gifts, who best
> Bear his milde yoak, they serve him best, his State
> Is Kingly. Thousands at his bidding speed
> And post o're Land and Ocean without rest:
> They also serve who only stand and waite.
>
> (8–14)

What the "eye" cannot see, the "ear" hears: foolish discourse is arrested and superseded by words whispered in the ear. But this whispering, the reply of patience personified, is an act of imagination and this act, the imagined voice and the vision of God's glory that its words unfold, operate as a persuasion to believe—hence the conviction of the closing statement: "They also serve who only stand and waite."

So here in the invocation, the meditation on his blindness becomes the occasion of a prayer for faith. "So much the rather thou Celestial light / Shine inward" depends for its full significance on the switch from the literal to the figurative meaning of the loss of sight in the preceding lines. Hence the preparatory emphasis on the sensible world as "the Book of knowledg fair," the "ground" or object of discursive knowledge—a book now closed "And wisdome at one entrance quite shut out" (III.50). The pivotal "So much the rather" indicates the superiority of the new wisdom. The new seeing, the eyes with which Milton hopes to see "things invisible to mortal sight" are planted, "there plant eyes," just as faith itself is "A FIRM PERSUASION IMPLANTED," or fame in *Lycidas* is "no plant that grows in mortal soil" (78). True fame ("eternal life, which will never allow the memory of the good deeds we performed on earth to perish"[70]) is the fruit of faith; it "lives and spreds aloft by those pure eyes, / And perfet witness of all-judging *Jove*" (81–82), that is, true fame lives by "pure-ey'd Faith" (*Mask* 212). Thus, "things invisible to mortal sight" refers to both what the imagination reflects and what faith sees—what is reflected in the imagination is what faith sees. The persuasion that is faith turns on what the imagination reflects: the icastic imagination thus provides the ground or evidence of faith, or as Bacon puts it, grace uses the motions of the imagination as an instrument of illumination.

In the invocation to Book I there is, as we shall see, something similar. Faith, the new seeing, is apprehended through the ear: so in *Lycidas*, after the poet has exhausted foolish discourse, Phoebus "touch'd my trembling ears" (77) and whispers the revelation of faith. The trembling ears may refer to the ass's ears that Midas earns from Apollo by his inability to distinguish the divine art of Apollo from the gross pipe-playing of Pan.[71] Sandys explains the "healthfull doctrine" figured in this story:

there is a twofold harmony or musick; the one of divine providence, and the other of humane reason. To humane judgment (which is as it were to mortall eares) the administration of the World, of the creature, and the more secret decrees of the highest, sound harsh and disconsonant; which ignorance though it be deservedly markt with eares of an asse, yet is it not apparent, or noted for a deforming by the vulgar.[72]

Our ears cease to be ass's and become the symbols of faith once we distinguish Pan from Apollo, once we realize that "That strain I heard was of a higher mood" (87), once we see the revelation planted

70. *Prolusion* VII (Yale, I, 302).
71. See *Metamorphoses* XI.146–93. The more obvious allusion is to Virgil, *Eclogues* VI.3–4: "Cynthius aurem uellit et admonuit."
72. Sandys, p. 524.

in the mind through our ears. In *Paradise Lost*, the seeds of the new
seeing are also planted through the ear. In the prologue to Book IX,
the heavenly muse brings the substance of things seen "nightly to
my Ear" (IX.47). She is able to do this because Milton reads the
Scriptures nightly:

> Yet not the more
> Cease I to wander where the Muses haunt
> Cleer Spring, or shadie Grove, or Sunnie Hill,
> Smit with the love of sacred Song; but chief
> Thee *Sion* and the flowerie Brooks beneath
> That wash thy hallowed feet, and warbling flow,
> Nightly I visit.
>
> (III.26–32)

The heavenly muse is the Holy Spirit,[73] that is, the indwelling spirit
of prophecy in Milton imaginatively re-creating the prophecy of revelation as he nightly broods over the Scriptures[74]—just as the Holy
Spirit itself "that dost prefer / Before all Temples th'upright heart
and pure . . . satst brooding on the vast Abyss / And mad'st it pregnant" (I.17–18, 21–22).

The references to Sion and its flowery brooks explains why in the
invocation to Book I, "*Sion* Hill . . . and *Siloa*'s Brook that flow'd /
Fast by the Oracle of God" (I.10–12) might "Delight" the heavenly
muse more than the revelation to Moses on Oreb and Sinai. Though
the sequence of biblical place-names certainly "summarizes the progressive revelation of God to His people,"[75] Kerrigan's observation
does not really explain either the emphasis on "Delight" or the opposition between the two pairs of place-names. Sion Hill and its
brooks, as their context in Book III amplify, are associated with the
most poetical or imaginative parts of prophecy—the Psalms, Isaiah—
while the word "delight" has obvious associations with poetry and
the imagination—ever since Horace the end of poetry has been "to
teach and delight." "Delight thee more" thus suggests the poetic or
the imaginative as the instrument of illumination. In the *Purgatorio*
(xxviii.80–81), Matilda explains the effect of Sion's songs:

> ma luce rende il salmo *Delectasti*,
> che puote disnebbiar vostro intelletto.

73. For a different view, see Hill, pp. 110–11.
74. Not forgetting the classics, because, as Nohrnberg points out, "all good words
are an analogy for this Word" (p. 105).
75. Kerrigan, p. 126.

But the psalm *Delectasti* gives light that may dispel the cloud from your minds.

This states in microcosm the process described by Milton in Book III. How reading the Scriptures—the delight of Sion hill and its flowery brooks—gives the light that moves imagination which in turn moves faith: "there plant eyes, all mist from thence / Purge and disperse." It also explains what Sidney means by "the eyes of the mind, only cleared by faith" when he talks of the "heavenly poesy" of the Psalmist "wherein almost he showeth himself a passionate lover of that unspeakable and everlasting beauty to be seen by the eyes of the mind, only cleared by faith."[76] Poetry at its highest potential is the ground of faith: the pictures imagined by the Psalmist are conceived as part of the process of faith clearing the eyes of the mind, a process which will finally result in the sight of that unspeakable and everlasting beauty.

The final and most important opposition between Sinai and Sion is of course the opposition between the law and the gospel—or as Vaughan puts it, "thy *Gospel*, and thy *Law* . . . *Faith*, and *Awe*."[77] Sion is associated with the gospel because through Christ we "are come unto Mount Sion" (Hebrews 12:22)—"but now since we to Sion came, / And through thy cloud thy glory see."[78] The gospel delights Milton's muse more because it is poetic, poetic in the very precise sense that the gospel fulfils and replaces the law with faith, and faith requires the activity of the icastic imagination—Siloa's brook is not only the place where Christ gave new sight to the faithful (John 9), but one of Sion's flowery brooks.

76. *Apology*, p. 99.
77. "The Law, and the Gospel" 27–28. Cf. James Hoyle, "'If Sion Hill Delight Thee More': The Muse's Choice in *Paradise Lost*," *ELN* 12 (1974–75): 20–26.
78. "The Law, and the Gospel" 11–12.

PART TWO

Imagination and the Reader in *Paradise Lost*

CHAPTER THREE

Phantastike Poetry and Our Deception

BEHOLD A WONDER:
THE WARNING ALLUSION TO
A MIDSUMMER NIGHT'S DREAM

> To adde unto the delusion of dreames, the phan-
> tasticall objects seeme greater then they are, and
> being beheld in the vaporous state of sleepe, enlarge
> their diameters unto us; whereby it may prove more
> easie to dreame of Gyants then pygmies.
>
> Sir Thomas Browne, "On Dreams"[1]

In *Paradise Lost*, the great example of *phantastike* poetry, the kind of poetry that is both the creation and creator of delusion, of fancy ungoverned by reason, is concentrated in the first two books of the poem, in what might be called the Satanic epic.[2] This is the point of the extended, climactic allusion to *A Midsummer Night's Dream* at the end of Book I, the allusion which is meant to penetrate illusion:

> So thick the aerie crowd
> Swarm'd and were straitn'd; till the Signal giv'n,
> Behold a wonder! they but now who seemd
> In bigness to surpass Earths Giants sons
> Now less then smallest Dwarfs, in narrow room
> Throng numberless, like that Pigmean Race
> Beyond the *Indian* Mount, or Faerie Elves,

---

1. Quoted from Sir Thomas Browne, *Selected Writings*, ed. Sir Geoffrey Keynes (Chicago: University of Chicago Press, 1968), pp. 400–401.

2. Cf. Fowler who, following Dennis H. Burden, *The Logical Epic* (London: Routledge and Kegan Paul, 1967), p. 64, suggests that Satan "sees himself as the hero of the sort of Satanic or pagan epic that the devils show a taste for at ii 549ff" (Carey and Fowler, p. 468n). Cf. also Francis C. Blessington, Paradise Lost *and the Classical Epic* (London: Routledge and Kegan Paul, 1979), pp. 1–18, and Quilligan, pp. 98–108. Guillory, pp. 108–13, interprets this representation of imagination ungoverned by reason as an attack on imagination itself.

Whose midnight Revels, by a Forrest side
Or Fountain some belated Peasant sees,
Or dreams he sees, while over-head the Moon
Sits Arbitress, and neerer to the Earth
Wheels her pale course, they on thir mirth and dance
Intent, with jocond Music charm his ear;
At once with joy and fear his heart rebounds.
                                          (I.775–883)[3]

The passage is full of the sounds of Shakespeare's fairyland: "Beyond the *Indian* Mount" echoes "from an Indian King" (II.i.22); "midnight Revels" "moonlight revels" (II.i.141); "Forrest side / Or Fountain" "in grove or green, / By fountain clear or spangled starlight sheen" (II.i.28–29). In this context the belated peasant who sees or dreams he sees suggests Bottom—"this Athenian swain" who may "think no more of this night's accidents / But as the fierce vexation of a dream" (IV.i.64–68). The perception of the reader is thus associated with that of Bottom—what we see is like what he saw. And because Bottom is an ass, the association is a warning. He is an ass in the very particular sense that his intelligence is only a little higher than the animals'. He is, according to Puck, "The shallowest thickskin of that barren sort" (III.ii.13): "shallowest" refers to his intelligence and "thickskin" to his "brutishness"—"Some . . . suppose creatures are brutish more or lesse, according as to their skin is thicker or thinner."[4] As animals have fancy but no reason, so Bottom's reason is ruled by fancy. Puck's misjoining of "shallow" and "thick" is deliberate: the ill-matching words imitate a state of mind where mimic fancy holds sway. The ascendency of fancy is apparent in Bottom from the outset—from the moment when he and the other mechanicals credit their prospective audience with their own inability to distinguish the imaginary from the real:

Bottom: Let me play the lion too. I will roar that I will do any man's heart good to hear me. I will roar that I will make the Duke say, 'Let him roar again; let him roar again.'
Quince: An you should do it too terribly, you would fright the Duchess and the ladies, that they would shriek; and that were enough to hang us all.
All: That would hang us, every mother's son.
Bottom: I grant you, friends, if you should fright the ladies out of their wits, they would have no more discretion but to hang us. But I will aggravate

3. Cf. Thaler, p. 197.
4. Holland's Pliny, quoted in Harold F. Brooks, ed., *A Midsummer Night's Dream*, The Arden Shakespeare (London: Methuen, 1979), p. 63n.

my voice so that I will roar you as gently as any sucking dove; I will roar you an'twere any nightingale.

(I.ii.64–76)

The point about human imagination, fancy informed by reason, is precisely that it can make the kind of distinctions that the mechanicals find impossible. Comparing the imagination of men to that of beasts, Shakespeare's contemporary, André du Laurens, points out that

Finally, the imagination of man seemeth to enter into some maner of discourse with the understanding. For hauing beheld a painted Lyon, it perceiueth that it is not a thing to be feared, and at the same time ioyning it selfe unto reason, doth confirme and make bolde.[5]

Though it is much less schematic, *A Midsummer Night's Dream* uses the same device of confronting the fancy-sick with the spectacle of their own misjoining imaginations that we encountered in *The Tempest*.[6] As with the other characters who are touched by either Oberon or Puck, with Bottom his "dream" is a projection or outward show of his own state of mind. His retort to Snout is ironic:

Snout: O Bottom, thou art changed. What do I see on thee?
Bottom: What do you see? You see an ass head of your own, do you?

(III.i.105–6)

It is ironic not simply because Bottom actually has an ass's head, but because the projection of one's own fancy that he attributes to Snout applies equally to himself once he begins his "dream." The self-reflective quality of Bottom's "dream" is evident from the ease with which he enters into the "endless absurdities" of the fairy world:

Monsieur Cobweb, good monsieur, get you your weapons in your hand, and kill me a red-hipped humble-bee on the top of a thistle; and, good monsieur, bring me the honey-bag.

(IV.i.10–13)

5. *A Discourse of the Preservation of Sight,* trans. Richard Surphlet (London, 1599), p. 75. Cf. Felicity A. Hughes, "Psychological Allegory in *The Faerie Queene* III.xi–xii," *RES,* n.s. 29 (1978): 134.
6. See pp. 22–25. Cf. Marjorie B. Garber, *Dream in Shakespeare* (New Haven: Yale University Press, 1974), p. 69: "The stage event has become a metaphor. This is . . . the special provenance of the dream world, that it presents the imagined as actual and that it does so by means of transformation."

The same kind of self-reflective projection is even more apparent in Titania's "dream." Her doting on the misjoined shape of Bottom is emblematic of the state of mind that leads her to dote on the "lovely boy" (II.i.22). Whereas Oberon would hold the boy in subordination as a "Knight of his train" (II.i.25), Titania subordinates herself to the boy. And she does so in almost exactly the same way that she does to Bottom:

> But she perforce withholds the lovèd boy,
> Crowns him with flowers, and makes him all her joy
> (II.i.26–27)

> For she his hairy temples then had rounded
> With coronet of fresh and fragrant flowers.
> (IV.i.50–51)

The "lovely boy" is, of course, like Puck, a personification of way-ward fancy. In Spenser's maske of Cupid the identification is explicit—"The first was *Fancy*, like a louely boy" (*FQ* III.xii.7)[7]—while in Marlowe's *Edward II* the lovely boy appears at the climax of Gaveston's fantastic reverie: "I must have wanton Poets . . . Italian maskes . . . Sometime a lovelie boye in *Dians* shape" (I.i.50–73).[8] In the play itself, the boy is conceived by imitation of a metaphor, an act of imagination: his mother

> sat with me on Neptune's yellow sands,
> Marking th'embarked traders on the flood;
> When we have laughed to see the sails conceive
> And grow big-bellied with the wanton wind;
> Which she, with pretty and with swimming gait
> Following (her womb then rich with my young squire),
> Would imitate, and sail upon the land
> To fetch me trifles.
> (II.i.126–33)

7. Spenser is quoted from *The Poetical Works of Edmund Spenser*, ed. Ernest de Selincourt and J. C. Smith, 3 vols. (1909–10; rpt. Oxford: Clarendon Press, 1960–61). For the association of the lovely boy with Fancy and Cupid, see Hughes, "Psychological Allegory," p. 141: "Precedents for the personification of 'fancy' abound in English love poetry from Wyatt onwards, where it often appears in the role given by Italian poets to Amor."

8. Marlowe is quoted from *The Complete Works of Christopher Marlowe*, ed. Fredson Bowers, 2 vols. (Cambridge: Cambridge University Press, 1973).

He is the issue of airy nothingness, the wanton wind. Once Titania, as a result of Oberon's taunts over her infatuation with Bottom, gives up the changeling child, then she is released from the delusions of fancy, "This hateful imperfection of her eyes" (IV.i.62).[9]

Unlike Titania and the others whose fancy is sick, Bottom is not cured, but merely returns to his natural, asinine state: "Now, when thou wak'st, with thine own fool's eyes peep" (IV.i.83). In *Paradise Lost*, Bottom's asslike state, his delusion by fancy, is the outward show of the reader's own mind. For the wondrous sights we see or dream we see are the creations of unrestrained fancy: just as Titania's "lovely boy" is "stolen from an Indian King" so the demons appear "like that Pigmean Race" imagined "Beyond the *Indian* Mount" (I.780–81). The sights we see with all the accuracy of Bottom's perception refer not only to the immediate metamorphosis of the devils, but to the whole demonic phantasmagoria of Book I. What the allusion to Bottom tells us—if our ears be true enough to hear the echoes—is that we have been deluded by our own fancy, just as Bottom is made the dupe of Puck's pranks.

The opening books of *Paradise Lost* are frequently compared to an antimasque: "we should also realize," says Northrop Frye, for instance, "the extent to which the dramatic form of the Jonsonian masque has informed these first three books, a dark and sinister antimasque being followed by a splendid vision of ordered glory."[10] But they comprise an antimasque in a sense much more specific than "dark and sinister." The "antic masque" is characterized by the misshaping of unrestrained fancy symbolized by the monstrous dancing forms of figures like Comus's followers. Felicity Hughes defines "antic" as "a grotesque typical of Mannerist art which was *capriccioso*—wilful product of the liberated fantasy or, as Florio translated it, 'toyish, humorous, fantasticall, conceited, wavering in minde.'"[11] In Jonson's *Vision of Delight*, for example, the association of antimasque and "liberated" fancy is explicit. After an antimasque in which there is "*a she-monster delivered of six burratines that dance with six pantaloons*" (17–18)[12] and before a "*second antimasque of*

---

9. The significance for Milton of the quarrel between Oberon and Titania is not quite as "inexplicable" as Guillory, p. 141, suggests.

10. *The Return of Eden* (Toronto: University of Toronto Press, 1965), p. 18. Cf. John J. Demaray, *Milton's Theatrical Epic* (Cambridge: Harvard University Press, 1980), esp. pp. 57–72.

11. "Psychological Allegory," p. 135.

12. *The Vision of Delight* is quoted from *Ben Jonson: The Complete Masques*, ed. Stephen Orgel, The Yale Ben Jonson (New Haven: Yale University Press, 1969).

phantasms" (107) Fant'sy himself offers *"a verbal antimasque."*[13] In the jingling sound of rhyming couplets, Fant'sy's swift diversity of associations accelerates into a riot of ill-matching words and mis-joining shapes:

> And Fant'sy, I tell you, has dreams that have wings,
> And dreams that have honey, and dreams that have stings;
> Dreams of the maker and dreams of the teller,
> Dreams of the kitchen and dreams of the cellar;
> Some that are tall, and some that are dwarfs,
> Some that are haltered, and some that wear scarfs;
> Some that are proper and signify o'thing,
> And some another, and some that are nothing.
> For say the French farthingale and the French hood
> Were here to dispute; must it be understood
> A feather, for a wisp, were a fit moderator?
> Your ostrich, believe it, 's no faithful translator
> Of perfect Utopian; and then it were an odd piece
> To see the conclusion peep forth at a codpiece.
>   The politic pudding hath still his two ends,
> Though the bellows and the bagpipe were nev'r so good
>   friends;
> And who can report what offence it would be
> For the squirrel to see a dog climb a tree?
>
>   (53–70)

Despite its nonsensical appearance, the speech does have a kind of coherence; but that coherence resolves itself into a debate between two of the masters of unrestrained fancy, the passions of gluttony and lechery:[14] the pudding, for instance, is politic because it can join either side of the debate—as a sausage or a phallus. After the second antimasque, referring both to it and to his own speech, Fant'sy checks himself and prepares the way for the masque's revelation:

> Why, this you will say was fantastical now,
> As the cock and the bull, the whale and the cow;
>   But vanish away; I have change to present you,
> And such as I hope will more truly content you.
>   Behold the gold-haired Hour descending here,
> That keeps the gate of heaven and turns the year,

13. Orgel, p. 486.
14. See ibid., pp. 486–87.

> Already with her sight how she doth cheer,
> And make another face of things appear.
> (109–16)

A confusion similar to that of Fant'sy's verbal antimasque is apparent in Bottom's language—with the obvious difference, though, that Fant'sy's confusion has all the deliberateness of a theatrical performance, whereas Bottom's, as we have seen, is genuine:

> I have had a most rare vision. I have had a dream, past the wit of man to say what dream it was. Man is but an ass if he go about to expound this dream. Methought I was—there is no man can tell what. Methought I was, and methought I had—But man is but a patched fool if he will offer to say what methought I had. The eye of man hath not heard, the ear of man hath not seen, man's hand is not able to taste, his tongue to conceive, nor his heart to report what my dream was. (IV.i.203–11)

Bottom's confusion is not simply a matter of overexcitement or a "burlesque of Scripture."[15] It suggests unrestrained fancy's parody of true revelation—for Bottom's muddle is a distorted allusion to St. Paul's account of the process of revelation:

> But as it is written, Eye hath not seen, nor ear heard, neither have entered into the heart of man, the things which God hath prepared for them that love him.
> But God hath revealed them unto us by his Spirit: for the Spirit searcheth all things, yea, the deep things of God.
> (I Cor. 2:9–10)

What imagination at its highest potential yields as "the deep things of God," imagination at its lowest yields as "'Bottom's Dream' because it hath no bottom" (IV.i.214–15). What we see in the Satanic poem of *Paradise Lost* is unrestrained fancy's parody of revelation. If we take it at face value and regard it as a Satanic epic—if, like the readers of an earlier age, we see Milton's poem as a "work of disillusion" and believe that "the embers of his projected heroic poem, the poem of hope and achievement, must be sought in the prose works, and (eminently of course) in the verse of the early books of *Paradise Lost* and in the character of Satan"[16]—then we are no better than

15. Brooks, p. 99n.
16. Willey, p. 203.

Bottom the ass—innocent enough but ruled by fancy. If, however, we shed our ass's ears and become aware of our susceptibility to fancy, then just as the demonic heroes are transformed into dwarves, so the Satanic epic suddenly appears as it actually is—an "antic masque."

SATAN'S UNSETTLED FANCY:
HOW THE READER LOSES HIS WAY

> O pittie and shame, that they who to live well
> Enterd so faire, should turn aside to tread
> Paths indirect, or in the mid way faint.
> *Paradise Lost* XI.629–31

Once we accept that the allusion to *A Midsummer Night's Dream* is a warning that we have been beguiled, then it becomes imperative to find out how exactly we allowed it to happen.

Just as the Lady's journey in the *Mask* begins in daylight, so the action of *Paradise Lost* opens where what seems and what is coincide. The poem begins where the Bible ends—with revelation. The Devil appears stripped of disguise as the great dragon of the Apocalypse. When the narrator asks the Holy Spirit to unravel the mystery of the Fall and say who first seduced mankind to "that foul revolt" (I.28–33), the plain answer is a restatement of Revelation 12:9:

> Th'infernal Serpent; he it was, whose guile
> Stird up with Envy and Revenge, deceiv'd
> The Mother of Mankind, what time his Pride
> Had cast him out from Heav'n, with all his Host
> of Rebel Angels.
> (I.34–38)

And the great dragon was cast out, that old serpent, called the Devil and Satan, who deceiveth the whole world: he was cast out into the earth, and his angels were cast out with him.

The relationship between the Holy Spirit's answer and its biblical source is one of mutual illumination. Not only is Milton's image informed by the Word, but the biblical image is informed by Milton's words. The biblical image is given a doctrinal context by a series of abstract words which explain why the Devil deceived (envy and revenge), how he deceived (guile), and why he himself fell (pride). At the same time, the Miltonic image is given the symbolic value of its biblical source. The importance of that source is that it symbolizes the separation and consolidation of evil: all the various archetypes of evil scattered throughout the Bible—Dragon, Serpent, Devil, Satan—are drawn together in the image and identified. In the language of the *Areopagitica*, no longer is the world a field in which good and evil grow up together almost inseparably, involved and interwoven in so many cunning resemblances as hardly to be discerned,[17] but here the demonic is made manifest, and by the power of the Word it is as though we see through the eyes of God: "for Heav'n hides nothing from thy view" (I.27):

> For the word of God is quick, and powerful . . . and is a discerner of the thoughts and intents of the heart.
> Neither is there any creature that is not manifest in his sight: but all things are naked and opened unto the eyes of him with whom we have to do.
>
> (Hebrews 4 : 12–13)

What we see is the consolidation of evil hoped for by the Elder Brother in the *Mask*—

> But evil on it self shall back recoyl,
> And mix no more with goodness, when at last
> Gather'd like scum, and setl'd to it self
> It shall be in eternal restless change
> Self-fed, and self-consum'd
>
> (592–96)

—and emphasized in the opening picture of Hell:

> but torture without end
> Still urges, and a fiery Deluge, fed
> With ever-burning Sulphur unconsum'd.
>
> (I.67–69)

It is the consolidation of evil foreseen by God the Father when he refers to Satan's "desparate reveng, that shall redound / Upon his own rebellious head" (III.85–86). Most important, it is the consolidation of evil the return to which is foreseen by the narrator at the point where evil has actually begun to "deconsolidate" or uncoil itself in the poem. The beginning of "deconsolidation" is symbolized by the physical movements of the reawakening monster—his

17. See Yale, II, 514.

thoughts and eyes (I.54–58), his bold words (I.84), his head uplift above the wave (I.193), and finally his whole body (I.221–22). These movements, however, as the narrator explains, are only possible because the will

> And high permission of all-ruling Heaven
> Left him at large to his own dark designs,
> That with reiterated crimes he might
> Heap on himself damnation, while he sought
> Evil to others, and enrag'd might see
> How all his malice serv'd but to bring forth
> Infinite goodness, grace and mercy shewn
> On Man by him seduc't, but on himself
> Treble confusion, wrath and vengeance pour'd.
>   (I.212–20)

Far from bearing the vindictiveness that an exclusively literal reading might suggest, in its fullest sense the passage is an act of faith like the Elder Brother's—that evil will finally recoil upon itself, and that what seems and what is will finally come together.

The Lady loses her way when night overtakes her and her brothers. In this context, night signifies a state in which what seems and what is no longer coincide—a state in which one's eyes are of little use, and which is registered by the phrase "night-founder'd" (*Mask* 483). This is the state which the reader in *Paradise Lost* comes to experience like "The Pilot of some small night-founder'd Skiff" (I.204) who mistakes Leviathan for the security of an island. In the *Mask*, oncoming night—"the gray-hooded Eev'n / Like a sad Votarist in Palmers weed" (187–88)—is represented in an image which is not only fanciful in itself but recalls the first, deceptive appearance at evening of Archimago, the chief manipulator of unrestrained fancy in *The Faerie Queene*:

> An aged Sire, in long blacke weedes yclad,
> His feete all bare, his beard all hoarie gray,
> . . . .
> Sober he seemde, and very sagely sad.
>   (I.i.29)[18]

And just as Archimago, once night falls, abuses the fantasy of Redcross with false shows, so "theevish night" precipitates a thousand

18. Cf. A. Burnett, "Milton's 'Paradise Regained,' I.314–19," *N&Q* 25 (1978): 509–10. For the connection between Archimago and Satan, see Quilligan, pp. 106–7.

fantasies that throng the Lady's memory with "calling shapes, and beckning shadows dire, / And airy tongues that syllable mens names" (206–7). The discontinuity between appearance and substance signified by night is then associated with the "liberation" of fancy. But the false shows of fancy, fancy's power to counterfeit, are not so much the consequence as the cause of this symbolic night. There is the suspicion that the false appearance of night as evening, of "envious darknes" (193) as "a sad Votarist," is the particular act of fancy that dulls the foresight of the Lady and her brothers and lulls them into separating at such a dangerous time: "they left me then, when the gray-hooded Eev'n . . . Rose from the hindmost wheels of *Phoebus* wain."

Redcross loses his way by a similar act of uninformed imagination. First, the rich diversity of lofty trees clad "with sommers pride" shuts out "heauens light" (I.i.7) and lulls the sense of Redcross and his companions—"Led with delight, they thus beguile the way" (I.i.10). The phrase "beguile the way" is double-edged; it means quite innocently that they divert their attention from the journey, imaginatively cataloguing the human associations of the trees, but it also means that, lost in the pleasures of imagination, they cheat themselves of the true path. Second, when Redcross has to choose some path, trusting to appearances, the broadest is imagined to be the safest: "That path they take, that beaten seemd most bare, / And like to lead the labyrinth about" (I.i.11). The path is of course the primrose path which Comus urges the Lady to take when his fancy begets on her youthful thoughts the image of "*April* buds in Primrose-season" (670).

Redcross's wandering into Error and his separation from Una, his parting from truth, are the same fall seen from different perspectives: Redcross wandering into Error begins the first canto's paradigm of the action of Book I, while his parting from truth begins the action of the Book itself.[19] His separation from Una at first suggests that he has been the victim of Comus's magic dust, "delusions the virtuous reason could not counter," hypocrisy being "a vice in the creature seen, not in the judgement behind the seeing eye—which is faulty but not guilty":[20] he is confronted by a sight over which he has no control and Archimago is referred to as "Hypocrisie" (epigraph Canto I). But Redcross's ambiguous reaction to this sight, the

19. Cf. Alastair Fowler, *Spenser and the Numbers of Time* (London: Routledge and Kegan Paul, 1964), p. 7: "The opening battle against Error and her horribly prolific spawn serves as a brief emblematic statement of the subject of Book I."

20. Tuve, *Images & Themes*, p. 128. See pp. 11–12.

image of Una and a squire knit in "*Venus* shamefull chaine" (I.ii.4),
suggests that he might not have seen it had it not been a projection
of his own secretly imagined desires—desires engendered by the earlier assault on his fancy: "which when he saw, he burnt with gealous
fire" (I.ii.5). "Gealous" means "vehement" and "furious"—without
mind, passionate—but it also, almost inescapably, means "covetous"
or "troubled by the belief that what one desires oneself is being given
to another."[21] His anger is followed by "bitter anguish of his guiltie
sight" (I.ii.6). Here the possessive "his" refers to both "guiltie" and
"sight": it means the guilty sight he saw, but also that the guilt of the
sight was his.

In *Paradise Lost*, the reader, like the Lady and Redcross before
him, loses his way through the uninformed operation of his own
imaginative powers—through the picture that the fancy of the demonic speeches and the demonic mind as it is reflected in the narrator's descriptions begets on our youthful thoughts.

The role of the narrator, Milton's "epic voice," in the reader's wandering is critical. The views of this role put forward by Anne Davidson
Ferry and Stanley Fish,[22] however, both require some qualification.
As postlapsarian readers, we certainly "stand in need of a guide to
correct our reading,"[23] and it is clear that some of the narrator's com-
ments do this, but the problem remains that the narrator's descriptions of what is seen have the power to mislead every bit as much as
they do to guide. The narrator's apparent admiration for Satan, for
instance—the grudging admiration with which he describes the
Devil's metamorphosis from sea-monster to heroic figure, whose
"form has yet not lost / All her Original brightness" (I.591–92), or
that of his followers from locusts to "Godlike shapes and forms / Ex-
celling human" (I.358–59)—cannot be dismissed in a parenthesis as
giving the Devil his due.[24] And if, as Fish ultimately accepts, the re-
liability of the narrator as a guide is "largely negative and hardly
comforting, extending to what Satan is not, to what the human mind
cannot do, to what cannot be trusted," then it is difficult to see how
the poem can be considered, even on "one level at least," as "a Platonic dialogue, with the epic voice taking the role of Socrates, and
the reader in the position of a Phaedrus or a Cratylus."[25]

21. Cf. *OED*, 1 and 4.
22. *Milton's Epic Voice* (Cambridge: Harvard University Press, 1963); and *Surprised by Sin.*
23. Ferry, p. 47.
24. Fish, *Surprised by Sin*, p. 49.
25. Ibid., pp. 70, 49.

Besides the internal evidence, the provision of such a foolproof guide as Ferry's narrator would scarcely conform with Milton's impassioned views on the superiority of poetry over prose discourse as a mode of teaching. Spenser is a better teacher than Scotus or Aquinas (*Paradise Lost* than the *Christian Doctrine*) because poetry unlike prose enables the reader to know good by evil, to confirm truth by scanning error: "a poem," as Ferry herself puts it, "'acts out' its meaning as an abstract argument does not."[26] Poetry is able to place the reader in a situation which simulates the field of this world where "the knowledge of good is so involv'd and interwoven with the knowledge of evill, and in so many cunning resemblances hardly to be discern'd"[27] that the reader is forced into the exercise of virtue: he is forced to reason, to choose, to read actively—otherwise he finds himself in the Devil's party without knowing it. Just as Guyon, according to Milton, is led through the Cave of Mammon and the Bower of Bliss with only his palmer "that he might see and know, and yet abstain,"[28] so is the reader led through Hell with only his own reason: not unaided reason, the weak mightiness of man's reasoning, but reason informed by the revelation of the Word, the mighty weakness of Christ's words—reason, as we shall see,[29] consistently illuminated by echoes of the Word throughout the text and only occasionally prompted by the overt checks of the narrator. Milton implies that this is how the Bible itself must be read because it

oftimes relates blasphemy not nicely, it describes the carnall sense of wicked men not unelegantly, it brings in holiest men passionately murmuring against providence through all the arguments of *Epicurus*: in other great disputes it answers dubiously and darkly to the common reader.[30]

The kind of narrator imagined by Ferry in the poem suggests an analogy with the kind of divine providence that would not suffer Adam to transgress in the world: "foolish tongues! when God gave him reason, he gave him reason to choose, for reason is but choosing; he had

26. Ferry, p. 9.
27. *Areopagitica* (Yale, II, 514).
28. For Milton's mistake—the palmer does not enter the Cave of Mammon—see Yale, II, 516n; Ernest Sirluck, "Milton Revises *The Faerie Queene*," *MP* 48 (1950): 90–96; Bloom, *Map of Misreading*, pp. 127–29; Guillory, pp. 130–39; and Quilligan, pp. 50–52.
29. See esp. pp. 122–27.
30. *Areopagitica* (Yale, II, 517). As far as reading the Bible itself is concerned, reason informed by revelation means ensuring that "interpretation is in agreement with faith" (*Christian Doctrine* I.xx [Yale, VI, 582]). For more on the "analogy of faith," see Yale, VI, 582n.

bin else a meer Artificiall *Adam*, such an *Adam* as he is in the motions."[31] The source of the confusion is the failure of Fish and Ferry
to emphasize the distinction between the narrator's overt checks and
the subtleties of his descriptions. For in as much as the narrator's descriptions simulate the fallen world's chaos of well-seeming forms,
his relation to the reader sometimes seems as much like that of
Comus or Archimago as any true guide.[32]

The uncoiling of evil, first registered by the tentative, awakening
movements of the Devil, and then by the mustering of the Demonic
host and the construction of Pandemonium, coincides with the engendering of illusions in the reader's imagination—illusions which
precipitate the disintegration of the opening picture of consolidated
evil. As the process begins to accelerate and the images multiply,
Satan appears for one significant moment as a magician: his spear
which in an image of considerable optical confusion[33] has already
been associated with a wand (I.294) is now likened to "the potent
Rod / Of *Amrams* Son" (I.338–39). The rod is not, however, Moses'
but Circe's and Comus's. For, as Sandys explains, the Circean wand is
the demonic counterfeit of Moses' rod: it is that "Wherein the devill
perhaps aped that rod of *Moses* wherewith hee performed such wonders."[34] As the Circean wand apes Moses' rod, so the narrator's simile
presents the Devil as Moses—the epic voice is hardly checking our
reading at this point. The importance of this particular act of uninformed fancy, the misjoining of the Devil and Moses, is apparent
in the significance of the "pitchy cloud / Of *Locusts*" (I.340–41)
that the Circean wand conjures up. The allusion is not just to the
locusts of Exodus, but to their reappearance as the devils of Revelation (9:3):[35]

And there came out of the smoke locusts upon the earth: and unto them was
given power, as the scorpions of the earth have power.

As Milton makes clear in *Of Reformation*, this is a major image of
the "deconsolidation" or reinvolvement of evil. Referring to those

31. *Areopagitica* (Yale, II, 527).
32. Cf. Boyd M. Berry, "Melodramatic Faking in the Narrator's Voice, *Paradise Lost*," *MiltonQ* 10 (1976): 1–5.
33. See Fish, *Surprised by Sin*, pp. 22–27.
34. Sandys, p. 652. For more on magical Moses' rods, see Thomas, pp. 235–36.
35. Cf. J. B. Broadbent, *Some Graver Subject* (London: Chatto and Windus, 1960), p. 87.

who would deck out the divine intercourse between God and the soul in the "deformed, and fantastick dresses" of liturgy, he prays:

> O let them not bring about their damned *designes* that stand now at the entrance of the bottomlesse pit expecting the Watch-word to open and let out those dreadfull *Locusts* and *Scorpions*, to *re-involve* us in that pitchy *Cloud* of infernall darknes, where we shall never more see the *Sunne* of thy *Truth* againe.[36]

The initial sequence of this reinvolvement begins with the almost imperceptible shift of tense into an immediate Hell[37]—

> But his doom
> Reserv'd him to more wrath; for now the thought
> Both of lost happiness and lasting pain
> Torments him
>
> (I.53–56)

—and concludes with the equally unobtrusive metamorphosis of the beast into a hero. The sequence is paradoxical: for the Devil's tentative movements and his reaction to the world in which he finds himself suggest an awakening or coming to consciousness— "as if emerging from a drug"[38]—while the "sleepy language" (*Tmp.* II.i.205) of his speeches and those of Beelzebub—"full of paradoxical expressions—antithesis, antimetabole, oxymoron,"[39] asinine self-contradictions like "endanger'd Heav'ns perpetual King" (I.131)— and the illogical and unremarked transitions, the adamantine chains that disappear and weapons that appear from nowhere, all give events the quality of a dream. The paradox is resolved as soon as we realize that the narrator is not only reporting what the devils say, he is imagining what they see—"round he throws his baleful eyes / That witness'd huge affliction . . . At once as far as Angels kenn he views / The dismal situation" (I.56–57, 59–60)—and that the devils' waking world is a dream world, a world where reason is fuled by fancy, where shapes are misjoined and words ill-matched.

Not only is the scene presented from the devils' point of view,[40] but when we enter hell we actually enter the Devil's mind. The tra-

---

36. Yale, I, 521, 614.
37. See Broadbent, *Some Graver Subject*, p. 69.
38. William Empson, *Milton's God*, rev. ed. (London: Chatto and Windus, 1965), p. 43.
39. Broadbent, *Some Graver Subject*, p. 71.
40. Cf. Empson, p. 43.

ditional typological identification of the mouth of hell with the mouth of the demonic dragon is captured in Spenser: "for his deepe deuouring iawes / Wide gaped, like the griesly mouth of hell" (*FQ* I.xi.12). Milton's leviathan whose "Eyes / That sparkling blaz'd" (I.193–94) is of course very much Spenser's dragon whose "blazing eyes . . . sparkled liuing fyre" (*FQ* I.xi.14), and the Spenserian dragon's "Three ranckes of yron teeth" (*FQ* I.xi.13) is perhaps remembered in hell-gate's "thrice threefold . . . three folds were Brass, / Three Iron, three of Adamantine Rock" (II.645–46). The geography of hell is created by fancy in the image of the Devil's own desire. In particular, the volcanic landscape is a symbolic manifestation of Satan's desire for glory, his own rebellious ambition: "To reign is worth ambition though in Hell" (I.262). In Sandys' Ovid, the giant Typhon, "the type of Ambition; ascending as all other vices, from hell,"[41] is pinned down by the weight of Sicily:

> *Ausonian Pelorus* his right hand
> Downe waighs . . .
> And *Aetna's* bases charge his horrid head:
> Where, lying on his back, his jawes expire
> Thick clouds of dust, and vomit flakes of fire.
> Oft times he struggles with his load below.
> (*Met.* V. 348–54)

Since Typhon becomes Aetna, and Typhon, in as much as he is the type of ambition, is Satan—"in bulk as huge / As . . . *Typhon*" (I.196–99)—then hell's volcanic landscape is an image of Satan's ambitious mind struggling to break free:

> And such appear'd in hue, as when the force
> Of subterranean wind transports a Hill
> Torn from *Pelorus*, or the shatter'd side
> Of thundring *Aetna*, whose combustible
> And fewel'd entrals thence conceiving Fire.
> (I.230–34)[42]

41. Sandys, p. 250.
42. For the association of Typhoean Aetna with the apocalyptic dragon, cf. Spenser:

> For griefe thereof, and diuelish despight,
> From his infernall fournace forth he threw
> Huge flames, that dimmed all the heauens light,
> Enrold in duskish smoke and brimstone blew;
> As burning *Aetna* from his boyling stew
> Doth belch out flames, and rockes in peeces broke,
> And ragged ribs of mountaines molten new,

Thus when Beelzebub talks of being "swallow'd up" in hell (I.142) he is unconsciously making the point that the devils are devoured by their own appetite. As the opening image of consolidated evil makes clear, the pain of hell is self-inflicted—it is the Devil's "Pride" that "cast him out from Heav'n" (I.36–37). What torments him is the burden of his own insatiable desire: "now the thought . . . Torments him" and

> torture without end
> Still urges, and a fiery Deluge, fed
> With ever-burning Sulphur unconsum'd.
> (I.67–69)

It is this torture of desire blowing on the coals of fancy that has transformed heaven into hell: even when confronted by Eve whose "look summs all Delight" (IX.454) still

> the hot Hell that alwayes in him burnes,
> Though in mid Heav'n, soon ended his delight,
> And tortures him now more, the more he sees.
> (IX.467–69)

The same metamorphosis of heaven into hell is experienced by the fancy-sick Hermia:

> Lysander and myself will fly this place.
> Before the time I did Lysander see,
> Seemed Athens as a paradise to me.
> O, then, what graces in my love do dwell
> That he hath turned a heaven unto a hell.
> (*MND* I.i.203–7)

The Devil, however, cannot "fly this place," because, as he later admits once the illusions of the Satanic poem have been penetrated, "Which way I flie is Hell; my self am Hell" (IV.75). This is the irony

---

Enwrapt in coleblacke clouds and filthy smoke,
That all the land with stench, and heauen with horror choke.
(*FQ* I.xi.44)

And with the Devil, cf. Milton: "tandem suspiria rupit / Tartareos ignes & luridum olentia sulphur. / Qualia Trinacriâ trux ab Jove clausus in Ætna / Efflat tabifico monstrosus ab ore Tiphoeus" ("In Quintum Novembris" 34–37; "at last he bursts forth sighs that reek of Tartarean fires and of lurid sulphur, sighs such as the grim creature, penned by Jove within Trinacrian Ætna, monstrous Typhoeus, breathes forth from his corruption-working mouth").

of Satan's great affirmation of the shaping power of the human mind. He claims to be

> One who brings
> A mind not to be chang'd by Place or Time.
> The mind is its own place, and in it self
> Can make a Heav'n of Hell, a Hell of Heav'n.
> (I.252–55)

The mind is indeed its own place and precisely because the Devil fails to recognize it as such—that the place in which he finds himself is the creation of his own mind, that hell is the work of his own vain fantasy, then it is vain fantasy to think he can make a heaven out of it. In a much less serious context, Helena suffers from the same delusion; but whereas Satan's delusion is expressed in language that spreads the contagion of his fancy, Helena's delusion is expressed in language that mocks itself and makes the absurdity of her fancy immediately manifest:

> I'll follow thee, and make a heaven of hell,
> To die upon the hand I love so well.
> (II.i.243–44)

The Devil claims for himself a "fixt mind" (I.97) in the sense that it is not to be distracted from its purpose by circumstance. The phrase is ironic; for his mind, unlike the "fixed mind" in "Il Penseroso," is only fixed in as much as it lacks the rational self-awareness that constitutes the consciousness or conscience and is consequently especially vulnerable to its own fantasies, "vain deluding joyes . . . fancies fond with gaudy shapes" ("Il Penseroso" 1–10).

It is clear then that hell is self-reflective: it is the fantastic creation of the Devil's own solipsistic mind. This is the point of the allusion to Galileo (I.287–91). What the Tuscan artist sees through his optic glass is no less imaginary than the heroic metamorphosis of the Devil that we witness at exactly the same moment through the glass of Satan's mind. For, as we discover later, the geography of the Moon is only "imagind" (V.263). It is in fact a geography created like any other artist's image in the likeness of the artist's mind. The "Rivers or Mountains" Galileo describes are imaginary projections of his own environment—the river valley of the Arno, "*Valdarno*," and the mountain "top of Fesole." The main thrust of the allusion is neither to indulge "fond memories"[43] nor to provide an analogue for

43. Carey and Fowler, p. 479n.

Milton's "transumptive vision,"[44] but to emphasize a tendency even in the best of minds to deceive itself—to mistake one's own fancy for objective reality.[45] And this is how the reader loses his way. The decisive moment is the narrator's almost imperceptible entrance into hell. There the image of consolidated evil begins to disintegrate and there words bear only a "Semblance of worth, not substance" (I.529). As Redcross "loses his way" once he fails to recognize Duessa as a counterfeit imitation sprung from his own fantasy, so the reader in *Paradise Lost* loses his way once he fails to recognize hell as a fantasy sprung from the human mind—a fantasy that starts as Satan's but soon becomes his own. The path to error is marked by an increasing tendency to read metaphors literally, to judge by appearances. For example, Satan's literal understanding of the monarchal metaphor of divinity leads him to declare that God deliberately led him and his followers into temptation and destruction:

> But He who reigns
> Monarch in Heav'n, till then as one secure
> Sat on His Throne, upheld by old repute,
> Consent or custome, and His Regal State,
> Put forth at full, but still his strength conceal'd,
> Which tempted our attempt, and wrought our fall.
>
> (I.637–42)

This fantasy becomes the reader's when by an equally literal understanding of the narrator's promise that evil (whose existence is the necessary corollary of free will) will finally recoil upon itself leads him to declare "that God's actions towards Satan were intended to lead him into greater evil."[46] What deludes both Redcross and the reader in *Paradise Lost* is what we have called uninformed fancy and what St. Augustine calls the "carnal" or sense-bound imagination:[47] while Redcross perceives the world according to appearances, the errant reader apprehends the word according to the letter; while

44. Bloom, *Map of Misreading*, p. 133. Guillory recognizes that "'imagin'd lands' hint at the distortion of the imagination itself" (p. 160), but fails to note that it invalidates Bloom's assertion that Galileo's "accurate" perception of what no one else has seen is intended to act as an image of the way Milton transumes his precursors.

45. For a different but related view of Milton's "curiously deprecatory" attitude to Galileo, see Frye, *Return of Eden*, pp. 57–59.

46. Empson, p. 42.

47. Cf. *Christian Doctrine* III.v (Dods, IX, 86): "For when what is said figuratively is taken as if it were said literally, it is understood in a carnal manner." Cf. also H. R. MacCallum, "Milton and Figurative Interpretation of the Bible," *UTQ* 31 (1961–62): 397–415.

Redcross believes what he sees as though it were actually present, the reader believes what he sees—pictures forged by the words in his imagination—as though they were actually true. He reads transparently: "as if words as words withdrew themselves from the focus of our attention and we were directly aware of a tissue of feelings and perceptions."[48] This is precisely the kind of imagination that would "bring the inward acts of the *Spirit* to outward and customary eyService of the body," that would reverse the *Phaedrus*-like ascent of the soul: "the Soule by this meanes of overbodying her selfe, given up justly to fleshly delights, bated her wing apace downeward."[49]

The history of Milton criticism is littered with the confusion precipitated by carnal imagination's hankering after sensation—the reader's reluctance "to lift the eye of the mind above the corporeal and created."[50] The Romantic inversion of *Paradise Lost*'s values is ultimately rooted in the eighteenth century's desire to visualize the poem—as though Milton were an artist who had simply decided to use words instead of paint: "it is astonishing with what gloomy pomp, with what a significant and expressive uncertainty of strokes and colouring, he has finished the portrait of the King of Terrors [Death]."[51] The problem with this kind of visualizing imagination is that admiration for the artistry of the picture has a habit of being transferred to its subject matter. The embryo of such a transference is evident in, for instance, Leonard Welsted's failure to recognize any difference between the representation of Satan in Book I and in Book IV: Homer's description of the goddess Discord is "undoubtedly very great; but to anyone who has read the prodigious description Milton gives us of Satan, as when he rises from the fiery surge, when he views the host of fallen angels, and particularly when he is apprehended in Paradise, this perhaps will seem but moderately sublime."[52] The reader loses his awareness that du Laurens' painted lion is only an image in his preoccupation with the particular qualities of the image and so arrives at Bottom's asslike level of perception. Even in fairly recent criticism the voice of carnal imagination itching after particularities can still be heard:

48. Leavis, pp. 48–49. See pp. 13–15, 17.

49. *Of Reformation* (Yale, I, 520, 522).

50. Augustine, *Christian Doctrine* III.v (Dods, IX, 86).

51. Edmund Burke, *A Philosophical Enquiry into the Origin of Our Ideas of the Sublime and Beautiful* (London, 1757), quoted in Arthur Barker, "'. . . And On His Crest Sat Horror': Eighteenth-Century Interpretations of Milton's Sublimity and His Satan," *UTQ* 11 (1941–42): 430–31.

52. Leonard Welsted, *The Works of Dionysius Longinus* (London, 1712), quoted in Barker, "'. . . And On His Crest Sat Horror,'" p. 429.

There is not much in *PL* of the *feel* of the Bible, or of Homer, anyway as I register it. I miss, for example, the practical details from both sources, the earthenware vessels, soldiers tightening straps, weapons breaking, animals being carefully butchered, sails set.[53]

It is after Michael checks this sense-bound imagination in Adam, his literal reading of the seduction of the Sons of God, with the warning "Judg not what is best / By pleasure, though to Nature seeming meet" (XI.603–4), that Adam, alluding to Redcross losing his way—

> A shadie groue not far away they spide,
>
> . . . .
>
> And all within were pathes and alleies wide,
> With footing worne, and leading inward farre:
> Faire harbour that them seemes; so in they entered arre
>
> (*FQ* I.i.7)

—laments mankind's recurring fall:

> O pittie and shame, that they who to live well
> Enterd so faire, should turn aside to tread
> Paths indirect, or in the mid way faint!
>
> (XI.629–31)[54]

BEHOLD A WONDER:
THE WARNING ALLUSION TO *THE FAERIE QUEENE*

> Because that, when they knew God, they glorified
> him not as God, neither were thankful; but became
> vain in their imaginations, and their foolish heart
> was darkened.
> Professing themselves to be wise, they became
> fools.
>
> Romans 1 : 21–22

The location of the warning allusion to *A Midsummer Night's Dream* is critical. It occurs at the entrance to Pandemonium—at

---

53. John Broadbent, Paradise Lost: *Introduction* (Cambridge: Cambridge University Press, 1972), p. 104. David Daiches' remark, presumably intended for T. S. Eliot, seems apposite here: "Criticism of Milton for not employing sufficiently precise visual imagery is peculiarly stupid; in *Paradise Lost* images are symbolic states of mind, and some degree of abstraction in them is absolutely necessary" (*Milton* [London, 1957; rpt. New York: Norton, 1966], p. 175).

54. There is also an allusion to Dante—*Inferno* i.1–3.

the moment the devils begin swarming into its "spacious Hall" (I.762). Through another extended allusion, this time to the house of Alma in *The Faerie Queene*,[55] it becomes apparent that the spacious hall of Pandemonium, the Devil's "high Capital" (I.756), is in fact Fancy's chamber: Pandemonium is not only a creation but a projection of the *cellula phantastica*. Through the bee simile, the demonic heroes who

> Thick swarm'd, both on the ground and in the air,
> Brusht with the hiss of rustling wings. As Bees
> In spring time, when the Sun with *Taurus* rides,
> Pour forth thir populous youth about the Hive
> In clusters
>
> (I.767–71)

are suddenly revealed as the idle thoughts and fantasies of uninformed imagination:

> And all the chamber filled was with flyes,
>   Which buzzed all about, and made such sound,
>   That they encombred all mens eares and eyes,
>   Like many swarmes of Bees assembled round,
>   After their hiues with honny do abound:
>   All those were idle thoughts and fantasies,
>   Deuices, dreames, opinions vnsound,
>   Shewes, visions, sooth-sayes, and prophesies;
> And all that fained is, as leasings, tales, and lies.
>
> (*FQ* II.ix.51)

Because the house of Alma represents a healthy mind, uninformed fancy appears as it is; because hell represents a mind where upstart passions have caught the government, fancy's cell appears in the guise of Pandemonium.[56] The allusion enables the reader to penetrate the illusion of the Devil's "high Capital"; and the climactic picture of Spenser's Phantastes—

> Emongst them all sate he, which wonned there,
>   That hight *Phantastes* by his nature trew
>
> (*FQ* II.ix.52)

55. The allusion to *FQ* II.ix.51 is, among eighteen other analogues, noted in James Whaler's "Animal Simile in *Paradise Lost*," *PMLA* 47 (1932): 539–53. Whaler concludes that the essence of the relationship between the two similes, Spenser's and Milton's, is one of "bewildering confusion" (p. 550).

56. See Hughes, "Psychological Allegory," on the relationship between the houses of Alma and Busyrane.

—enables him to penetrate the opening grandeur of Book II and see Satan as Phantastes:

> High on a Throne of Royal State, which far
> Outshon the wealth of *Ormus* and of *Ind,*
> Or where the gorgeous East with richest hand
> Showrs on her Kings *Barbaric* Pearl and Gold,
> Satan exalted sat.
>
> (II.1–5)[57]

As Satan's pride is obvious, so is our entrance into the house of Lucifera:

> High aboue all a cloth of State was spred,
> And a rich throne, as bright as sunny day,
> On which there sate most brave embellished
> With royall robes and gorgeous array,
> A mayden Queene.
>
> (*FQ* I.iv.8)

But as Satan's manipulation of our fancy is much less obvious, so is our entrance into Circe's "marble-covered frame" where in Sandys' Ovid

> On a throne of state,
> She in sumptuous inward chamber sate:
> With gold her undergarment richly shone;
> And over it a purple mantle thrown.
>
> (*Met.* XIV.262–65)

And so when Satan "His proud imaginations thus displaid" (II.10), it suggests that the infernal council and the Satanic epic of which the council is a part are, like Pandemonium itself, little more than the

---

57. The idolatrous image of Satan also recalls the idolatrous image of Rosaline in *Love's Labour's Lost:*

> Who sees the heavenly Rosaline,
> That, like a rude and savage man of Inde,
> At the first opening of the gorgeous east,
> Bows not his vassal head and, strooken blind,
> Kisses the base ground with obedient breast?
> (IV.iii.216–20)

In as much as both the devils and Berowne are ruled by fancy theirs is not, as Fowler (Carey and Fowler, p. 509n) suggests, "a different sort of idolatry." Cf. also Giles Fletcher, *Christs Victorie on Earth,* sts. 55ff.

airy fabric or "magic structure" of fancy: "She forms Imaginations, Aerie shapes" (V.105). But as with Comus and Eve's dream there is more to Satan's imaginations than unrestrained fancy and here that "addition strange" (V.116) is explained by the biblical associations of the word "imaginations."

Satan's "proud imaginations" suggests not the inoperation of the rational faculty, but its subversion by desire—that is, not an accidental but a deliberate misjoining, a pseudorational organization of fancy's images. In this it corresponds to the biblical meaning of "imaginations." Analyzing Genesis 8:21—"for the imagination of man's heart is evil from his youth"—William Perkins explains imagination as "that which the minde & understanding by thinking, plotteth, and deviseth"; it is "the naturall disposition of the understanding after the fall of man." The important word is "naturall"; it means that as soon as man tries to think independently of God, "naturally," then because his nature is fallen he is doomed to "deny God in his heart." He does this in one of two ways: either by turning the true God into an idol of his brain, or by replacing the true God with "somewhat that is not God."[58] For Perkins, a theologian like Aquinas would be guilty of the first form of denial, a scientist like Galileo the second. In *Paradise Lost*, the speculative reason that has no end but itself is seen as a form of idolatry that dooms Galileo to mistake his own valley for a moonscape and the astronomers to construct a mental Babel whose confusion finally reveals the operation of their own misjoining fancy—"apt the Mind or Fancie is to roave / Uncheckt" (VIII.188–89).[59] What Milton means by "the weak mightines of mans reasoning" and Satan's "proud imaginations" is ultimately the same. The weak mightiness of man's reasoning is the antithesis of God's strength, a strength "made perfect in weakness" (II Cor. 12:9), but in St. Paul that strength is itself the antithesis of the "imaginations, and every high thing that exalteth itself against the knowledge of God" (10:5).[60]

Just as the magic structures of Comus, the physical structure of his stately palace and the rhetorical structure of his stance as an Ovidian lover, are "imaginations" founded on lechery; so the Devil's magic structures, Pandemonium and his Satanic epic, are "imaginations" founded on pride. The movement from Book I to Book II, from the fantastic landscape of hell into the spacious hall of Pandemo-

58. *A Treatise of Man's Imaginations* (*Workes*, II, 458,459).
59. Cf. Frye, *The Return of Eden*, pp. 57–59; and Fish, *Surprised by Sin*, pp. 28–29.
60. For the way that towers and "every high thing" symbolize "the drive of evil to rival God and construct its own version of reality," see Anthony Low, "The Image of the Tower in *Paradise Lost*," *SEL* 10 (1970): 171–81.

nium, symbolizes the culmination of a movement from unrestrained fancy to "imaginations," the weak mightiness of man's reasoning. Thus, as the warning allusion to Bottom looks back to the illusions of unrestrained fancy, so the warning allusion to Phantastes looks forward to the prison house of "imaginations," the fully realized snare of the Satanic epic.

SATAN'S PROUD IMAGINATIONS:
THE SATANIC EPIC

> Thir Song was partial, but the harmony
> (What could it less when Spirits immortal sing?)
> Suspended Hell, and took with ravishment
> The thronging audience.
>
> *Paradise Lost* II.552–55

The importance of the infernal debate in trapping the reader in a web of proud imaginations is clear enough: as Fish puts it, it is man's reasoning, the "inquiring and discriminating mind" of the reader that betrays him in Book II "as he is led to distinguish between speeches which are united in blasphemy, a blasphemy he tacitly approves and shares if he judges them on any other basis."[61] The apparent freedom of the dialectic deflects the mind away from the assumptions upon which the debate is based, assumptions which reveal the devils' mental imprisonment, and failure to recognize which confirms our own. The debate is something like the "rigged council"[62] of the *Iliad*, Book II, which also originates in a false dream, a fantasy that Agamemnon mistakes for revelation:

> 'Heare, friends, a dreame divine
> Amids the calme night in my sleepe did through my shut eyes shine
> Within my fantasie.
>
> (II.43–45)[63]

Whereas in the *Iliad* as the nobles conspire with Agamemnon to manipulate the Greeks, it is easy to lose sight of the fact that Agamemnon is himself being manipulated by Jove; so here as Beelzebub

---

61. Fish, *Surprised by Sin*, p. 241.
62. Blessington, p. 1.
63. Homer is quoted from *Chapman's Homer: The Iliad, The Odyssey, and The Lesser Homerica*, ed. Allardyce Nicol, 2d ed., 2 vols. (Princeton: Princeton University Press, 1967).

conspires with Satan to manipulate the other devils, it is easy to lose sight of the fact that Satan is like Agamemnon a "foole," "Repeating in discourse his dreame and dreaming still, awake" (II.28, 27), a fool the workings of whose pride, if not manipulated by God, are certainly transformed by him—"That all this good of evil shall produce" (XII.470).[64] In our failure, the speeches conspire with our own "imaginations" to manipulate us. The debate is, however, only one very effective part of a total, mental structure that increasingly closes in on the reader, a transforming structure or system that demands a particular understanding of events. That structure is the miniature epic into which the Devil shapes his experience—a trap that has snapped shut once we begin to appreciate the coherence of the Devil's story, his perseverence and sense of purpose, once we can assert that

Nothing can exceed the grandeur and the energy of the character of the Devil as expressed in Paradise Lost. . . .
    Milton's Devil as a moral being is as far superior to his God, as one who perseveres in some purpose which he has conceived to be excellent, in spite of adversity and torture, is to one who in the cold security of undoubted triumph inflicts the most horrible revenge upon his enemy.[65]

Shelley is in fact describing the role that the Devil's own fancy assigns to himself.
    The construction of the epic culminates with the climax of the debate when Satan, echoing the Sybil's warning to Anchises' son—

> facilis descensus Auerno:
> sed reuocare gradum superasque euadere ad auras,
> hoc opus, hic labor est . . .
>
> (*Aeneid* VI.126–29)

the descent to Avernus is not hard. . . . But to retrace the steps and escape back to upper airs, that is the task and that is the toil

—assumes the role of an Aeneas who will seek out a new Troy, "this new world" (II.403): "long is the way / And hard, that out of Hell leads up to light" (II.432–33). With this, revealing himself a much more realistic and profound hero than Moloch who in his fury casts

---

64. Cf. II Thess. 2:10–11: "they received not the love of truth. . . . And for this cause God shall send them strong delusion, that they should believe a lie."
    65. Shelley, *On the Devil, and Devils*, quoted from Joseph Anthony Wittreich, Jr., ed., *The Romantics on Milton* (Cleveland: The Press of Case Western Reserve University, 1970), pp. 534–35.

aside the Sybil's warning—"Th'ascent is easie then" (II.81)—Satan precipitates the story of the Fall of Man. The construction of the epic, however, begins with the initial uncoiling of evil. Even before we enter the demonic mind the first classical allusion of the action is ominous: "Him the Almighty Power / Hurld headlong flaming from th'Ethereal skie" (I.44–45) identifies the Devil with the figure of Hephaestus-Vulcan-Mulciber whom Jove took "by the heele / And hurld . . . out of heaven" (*Iliad* I.572–73). If classical stories are read typologically, this allusion simply extends the biblical view of consolidated evil to embrace the truths implicit in classical myth—truths which the Attendant Spirit in the *Mask* attributes to divine inspiration—

> Ile tell ye, 'tis not vain or fabulous,
> (Though so esteem'd by shallow ignorance)
> What the sage Poets taught by th'heav'nly Muse,
> Storied of old in high immortal vers
>
> (512–15)

—and truths which Christ in *Paradise Regained*, thinking of the classics as a whole, attributes to divine inspiration working through natural revelation: "where moral vertue is express't / By light of Nature" (IV.351–52). If, however, there is a failure to read classical myth typologically, if it appears independent or suggests an alternative to Christian revelation, if one begins to sympathize with "heaven's great both-foote-halting God" (*Iliad* I.587) and resent Jove's anger, then the allusion breaks the unity of the biblical vision and raises the dangers of the classics' fabulous, distracting appeal to the imagination. Barbara Lewalski's assertion that Milton "used classical myth typologically" overstates the case.[66] Here there is an ambiguity in his use that tests the reader, while elsewhere classical myth is used explicitly as both alternative and type: it is for this reason that Jove can be both numbered among the devils (I.506–21) and identified with Messiah (VI.760–66).

When the classics (or any other form of literature, including Shakespeare's stories) appear as an alternative to Christianity, then, as Milton's Christ explains, it is clear that they are *phantastike*, the productions of fancy uninformed by reason or fancy having subverted the rational faculty—"little else but dreams, / Conjectures,

66. "Typological Symbolism and 'The Progress of the Soul' in Seventeenth-Century Literature," in *The Literary Uses of Typology*, ed. Earl Miner (Princeton: Princeton University Press, 1977), p. 103.

fancies, built on nothing firm" (*PR* IV.291–92)—and their wisdom is an illusion:

> Who therefore seeks in these
> True wisdom, finds her not, or by delusion
> Far worse, her false resemblance only meets,
> An empty cloud.
>
> (*PR* IV.318–21)

In this context, it becomes apparent that the choice of an allusion to Vulcan is a very careful one: for in *Paradise Lost*, Vulcan signifies the maker who considers himself independent of God—the creative imagination that denies the origin of its own creativity and in consequence only creates parodies of the good.[67] Though Mammon or greed precipitates the construction of Pandemonium, its actual design originates in the imagination of Vulcan or Mulciber. He is the architect of the demons' parody of heaven, the "physical" manifestation of the Devil's solipsism that "the mind is its own place, and in it self / Can make a Heav'n of Hell" (I.254–55). He is the sense-bound artist who brings the inward temple of the spirit to the outward and customary eye-service of the body, constructing a concrete temple which, like all the creations of fancy divorced from true reason—the tower of Babel, St. Peter's at Rome,[68] Virgil's palace of Dido,[69] Ovid's palace of the Sun,[70] "the machinery of a masque—artificial, tem-

67. For the "Satanic predicament" in general, see C. S. Lewis, *A Preface to* Paradise Lost (1942; rpt. London: Oxford University Press, 1960), pp. 96–97: "a creature revolting against a creator is revolting against the source of his own powers—including even his power to revolt"; and Frye, *The Return of Eden*, p. 33: "This may be the Son of God's first epiphany, or manifestation as an objective fact of personality, to the angels, but what the angels are really looking at, including those who are later to revolt, is their own creative principle."

68. The refutation in Carey and Fowler, p. 503n, of R. W. Smith's suggestion that Pandemonium may be modeled on St. Peter's in Rome ("The Source of Milton's Pandemonium," *MP* 29 [1931]: 187–98) is expanded in Roland Mushat Frye, *Milton's Imagery and the Visual Arts* (Princeton: Princeton University Press, 1978), pp. 133–38. Both refutations depend on close attention to architectural detail. Allusion, however, hardly depends on precise and complete reproduction: as Hollander, p. 64, points out, allusion "may be fragmentary or periphrastic." And in any case, given Milton's very well known views on the eye-service of the body—on the way the Holy Spirit prefers "Before all Temples th'upright heart and pure" (I.18), on the fact that Eden was destroyed "To teach thee that God attributes to place / No sanctitie" (XI.836–37)—it is hard to imagine what else he could have thought of "the chief church of Roman Catholicism" (R. M. Frye, p. 135) than that it was demonic. Cf. also Patrick Cullen, *Infernal Triad* (Princeton: Princeton University Press, 1974), p. 100n.

69. See Blessington, pp. 7–8.

70. Rather like our entrance to Book II through Pandemonium, "The entrance unto

porary, illusory"[71]—is built on nothing firm, only the empty breath of human wisdom as it appears in Ecclesiastes: "out of the earth a Fabrick huge / Rose like an Exhalation" (I.710–11). Pandemonium is one of those Miltonic symbols that assimilate an array of associations, almost infinite in their variety but all governed by one idea— in this case the vanity of human structures or systems built "naturally" or independent of God.

One of the verbal equivalents of physical "imaginations" like Pandemonium is fable. Fable is a verbal structure that through fancy controlling reason roves from the truth, just as classical myth itself was thought to be a fanciful distortion of the original Mosaic revelation. In order to emphasize the relationship between the physical and verbal manifestations of man's imaginations, Mulciber is represented not only as the architect of Pandemonium, but as a source of fable. After the narrator implies the value of Mulciber's creativity when it knew its source—"his hand was known / In Heav'n by many a Towred structure high" (I.732–33)—Mulciber himself becomes the subject of spiraling imagination:

> Nor was his name unheard or unador'd
> In ancient *Greece*; and in *Ausonian* land
> Men call'd him *Mulciber*; and how he fell
> From Heav'n, they fabl'd, thrown by angry *Jove*
> Sheer o're the Chrystal Battlements; from morn
> To Noon he fell, from Noon to dewy Eve,
> A Summers day; and with the setting Sun
> Dropt from the Zenith like a falling Star,
> On *Lemnos* th'*Aegaean* Ile.
>
> (I.738–46)

With his unerring flair for losing his way in fancy's labyrinths, F. R. Leavis declares that here the "verse glows with an unusual life."[72] And so it does until the narrator snuffs it out—"thus they relate / Erring" (I.746–47). The passage together with Leavis's response demonstrates in microcosm the seductiveness of the narrator's fabulous imaginations and how relatively ineffective his checks can be. More important, it indicates the fabulous nature of Satan's epic structure: both the passage and the epic wander from the truth, establishing myth as an alternative to revelation.

this second booke [of the *Metamorphoses*] is through the glorious pallace of the Sunne" (Sandys, p. 104).

71. Broadbent, *Some Graver Subject*, p. 101.

72. Leavis, p. 44.

Vulcan's role as the representative of the maker independent of God and the way in which that maker's creations are rooted in self-regarding desire is confirmed once we read typologically, once the classical type is assimilated into its biblical antitype. Besides the Devil, the biblical antitype of Vulcan is Tubalcain:

> Now *Vulcan* was truely that *Tuball-Caine* recorded by *Moses;* there being no small conformity in the name; who invented the art of working in Brasse and Iron.[73]

In *Paradise Lost,* Tubalcain is immediately established as the "natural" maker, the creator who denies the divine source of his creativity: he and his kin appear studious

> Of Arts that polish Life, Inventers rare,
> Unmindful of thir Maker, though his Spirit
> Taught them, but they his gifts acknowledg'd none.
>   (XI.610–12)

Because their works are "natural," they are, it is hinted, idolatrous— "grav'n in mettle" (XI.573). At the same time, their offspring are the provoking objects that ensnare the Sons of God: the Sons of God

> though grave, ey'd them, and let thir eyes
> Rove without rein, till in the amorous Net
> Fast caught, they lik'd, and each his liking chose.
>   (XI.585–87)

The juxtaposition of Tubalcain's works and his offspring, that the Sons of God are ensnared with the same "amorous Net" with which Tubalcain's classical type ensnared Mars and Venus,[74] suggests that the ways in which the works of imagination entangle the mind are rooted in the ways in which this "Beavie of fair Women, richly gay / In Gems and wanton dress" (XI.582–83) inflame desire.

The net that ensnares the Sons of God brings us back to Satan's shield: both are forged by Vulcan and both symbolize the com-

---

73. Sandys, p. 203.
74. Literally, Vulcan's net terminates the amorous activities of Mars and Venus. But figuratively, according to Sandys, it is otherwise. Because Vulcan's net is forged in the same fire that signifies the desire of Mars and Venus, the net comes to mean something similar to Venus' shameful chain: "Mars and Venus are prone to inordinate affections . . . Vulcan bindes them in a net: that is, with too much fervor subdues their operations" (p. 202).

prehensiveness of those false structures that completely entangle the mind. Satan's shield—"the broad circumference / Hung on his shoulders like the Moon" (I.286–87)—is associated with the shield of Achilles—"About the whole circumference, in which his hand did shew . . . the Moone exactly round" (*Iliad* XVIII.434–37).[75] Inside the circumference of Achilles' shield is the world: *"for what is here prefigurde by our miraculous Artist but the universall world, which being so spatious and almost unmeasurable, one circlet of a Shield representes and imbraceth?"*[76] Inside the circumference of Satan's shield is simply the moon, the arbitress of fancy. But, as Galileo's imaginary landscape suggests, it seems to contain a whole world.

As the Devil begins to speak, as soon as he is given a name and with it a human identity, as soon as he begins to use the most human of attributes, language, then he begins to forge the net of his epic structure. The Satanic poem immediately begins to reverse one of the fundamental impulses of Milton's poem. As *Paradise Lost* seeks to assimilate the classics into the Christian scheme of things, so Satan's poem seeks to assimilate the events of Scripture into a classical epic. We are confronted with the extraordinaryy drama of two poems, one inside the other, moving in diametrically opposite directions. Satan, like Faustus, seeks to establish the classics as an alternative world-picture to Scripture:[77] as Faustus would confound hell in Elysium (I.iii.287), so the devils attempt to confound the reality of hell—a universe of death created by their own perverted fancy, "worse / Than Fables yet have feign'd, or fear conceiv'd" (II.626–27)—in an imitation of Virgil's Elysium (*Aeneid* VI.642–59)—"Part on the Plain, or in the Air sublime / Upon the wing, or in swift Race contend" (II.528–29). There is no genuine opposition between classical myth and Christianity—the tension only exists in the desires of Satan's mind. In terms of Milton's poem, as we have seen, once classical myth is divorced from Christianity it becomes fable; its only true value depends upon its being used as a shadowy type of the truth which is by definition Christian.

75. Cf. Blessington, p. 10; Frye, *The Return of Eden*, p. 58. Fowler (Carey and Fowler, pp. 478–79n) underestimates the importance of the allusion because he thinks the primary reference is to *Iliad* XIX.373 (359 in Chapman): "his shield, that cast a brightnesse from it like the Moone."

76. Chapman, "To the Most Honored Earle, Earle Marshall," *Achilles Shield*, in *Chapman's Homer*, p. 543.

77. For Satan and Faustus as Elizabethan tragic heroes, see Helen Gardner, "Milton's 'Satan' and the Theme of Damnation in Elizabethan Tragedy," in *Milton: Modern Es-*

The divisiveness of Satan's language, his role as Typhon, this time Typhon as the "type of those that dismember truth,"[78] is epitomized in the double-faced allusion of his opening lines. His exclamation, "If thou beest he; But O how fall'n! how chang'd / From him, who . . ." (I.84–85), appears to confirm the Apocalyptic view of evil consolidated by referring to the other major biblical source for the fall of the angels in Isaiah: "How art thou fallen from heaven, O Lucifer, son of the morning!" (14:12). But Satan's true direction is contained in the simultaneous reference to the *Aeneid*. Satan sees Beelzebub not as a reflection of himself as the fallen Lucifer, but as the image of Hector's ghost that appears to Aeneas: "ei mihi, qualis erat, quantum mutatus ab illo / Hectore" (*Aeneid* II.274–75; "And, oh, how harrowing was the sight of him; how changed he was from the old Hector"). Although the ghost brings news of Troy's fall, much more important, he is a sign of hope, of victory brought forth out of defeat, for it is the ghost that gives Aeneas his epic purpose:

> sacra suosque tibi commendat Troia penatis;
> Hos cape fatorum comites, his moenia quaere
> Magna pererrato statues quae denique ponto.
> (*Aeneid* II.293–95)

But now Troy entrusts to you her sanctities and her Guardians of the Home. Take them with you to face your destiny, and find for them the walled city which one day after ocean-wandering you shall build to be great like them.

In Satan's imagination, the flames of hell are like those of Troy, and the tenor of his heroic resolve—his "unconquerable Will," "courage never to submit or yield," and determination "not to be overcome" (I.106–9)—recalls that of Aeneas: "una salus uictis nullam sperare salutem" (*Aeneid* II.354; "Nothing can save the conquered but the knowledge that they cannot now be saved"). Satan disguises his "deep despare" (I.126) as desperation, and just as Aeneas's words gave his followers' "proud hearts the strength of desperation" (*Aeneid* II.355; "sic animis iuuenum furor additus"), so Satan seeks "resolu-

---

says in Criticism, ed. Arthur E. Barker (New York: Oxford University Press, 1965), pp. 205–17.

78. Carey and Fowler, p. 474n. Cf. *Areopagitica*: "Truth indeed came once into the world with her divine Master, and was a perfect shape most glorious to look on: but when he ascended, and his Apostles after him were laid asleep, then strait arose a wicked race of deceivers, who as that story goes of the *AEgyptian Typhon* with his conspirators, how they dealt with the good *Osiris*, took the Virgin Truth, hewd her lovely form into a thousand peeces, and scatterd them to the four winds" (Yale, II, 549).

tion from despare" (I.191). The emotional appeal of this kind of heroic resolve is hard not to admire; but when it is "Baited with reasons not unplausible" (*Mask* 162), when it occurs inside a structure,
partial but harmonious, that is, a structure which judged by the measure of its own internal coherence appears rationally plausible, then
out of our own virtue or admiration for virtue, Satan, like Iago,
makes the net that will enmesh us.[79] Once we accept a part of Satan's
scheme of things, even his apparent courage, then the comprehen-
siveness and apparent coherence of his system is such that we are
drawn in to accept the whole. It is for this reason, to catch our conscience with his courage, that Satan begins to disguise his purpose in
Aeneas's.

Once Satan has established himself as the new Aeneas, once he
has established the heroic direction of his account of things, the main
lines of the Satanic epic's shape are predictable enough: the demonic
host is mustered much like the Greek army in the second book of the
Iliad; the infernal council follows the action of Agamemnon's council
in the same book; the devils' activities in hell are modeled on those
of the glorious dead in the sixth book of the *Aeneid*; Satan's journey
is related to that of Odysseus in the first half of the *Odyssey*. But
what is startling is not the main lines but the detail. For it is in the
detail that the transformational power of Satan's epic structure, the
power "whereby new material is constantly processed by and through
it,"[80] becomes fully apparent. In Satan's poem the events of Scripture,
for instance, become types of his own story. Most obvious perhaps,
the story of the Exodus, a story which prefigures Christ's life in the
gospels,[81] is assimilated into the pagan epic.

In Book I, the allusions to Exodus begin with the rebel angels pic-
tured as the debris of Pharaoh's defeated army:

> His legions, Angel Forms, who lay intrans't
> Thick as Autumnal Leaves . . .
> . . . or scattered sedge
> Afloat, when with fierce Winds *Orion* arm'd
> Hath vext the Red-Sea Coast, whose waves orethrew
> *Busiris* and his *Memphian* Chivalry,

---

79. Cf. *Othello* II.iii.343–46.

80. Terence Hawkes, *Structuralism and Semiotics* (London: Methuen, 1977), p. 16.

81. For convenient summary, see Frye, *The Return of Eden*, pp. 118–43, esp.
pp. 122–24; for more detail, see A. C. Charity, *Events and Their Afterlife* (Cambridge:
Cambridge University Press, 1966), esp. pp. 83–148. Cf. also John T. Shawcross, *With
Mortal Voice* (Lexington: University Press of Kentucky, 1982), pp. 119–38.

> While with perfidious hatred they pursu'd
> The Sojourners of *Goshen*, who beheld
> From the safe shore thir floating Carkases
> And broken Chariot Wheels.
>
> (I.301–11)

Since Pharaoh is a type of the Devil, this picture confirms the biblical view, but the line "while with perfidious hatred they pursu'd" prepares the way for a sudden reversal of roles. From the devils' point of view it is they who have been pursued with perfidious hatred— "But see the angry Victor hath recall'd / His Ministers of vengeance and pursuit" (I.169–70)—and Satan raises the demons from the flood by warning them against the threat of God's "swift pursuers" (I.326). As he does so, in an epic simile, he himself becomes Moses and the rebel angels the locusts with which God punishes Pharaoh:

> As when the potent Rod
> Of *Amrams* Son in *Egypts* evill day
> Wav'd round the Coast, up call'd a pitchy cloud
> Of *Locusts*, warping on the Eastern Wind,
> That ore the Realm of impious *Pharaoh* hung.
>
> (I.338–42)

As the demons emerge from the flood, they now become the Israelites emerging from their crossing of the Red Sea, a prefiguration of Christ's baptism in the Jordan. In Isaiah, when the dispersed nations of Israel are reunited, the imagery of Exodus is used:

> And he shall set up an ensign for the nations, and shall assemble the outcasts of Israel, and gather together the dispersed of Judah. . . .
> And the Lord shall utterly destroy the tongue of the Egyptian sea . . . and make men go over dryshod.
>
> (11:12, 15)

In much the same way, Satan's legions are reunited: these outcasts, under twelve chief gods like the twelve tribes, "All these and more came flocking; but with looks / Down cast and damp" (I.522–23) and assembled beneath "Th'Imperial Ensign, which full high advanc't" (I.536). In Book II, the process intensifies with Satan carefully assigning to himself the role of the Mosaic deliverer, a prefiguration of Christ the redeemer: as he explains to his followers, he seeks "Deliverance for us all" (II.465); as he explains to Sin and Death, he seeks deliverance from the house of bondage—"I come no enemie, but to set free / From out this dark and dismal house of pain" (II.822–23); he wanders the "darksome Desart" (II.973) of Chaos to discover the promised land, "To search with wandering quest a place foretold . . . a place of bliss" (II.830–32). In Book III when he catches sight of the earth, like the spies of Numbers (13), he has discovered the promised land:

> As when a Scout
> Through dark and desart wayes with peril gone
> All night; at last by break of chearful dawne
> Obtains the brow of some high-climbing Hill,
> Which to his eye discovers unaware
> The goodly prospect of some forein land
> First-seen
>
> (III.543–49)

Thus, at the end of the infernal debate, the climax of the Satanic epic, Satan offers himself not only as Aeneas but as Moses and Christ. His role as Christ is emphasized by the parallel responses of the infernal and divine councils to their heroes' undertakings: in heaven "all . . . stood mute" (III.217), while in hell "all sate mute" (II.420). It is a measure of the comprehensive, synthesizing power of the verbal structure built by Satan that all these roles can be assimilated—even that of the reader himself, the aspiring Christian soul; for when Satan represents himself as Aeneas—"long is the way / And hard, that out of Hell leads up to light" (II.432–33)—he also identifies himself with Dante: "la via è lunga e 'l cammino è malvagio" (*Inferno* xxxiv.94; "The way is long and the road is hard"). The true power of evil consists in the direction of the creative power of the "rationall Fancie"[82] away from its source. This brings us to Sin.

Satan's "fixed mind," his inability to change morally, his lack of conscience, consciousness, self-knowledge, is evident in his inability to recognize the outward shows of his own mind. Ironically enough, Stanley Fish's affirmation that "the devil is always given his due . . . his courage is never denied" is more accurate than one might imagine.[83] The Devil is given his due because his courage is nonexistent. His "courage" is in fact the measure of his moral stupidity: the Devil is an ass precisely because he makes a virtue of remaining unterrified, undaunted before figments of his own imagination. Like Bottom, he

82. Reynolds, *A Treatise of the Passions and Faculties*, p. 240.
83. Fish, *Surprised by Sin*, p. 49.

cannot distinguish a painted lion from a real one. As we enter hell he fails to recognize the place as the lively image of his own unrestrained fancy, and as we leave hell he fails to recognize Sin as the lively image of his proud imaginations. The monstrous misjoining of fair appearance and foul substance in Sin is the true emblem of Satan's epic structure.

Like Spenser's Error, Milton's Sin is modeled on the monstrous figure of Scylla.[84] According to Sandys, Scylla signifies human wisdom and intelligence "polluted by the sorceries of *Circe*,"[85] that is, reason subverted by the magic of fancy. Sin is also the negative inversion of Minerva: Minerva came forth, says Cartari's translator, Richard Linche,

> into the world out of the head of Iupiter (according to the opinion of all fantasticke Poets.) By which is meant & vnderstood, that all human knowledge and understanding proceedeth from the superior and diuine guidance aboue.[86]

Sin proceeds from an inferior and demonic urge below: she proceeds from the imagination when, instead of operating as a mirror of the good, it operates as a common carrier of carnal desire. In the Satanic version of the Trinity,[87] she is the counterfeit Holy Spirit—"O Father, what intends thy hand, she cry'd, / Against thy only Son?" (II.727–28)—that is, the negative inversion of the true spirit of creativity. She is conceived in Satan's fancy: just as Ariel infects reason with the fantasy of a tempest—"I flamed amazement" (*Tmp.* I.ii.198)—so Sin's birth is a "sign / Portentous" (II.760–61) of the infection of Satan's reason—"while thy head flames thick and fast / Threw forth . . . amazement seis'd / All th'Host of Heav'n" (II.754–59). She is conceived in the image and likeness of her creator, but even at this stage Satan treats his "imagination" as though it were actual: "Thy self in me thy perfect image viewing / Becam'st enamour'd" (II.764–65). And just like the Sons of God with the offspring of Tubalcain, the maker independent of God, the issue is monstrous. The foul distortion of Sin, the Scylla-like issue of Satan's self-love, is the true reflection of his creativity. For, as Burton explains, monstrous births bear the stamp of their mothers' imagination (Satan is of course both the mother and father of Sin):

---

84. For more on Sin and Error, see Quilligan, pp. 80–98.

85. Sandys, p. 645.

86. Vincenzo Cartari, *The Fountaine of Ancient Fiction*, trans. Richard Linche (London, 1599; rpt. New York: Da Capo Press, 1973), s.v. Minerva.

87. See B. Rajan, Paradise Lost & *the Seventeenth Century Reader* (London: Chatto and Windus, 1947), p. 50; and Cullen, p. 104n.

Great-bellied women, when they long, yield us prodigious examples in this kind, as moles, warts, scars, harelips, monsters, especially caused in their children by force of a depraved phantasy in them. She imprints that stamp upon her child, which she conceives unto herself.[88]

This is the point of the birth of Eve: she is the image and issue of true creativity. She bears the stamp of Adam's imagination free from carnal desire, reflecting the design of God:

> Mine eyes he clos'd, but op'n left the Cell
> Of Fancie my internal sight, by which
> Abstract as in a transe methought I saw,
> Though sleeping, where I lay, and saw the shape
> Still glorious before whom awake I stood;
> Who stooping op'nd my left side, and took
> From thence a Rib, with cordial spirits warme,
> And Life-blood streaming fresh; wide was the wound,
> But suddenly with flesh fill'd up and heal'd:
> The Rib he formd and fashiond with his hands;
> Under his forming hands a Creature grew,
> Manlike, but different Sex, so lovly faire,
> That what seemd fair in all the World, seemd now
> Mean, or in her summd up, in her containd
> And in her looks, which from that time infus'd
> Sweetness into my heart, unfelt before,
> And into all things from her Aire inspir'd
> The spirit of love and amorous delight.
> Shee disappeerd, and left me dark, I wak'd
> . . . .
> When out of hope, behold her, not farr off,
> Such as I saw her in my dream.
>
> (VIII.460–82)

Eve's birth is an affirmation of human art. Its metaphoric value is as an image of human art, the process whereby the imagination guided by God translates its perception of the ideal into the actual. Eve's birth is the model of human creativity that is parodied by the construction of Pandemonium—Mammon's crew had soon "Op'nd into the Hill a spacious wound / And dig'd out ribs of Gold" (I.689–90)—and the birth of Sin:

> All on a sudden miserable pain
> Surpris'd thee, dim thine eyes, and dizzie swumm
> In darkness, while thy head flames thick and fast

88. *Anatomy of Melancholy* 1.2.3.2 (p. 221).

> Threw forth, till on the left side op'ning wide,
> Likest to thee in shape and count'nance bright,
> Then shining heav'nly fair, a Godess arm'd
> Out of thy head I sprung.
>
> (II.752–58)

Sin is then the counterfeit Eve and this, as we shall see, is another reason why she is represented as Scylla—a virgin poisoned by Circe. In creating Sin in the image of Scylla, Milton is not only enlisting all the associations of the moralized Ovid and Spenser's Error, but also of Bacon's scholastic philosophy:

> the fable and fiction of Scylla seemeth to be a lively image of this kind of philosophy or knowledge; which was transformed into a comely virgin for the upper parts; but then *Candida succinctam latrantibus inguina monstris* . . . so the generalities of the schoolmen are for a while good and proportionable; but then when you descend into their distinctions and decisions, instead of a fruitful womb for the use and benefit of man's life, they end in monstrous altercations and barking questions.[89]

As early as Prolusion IV, Error and scholastic philosophy are identified in Milton's mind: "and now foul Error reigns supreme in all the schools."[90] Like Sin, both Error and scholasticism are conceived in the fancy. According to Bacon, scholasticism is conceived by wit: the schoolmen "did out of no great quantity of matter, and infinite agitation of wit, spin out unto us those laborious webs of learning that are extant in their books." But wit divorced from judgment means much the same as fancy divorced from reason. Here, wit, like unrestrained fancy, is a matter of appearance not substance: if wit "works upon itself, as the spider worketh his web, then it is endless, and brings forth indeed cobwebs of learning, admirable for the fineness of thread and work, but of no substance or profit." The carnal desire that animates the "imaginations" of the schoolmen is pride: "but as in the inquiry of the divine truth their pride inclined to leave the oracle of God's word and to vanish in the mixture of their own inventions." Their understanding of things, the mental structure that they create, turns out to be, like Milton's view of Galileo's science, a projection of their own minds: "in the inquisition of nature they ever left the oracle of God's works and adored the deceiving and deformed images which the unequal mirror of their own minds or a few received authors or principles did represent unto them."

89. *Advancement of Learning* I (Spedding, III, 286–87).
90. Yale, I, 250.

It becomes increasingly clear that Satan's epic structure, his proud "imagination" and its symbol, the Scylla-like figure of Sin, have much in common with the nature of Bacon's scholasticism. Like scholasticism, the "generalities" of his structure for a while appear "good and proportionable" but when you descend to its "distinctions and decisions," the monstrous misjoining of subverted fancy becomes apparent. In particular, the dialectical sequences of Book II— sequences like Belial's speech where answering his questions only confirms the errors upon which they are based—putrify and dissolve on analysis "into a number of subtle, idle, and unwholesome, and (as I may term them) vermiculate questions, which have indeed a kind of quickness and life of spirit, but no soundness of matter or goodness of quality."[91] Most important, like scholasticism, Satan's epic is a web or comprehensive structure in which the unwary reader becomes enmeshed through his own fancy-subverted reasoning.

91. *Advancement of Learning* I (Spedding, III, 285–87).

CHAPTER FOUR

Eikastike Poetry and Revelation

THE DISSOLUTION OF THE SATANIC EPIC

> The charm dissolves apace;
> And as the morning steals upon the night,
> Melting the darkness, so their rising senses
> Begin to chase the ignorant fumes that mantle
> Their clearer reason.
>
> *The Tempest* V.i.64–68

Although the Satanic epic of the first two books provides the great example of *phantastike* poetry in *Paradise Lost*, it is also an example of *eikastike* poetry in as much as it is an exact verbal representation or imitation of a mind where reason has been subverted by carnal desire through fancy. In order to see this it is necessary to read not with our eyes, but with our ears, that is, visualization must be qualified by analysis. The phantasmagoria of the opening books is reduced to order, its illusions penetrated, by attention to the echoes and allusions, both the unintended and intended recurrence of word-sounds and patterns of word-sounds. The analysis of the previous chapter depends upon just this: attention to sounds recurring from within the poem, from within the body of Milton's work, and from within the literary traditions he was most familiar with—the good words that bear an analogous relationship to the Word. The echoes range from very conscious warning allusions, like those to *A Midsummer Night's Dream* and *The Faerie Queene*, to fragments of barely conscious association like Livingston Lowes's "hooked atoms." For example, just after Satan, lamenting the loss of his former state, begins to identify himself with Aeneas at the fall of Troy, he points out a "dreary Plain" to Beelzebub: "Thither let us tend / From off the tossing of these fiery waves, / There rest, if any rest can harbour there" (I.180, 183–85). This, according to Fowler, recalls the words of Richard II's queen: "Here let us rest, if this rebellious earth / Have any resting for her true king's queen" (*Richard II* V.i.5–6). This is appropriate enough—"since Earth was rebellious because mother of the Giants, the 'Earth-born' of 1.198 below"[1]—but it was probably remembered because it occurs as part of an extremely fanciful speech in which the fallen king is compared to "the model where old Troy did stand" (V.i.11) and to which the king responds with this piece of common sense:

> Learn, good soul,
> To think our former state a happy dream;
> From which awaked, the truth of what we are
> Shows us but this.
>
> (V.i.17–20)

There is, however, one pattern of echoic allusions, deliberate references that echo in our memory, which immediately and very consciously explodes the inflated imaginations of the Satanic epic, and that is of course the Word itself. Just as fantasy is reduced to order once fancy's misjoined images are framed by reason, so the demonic illusion is penetrated once Satan's proud imaginations are framed by the Bible—once image is informed by the Word, and once we remember that the Word scatters "the proud in the imagination of their hearts" (Luke 1:51).

The ironic commentary that dissolves the Satanic epic proceeds not from the narrator or the "epic voice" but from the biblical echoes woven into the very fabric of the poem. The echoes are put there deliberately by Milton so that the reader guided by conscience, reason informed by revelation, will find them, and so "Light after light well us'd they shall attain, / And to the end persisting, safe arrive" (III.196–97). In this, Scripture is made to imitate the *filia vocis*—a voice heard by the Jews "descending from heaven, directing them in any affair as occasion served," a kind of revelation which "might be made to one . . . that was no way prepared for prophecy."[2] The *filia vocis* is identified by Eve with the sole command of God not available to reason:

> But of this Tree we may not taste nor touch;
> God so commanded, and left that Command
> Sole Daughter of his voice; the rest, we live
> Law to our selves, our Reason is our Law.
>
> (IX.651–54)

---

1. Carey and Fowler, p. 473n.
2. Smith, *Of Prophecy* (*Select Discourses*, p. 268).

The *filia vocis* is identified by Henry Reynolds with Echo, a reflection of the breath of God, "*the daughter of the divine voice.*"[3] For Eve the *filia vocis* becomes a test of faith, for the Lady in the *Mask* she becomes the gracious echo of faith. As we have seen,[4] the Lady's faith, her invocation to Echo, the "*Daughter of the Sphear*"—"*give resounding grace to all Heav'ns Harmonies*" (240, 242)—is answered by the Attendant Spirit's rescue: "Com Lady while Heaven lends us grace" (937). So here, for the faithful, for those who understand that "the worlds were framed by the word of God" (Hebrews 11 : 3), Satan's proud imaginations are cast down by the weak mightiness of Scripture: the Satanic images are systematically counterpointed by biblical allusions, echoes that reflect the sound but reverse the sense.

Besides those biblical allusions consciously employed by Satan in his epic speeches, or by the narrator in some of his epic similes— allusions which suggest the Satanic epic's attempt to assimilate Scripture—the great mass of the Devil's scriptural reference is unconscious and not controlled by him. The allusions unconsciously embedded in the language of Satan and the narrator's reflections of the Satanic mind appear at first simply to confirm the biblical view of things. Satan's opening words—"If thou beest he; But O how fall'n! how chang'd / From him, who in the happy Realms of Light" (I.84–85)—suggest the consummation of Isaiah's prophecy of the destruction of the Satanic kingdoms:

> And Babylon, the glory of kingdoms, the beauty of the Chaldees' excellency, shall be as when God overthrew Sodom and Gomorrah. . . .
> How art thou fallen from heaven, O Lucifer, son of the morning!
> (Isa. 13 : 19; 14 : 12)

The narrator's description of the defeated demonic host—"Angel Forms, who lay intrans't / Thick as Autumnal Leaves" (I.301–2)— recalls the same prophecy—"and all their host shall fall down, as the leaf falleth off from the vine" (Isa. 34 : 4). However, as evil uncoils itself and the demonic phantasmagoria accelerates, the biblical allusions register the extent to which the words of Satan and the narrator diverge from the Word. Satan's imaginary claim to have endangered heaven's perpetual king is answered and rejected by Isaiah:

> His utmost power with adverse power oppos'd
> In dubious Battel on the Plains of Heav'n,
> And shook his throne
> (I.103–5)

3. *Mythomystes*, p. 110.
4. See pp. 35–36.

Yet thou shalt be brought down to hell, to the sides of the pit.
They that seek thee shall narrowly look upon thee, and consider thee,
saying, Is this the man that made the earth to tremble, that did shake
kingdoms.

(Isa. 14:15–16)

At the height of Satan's fantastic dream the narrator's description reflects the Devil's picture of himself:

And now his heart
Distends with pride, and hardning in his strength
Glories. . . .
. . . he above the rest
In shape and gesture proudly eminent
Stood like a Towr.

(I.571–73, 589–91)

But the language is deeply ironic. As Exodus makes clear, the harden-
ing of Satan's heart is an essential part of God's revelation of himself:

And I will harden Pharaoh's heart, and multiply my signs and my wonders
in the land of Egypt. . . .
And the Egyptians shall know that I am the Lord.

(Exod. 7:3–5)

And as Isaiah makes clear, the power of evil is an illusion:

For the day of the Lord of hosts shall be upon every one that is proud and
lofty. . . .
And upon every high tower.

(Isa. 2:12, 15)

Perhaps most important, Satan's assertion of his own independence,
of the independence of evil—"Evil be thou my Good" (IV.110)—is
shown to be an illusion of the self-regarding imagination:

Woe unto them who call evil good, and good evil; that put darkness for
light, and light for darkness. . . .
Woe unto them that are wise in their own eyes, and prudent in their own
sight!

(Isa. 5:20–21)

The examples are legion,[5] but the principle remains the same: language, especially when it is the verbal manifestation of unrestrained

5. The "Index of Biblical References" in James H. Sims, *The Bible in Milton's Epics*

or perverted fancy, read transparently, as though words were pictures of the actual world, leads to illusion, but language read analytically, the reader remaining conscious that words are words and words that echo the Word, leads to the dissolution of that illusion.

Uriel provides an example of the way in which Satan and his works are to be read. Uriel is at first deluded by Satan, just as the Lady is deluded by Comus's magic dust—she mistakes him for a true guide. As we have seen, the magic dust signifies delusions the virtuous reason could not counter, because they are delusions created by hypocrisy and hypocrisy is a vice in the creature seen, not in the judgment behind the seeing eye. Uriel is deluded by the same hypocrisy:

> So spake the false dissembler unperceivd;
> For neither Man nor Angel can discern
> Hypocrisie . . .
> . . . which now for once beguil'd
> *Uriel*, though Regent of the Sun, and held
> The sharpest sighted Spirit of all in Heav'n.
> (III.681–83, 689–91)

But Uriel does penetrate Satan's disguise, he does discover his hypocrisy. By watching Satan descend and land on Niphates' top, Uriel sees the perturbations of passion distort Satan's face—he "Saw him disfigur'd, more then could befall / Spirit of happie sort" (IV.127–28). He watches Satan because he has been warned: Satan "not anough had practisd to deceive / *Uriel* once warnd; whose eye pursu'd him down / The way he went, and on th'*Assyrian* mount / Saw him disfigur'd" (IV.124–27). It is not immediately apparent by whom or of what Uriel has been warned.[6] Uriel is in fact warned in the same way that the reader is—he is "Admonisht by his ear" (III.647). Literally, the phrase refers to the way Uriel discovers Satan's approach, but figuratively, it suggests the way he discovers Satan's hypocrisy—by attention to Satan's words. At first Uriel is completely taken in, but the fact that his suspicion is aroused, that he is warned before Satan leaves the Sun suggests that it is something Satan says that warns him. And sure enough, on analysis it becomes clear that Satan's words betray him as a type of Herod, for Satan's words—

(Gainesville: University of Florida Press, 1962), pp. 259–73, gives some indication of the extensiveness of the scriptural commentary on the poem.

6. Cf. Carey and Fowler, p. 615n.

> Brightest Seraph tell
> . . . .
> That I may find him, and with secret gaze,
> Or open admiration him behold
> On whom the great Creator hath bestowd
> Worlds, and on whom hath all these graces powerd
> (III.667, 671–74)

—recall Herod's—

> Go and search diligently for the young child; and when ye have found him,
> bring me word again, that I may come and worship him also.
> (Matt. 2:8)

The echoic allusions, especially the allusions to Scripture, make it clear then that the great example of *phantastike* poetry is also a work of *eikastike* poetry. With the opening of Book III, however, the poem ceases to be only implicitly icastic and becomes explicitly so. As Satan's epic journey from Pandemonium to Mount Niphates is interrupted by the poet's invocation to the celestial Light that plants the eyes of faith and the consequent revelation of the divine council, so the illusory structure of Satan's fantastic imagination is interrupted and transformed by the vision of the icastic imagination. The invocation and revelation take the form of a hymn:

> Hail holy Light, ofspring of Heav'n first-born
> . . . .
> Hail Son of God, Saviour of Men, thy Name
> Shall be the copious matter of my Song
> Henceforth, and never shall my Harp thy praise
> Forget, nor from thy Fathers praise disjoine.
> (III.1, 412–15)

In this the poet imitates the "sacred Song" (III.369) of the angels, just as Satan's epic "song" imitates the partial songs of the devils. The unrestrained fancy that moves the demonic songs is associated with the "inspired" madness of *furor poeticus*. Just as Circe's songs "in pleasing slumber lull'd the sense, / And in sweet madnes rob'd it of it self" (*Mask* 259–60), so the devils' songs "Suspended Hell, and took with ravishment / The thronging audience" (II.554–55). God the Father's remark, "seest thou what rage / Transports our adversarie" (III.80–81), penetrates the appearance of the opening books and suggests the illusory nature of Satan's escape. The emphasis on Satan transported by rage, moved by fury, not only indicates his motivation, but it identifies the events of the Satanic epic with the work of poetic frenzy: both are fantasies born of carnal desire. The poet's hymn, however, is like the Lady's song to Echo—it arouses "such sober certainty of waking bliss" (*Mask* 262). And the Lady's song, like Adam's dream of Eve, because it is moved by God, suggests the imagination at its most truly creative: the strains of her song "might create a soul / Under the ribs of Death" (561–62). Just as the Lady's song counters the "thousand fantasies" that "throng into my memory" (204–5) and the Attendant Spirit's song raises Sabrina to heal the contamination of malignant fancy, the "urchin blasts, and ill luck signes / That the shrewd medling Elfe delights to make" (844–45), and to dissolve the "gumms of glutenous heat" (916), just as the songs of morning clear the fancy infected reason in *The Tempest*—"A solemn air, and the best comforter / To an unsettled fancy" (V.i.58–59)—so here the poet's hymn dissolves the demonic phantasmagoria of the opening books.[7] It is for this reason that "Everybody feels that the Satan of the first two books stands alone; after them comes a break, and he is never as impressive again."[8] The image of Satan changes not because Satan has been subjected to some "technique of degradation"[9] but because our eyes have been freed from the blear illusion of fancy's magic dust.

The rising sense of the poet's hymn is both associated with and dissociated from Orpheus's return from the underworld: "borne / With other notes then to th'*Orphean* Lyre" (III.16–17). The poet dissociates himself from Orpheus not only because he is claiming "not to have lost his Eurydice,"[10] but because Orphic poetry is ultimately the work of *furor poeticus*. The demonic song that "charms the Sense" (II.556), that "Suspended Hell, and took with ravishment / The thronging audience" is an allusion to the impact of Orpheus on the divinities of the underworld.[11] The inspiration of Orphic poetry

7. Cf. Broadbent, *Some Graver Subject*, p. 162: "In contact with other devils and angels—Uriel, Gabriel—Satan remains splendid, asserting the cosmic scale of the issue between evil and good; but 'alone bent on his prey' he is bestial, vulture or toad, like tragic villains in soliloquy. The episode in Heaven has made this alteration possible, its impervious perfection insulating the dark fantasy of Hell from the bright reality of the created world."

8. A. J. A. Waldock, Paradise Lost *and Its Critics* (1947; rpt. Cambridge: Cambridge University Press, 1964), p. 81.

9. Ibid., pp. 65–96.

10. Carey and Fowler, p. 561n.

11. Cf. Ovid, *Metamorphoses* X.40–48.

is a fantasy: Orpheus's muse is "an empty dreame" (VII.39). The poet associates himself with Orpheus, however, because, although Orphic poetry in itself is illusory, it may be used, as we have seen in the *Mask*, as the classical shadow or type of divine poetry. This is the implication of Sandys' identification of Orpheus with Moses: the true and original use of poetry is "to sing the praises of the Highest, and to inflame the mind with zeale and devotion. Such *Moses* among the *Hebrewes*, among the *Grecians*, *Orpheus*."[12] Sandys offers a psychological explanation of Orpheus's return from the underworld which suggests that he is thinking of it as an allegory of the effects of Orphic song: "Hell, the Furies, and infernall torments" are "no other then the perturbations of his [Orpheus's] mind," while his return signifies the allaying of those perturbations—they are "pacified, and at length composed by the harmony of reason."[13] In this the Orphic song resembles the music that crept by Ferdinand on the waters "Allaying both their fury and my passion / With its sweet air" and fulfils one of the chief functions of poetry set out in the *Reason of Church-Government*—"to allay the perturbations of the mind, and set the affections in right tune."[14] Not only does the poet's hymn achieve this return to the harmony of reason, but it also does what the actual Orphic song seeks to do but cannot: it enables the reader to "*see the onely king of Heaven and Earth; / . . . unseene by mortall eyes; / Yet nothing from his sight concealed lies.*"[15]

We shall return to the sight unseen by mortal eyes in the second half of the chapter; in this half I wish to concentrate on the effect that this sight has on our perception of Satan.

With this return to reason, with the clearing of fancy's glass, there is a formal return to the divine perspective with which the poem opened. At the opening of Book I we are reminded that "Heav'n hides nothing from thy [the Holy Spirit's] view / Nor the deep Tract of Hell" (I.27–28), and at the opening of Book III, "High Thron'd above all highth, [the Father] bent down his eye" (III.58). Although the consolidated view of Satan is not fully recovered until the beginning of Book IV, it now becomes apparent that it is not Satan, but the poet and reader who have escaped from hell. As the narrator's almost imperceptible shift into hell (I.54–56) marks our entrance into the Devil's mind and the beginning of his fantastic epic, so the poet's

12. Sandys, p. 479. Cf. Edgar Wind, *Pagan Mysteries in the Renaissance*, rev. ed. (New York: Norton, 1968), esp. pp. 17–25; Clifford Davidson, "The Young Milton, Orpheus, and Poetry," *ES* 59 (1978): 27–34.
13. Sandys, p. 476.
14. Yale, I, 816–17.
15. Orphic fragment translated and quoted by Sandys, p. 479.

exit, his escape from "the *Stygian* Pool" (III.14), marks its end. As Fowler points out,[16] the phrase "Escap't the *Stygian* Pool" in the context of a prayer for sight recalls Dante's prayer at the height of heaven:

> Or questi, che da l'infima lacuna
> de l'universo infin qui ha vedute
> le vita spiritali ad una ad una,
> supplica a te, per grazia, di virtute
> tanto, che possa con li occhi levarsi
> più alto verso l'ultima salute.
> (*Paradiso* xxxiii.22–27)

Now this man, who from the lowest pit of the universe even to here has seen one by one the spiritual lives, implores thee of thy grace for power such that he may be able with his eyes to rise still higher toward the last salvation.

The arduous ascent of Dante ("la via è lunga e 'l cammino è malvagio") echoes the Sibyl's words to Aeneas: "facilis discensus Auerno . . . Sed reuocare gradum superasque euadere ad auras, / hoc opus, hic labor est" (*Aeneid* VI.126–29; "the descent to Avernus is not hard. . . . But to retrace the steps and escape back to upper airs, that is the task and that is the toil"). As we have seen, this ascent is underestimated by Moloch ("Th'ascent is easie then"; II.81), and appropriated by Satan—"long is the way / And hard, that out of Hell leads up to light" (II.432–33). It is now revealed as the poet's:

> Taught by the heav'nly Muse to venture down
> The dark descent, and up to reascend,
> Though hard and rare.
> (III.19–21)

This signal refrain occurs in the *Inferno* just after Dante passes the heart of darkness, the Devil fixed in ice at the center of the world. Suddenly, as Virgil commands Dante, "Lèvati sù . . . in piede: / la via è lunga e 'l cammino è malvagio" (*Inferno* xxxiv.94–95; "Rise to your feet. The way is long and the road is hard"), the descent of the aspiring soul is transformed into an ascent. The change in direction is first registered by a change in Dante's view of the Devil:

> Io levai li occhi e credetti vedere
> Lucifero com'io l'avea lasciato,
> e vidili le gambe in sù tenere.
> (*Inferno* xxxiv.88–90)

---

16. Carey and Fowler, p. 561n.

I raised my eyes and thought to see Lucifer as I had left him, and saw him
with his legs held upwards.

In *Paradise Lost* something similar occurs: the signal refrain indicates the transformation of the poet's descent into an ascent, and the
change in direction is further registered by a change in our view of
Satan. From Dante's new perspective, Lucifer appears upside down;
so from our recovered perspective, Satan's ascent now appears as a
descent. At the end of Book II, we left him ascending: Satan "With
fresh alacritie and force renew'd / Springs upward like a Pyramid of
fire" (II.1012–13), towards the world "he hies" (II.1055). When next
we see him he is descending: "ready now / To stoop with wearied
wings and willing feet" (III.72–73). Satan's deflation is similar to that
of Eve at the end of her demonic dream: "wondring at my flight and
change / To this high exaltation; suddenly / My Guide was gon,
and I, me thought, sunk down" (V.89–91). As in Dante the physical
change in perspective reflects a moral one. Dante's journey up towards the stars indicates the true direction of his soul; Satan's journey down to Earth symbolizes the descent of his soul.

The device of ascent being reversed into descent recurs throughout Book III. Satan's journey from the edge of the world to Mount
Niphates is punctuated by three stops: "he first finds a place since
call'd The Lymbo of Vanity . . . thence comes to the Gate of Heaven
. . . thence to the Orb of the Sun" (Argument, Book III). At each of
these stops the theme of ascent-into-descent is repeated, all contrib-
uting to the impression that, though still "bold, / Far off and fear-
less" (IV.13–14), Satan's descent is meant to suggest the sinking
or deflation of his fantastic reverie. This becomes clear when he
reaches Niphates' top and our original consolidated view of evil is
wholly recovered. It becomes clear that Satan's journey in Book III is
the icastic palindrome of his fantastic journey in Book II. It is the
symbolic dissolution of the epic.

In *The Tempest*, as we have seen, unrestrained fancy is revealed as
the common carrier of passion by emphasis on the idea of fury. The
outward show of those passions that move the malignant fancy of
Caliban and his confederates is revealed to them as the fury of barking dogs, while the outward show of those passions that move the
strong imagination of Alonso and the courtiers is revealed to them as
a harpy, the chief of the furies. With Satan there is a similar emphasis on fury. Not only is his epic identified as the work of *furor poeticus*, but the outward show of those passions that animate his fancy
is revealed over and over again as the exploding fury of gunpowder

and volcanoes.[17] We have already seen how the infernal landscape, the image of Satan's mind, is like Aetna "Sublim'd with Mineral fury" (I.235) and how this image is a reworking of one that appears in the longest of Milton's Gunpowder Plot poems: the Father of the Furies

> suspiria rupit
> Tartareos ignes & luridum olentia sulphur.
> Qualia Trinacriâ trux ab Jove clausus in AEtna
> Efflat tabifico monstrosus ab ore Tiphoeus.
> ("In Quintum Novembris" 8, 34–37)

bursts forth sighs that reek of Tartarean fires and of lurid sulphur, sighs such as the grim creature, penned by Jove within Trinacrian AEtna, monstrous Typhœus, breathes forth from his corruption-working mouth.

The Paradise of Fools belongs to the same pattern of exploding images. The foolish and vain are blown up and blown away in an anal exhalation of wind—"all these upwhirld aloft / Fly o're the backside of the World" (III.493–95)—a cosmic fart that suggests the "impetuous furie" (VI.591), the belching, defecating operation of the Devil's cannon, itself, according to Spenser, "framd by *Furies* skill" (*FQ* I.vii.13). The Paradise of Fools is identified with Ariosto's lunar limbo of vanity: the true limbo of vanity is here, Milton insists, and not "in the neighbouring Moon, as some have dreamd" (III.459). Just as Ariosto's Astolfo, once he has subdued a plague of harpies, is shown the limbo of vanity that he "may be taught / How to his wits *Orlando* may be brought" (*Orlando Furioso* XXXIV.60),[18] so here the reader, once Satan's *furor poeticus* has been pointed out in the poet's hymn— "seest thou what rage / Transports our adversarie"—is shown the Paradise of Fools that he may continue to recover his wits and truly see what he has been admiring.

While the ambition that animates Satan's epic is revealed as fury, so its object, glory, is shown to be vain and its medium, mimic fancy, misjoining and ill-matching. In the Paradise of Fools glory appears empty, the hot air or fume of vanity: "Up hither like Aereal vapours flew / . . . all things vain, and all who in vain things / Built thir fond hopes of Glorie" (III.445–49). And mimic fancy only results in dislocation and distortion: it is responsible for "All th'unaccomplisht

17. See Frye, *Return of Eden*, pp. 30–31; Stella Purce Revard, *The War in Heaven* (Ithaca: Cornell University Press, 1980), pp. 86–107.

18. *Orlando Furioso* is quoted from Ludovico Ariosto, *Sir John Harington's Translation of Orlando Furioso*, ed. Graham Hough (London: Centaur Press, 1962).

works of Natures hand, / Abortive, monstrous, or unkindly mixt" (III.455–56). The fume of vanity refers back to the building of Pandemonium which "Rose like an Exhalation" (I.711) and the dislocation and distortion of fancy refers back to the monstrous birth of Death by Sin. As Burton explains, monstrous births—"moles, warts, scars, harelips, monsters"—are produced "by force of a depraved phantasy" in the mother.[19] In *A Midsummer Night's Dream* the blessing of Oberon and Titania, the nuptial song of fancy tempered by reason, is explicitly intended to exorcise the danger of such misjoinings:

> So shall all the couples three
> Ever true in loving be;
> And the blots of Nature's hand
> Shall not in their issue stand.
> Never mole, harelip, nor scar,
> Nor mark prodigious, such as are
> Despisèd in nativity,
> Shall upon their children be.
>   (V.i.396–403)

The "mark prodigious" indicates the ambiguity of Sin's birth being held for a "Sign / Portentous" (II.760–61): to the literal-minded and vainglorious devils the phrase suggests her birth as an awesome portent, but to those who have ears to hear it punctures the devils' vanity and suggests that the birth of Sin herself is monstrous. Both Pandemonium and Sin symbolize Satan's epic, Pandemonium the emptiness of the works of fancy when divorced from reason, and Sin the monstrosity of those works because they come from minds, like those of Bacon's Schoolmen, that feed upon themselves. Pandemonium is the result of Sin just as the Paradise of Fools is only occupied after "Sin / With vanity had filld the works of men" (III.446–47). The Paradise of Fools is neither morally neutral[20] nor does it shift

19. *Anatomy* 1.2.3.2 (p. 221).

20. The emphasis on the similarity between the Paradise of Fools and Dante's vestibule of hell (*Inferno* iii) in Norma Phillips, "Milton's Limbo of Vanity and Dante's Vestibule," *ELN* 3 (1965–66): 177–82, Irene Samuel, *Dante and Milton* (Ithaca: Cornell University Press, 1966), pp. 85–93, and Merrit Y. Hughes, "Milton's Limbo of Vanity," in *Th'Upright Heart and Pure*, ed. Amadeus P. Fiore (Pittsburgh: Duquesne University Press, 1967), pp. 7–24, is misleading. The similarity is certainly there, but it is so because Milton is distinguishing not identifying his Paradise of Fools. The symbolic position of Dante's vestibule, its distance from Satan fixed at the heart of darkness, does suggest that "The 'viltà' of those in the anteroom of Hell is the emptiness of the mass of men, who belong with neither the saved nor the damned" (Samuel,

"guilt for the Fall from evil onto stupidity."[21] The opposition between evil and stupidity is a false one. For Milton virtue and intelligence, the practice of reason, or the action of mentally apprehending
something, are indissolubly linked: God does not captivate mankind
"under a perpetuall childhood of prescription, but trusts him with
the gift of reason to be his own chooser. . . . He that can apprehend
and consider vice with all her baits and seeming pleasures, and yet
abstain, and yet distinguish, and yet prefer that which is truly better,
he is the true warfaring Christian."[22] Being good means reasoning
and the failure to reason is not merely stupid, it is wicked. Though it
does not shift the guilt for the Fall from evil onto stupidity, the Paradise of Fools does refer forward to the process of the Fall. All three
elements apparent in the Paradise of Fools, the exploding fury of passion, the empty fume of vanity, and the dislocation of unrestrained
fancy, are equally apparent in Eve's dream, Satan's attempt to spread
the contagion of the *phantastike*: Satan tries to reach "The Organs
of her Fancie, and with them forge / Illusions as he list, Phantasms
and Dreams" in order to raise

> distemperd, discontented thoughts,
> Vaine hopes, vain aimes, inordinate desires
> Blown up with high conceits ingendring pride.
>   (IV.802-9)

The particular conception of vanity implicit in Pandemonium, the
Paradise of Fools, and Eve's dream is rooted in the wind metaphor of
Ecclesiastes: "The wind goeth toward the south, and turneth about
unto the north; it whirleth about continually, and the wind re-
turneth again according to his circuits. . . . all is vanity and vexation
of spirit" (Eccl. 1:6, 14). "Vexation of spirit" means "striving after
wind,"[23] and the "process of alternating inflation and deflation of the

---

Dante and Milton, p. 93). However, in Milton that Satan is the first to enter the Paradise of Fools and that it is populated through the work of Sin, the creation of Satan's
imagination, is clearly meant to move the emphasis away from the hierarchy of evil to
its unity. Fanciful distinctions between degrees of evil are a vanity and those that
make them tend to find their way into the Paradise of Fools. This is the point of the
juxtaposition of "Embryo's and Idiots, Eremits and Friers / White, Black and Grey,
with all thir trumperie" (III.474–75): as Fowler suggests, here Milton "satirizes a
Catholic tradition which consigned *idiots*, cretins and unbaptized infants to a much
debated *limbo infantum*" (Carey and Fowler, p. 589n).

21. Broadbent, *Some Graver Subject*, p. 163.
22. *Areopagitica* (Yale, II, 514–15).
23. Revised Standard Version.

devils begun in Book I, and continued for Satan all through the poem"[24] is symptomatic of this striving after wind. "All th'unaccomplisht works of Natures hand" (III.455), all natural creation, creation independent of God, is a striving after wind: "Then I looked on all the works that my hands had wrought, and on the labour that I had laboured to do: and behold, all was vanity and vexation of spirit" (Eccl. 2 : 11). This wind metaphor identifies the insubstantiality of inflated vanity not only with that of exploding fury, but also with that of fancy, in that fancy uninformed by reason forms "Aerie shapes" (V.105), or as Theseus puts it,

> And as imagination bodies forth
> The forms of things unknown, the poet's pen
> Turns them to shapes, and gives to airy nothing
> A local habitation and a name.
> Such tricks hath strong imagination.
> (*MND* V.i.14–18)

Just as Pandemonium and the *cellula phantastica* are identified in Book I, so here in the Paradise of Fools the fume of vanity and the airy nothingness of fancy become one. And so the deflation of vanity is also the deflation of fancy. This is the point of the long introductory simile (III.431–39). Just as the vain fondly imagine themselves ascending to heaven's gate where St. Peter "seems / To wait" (III.484–85), but are blown awry, descending in a welter of confusion—

> then might ye see
> Cowles, Hoods and Habits with thir wearers tost
> And flutterd into Raggs, then Reliques, Beads,
> Indulgences, Dispenses, Pardons, Bulls,
> The sport of Winds
> (III.489–93)

—so Satan's epic quest is represented as a flight "toward the Springs / Of *Ganges* or *Hydaspes, Indian* streams" that is interrupted by a descent to "the barren Plaines / Of *Sericana*, where *Chineses* drive / With Sails and Wind thir canie Waggons light" (III.435–39). When "India" is used negatively it is consistently associated with the deceptive, narcotic illusions of fancy. That this belongs to a tradition is indicated by Shakespeare: in *A Midsummer Night's Dream* Fancy is "A lovely boy, stolen from an Indian king" (II.i.22). So in the

24. Broadbent, *Some Graver Subject*, p. 110.

Areopagitica "all the contagion that foreine books can infuse, will finde a passage to the people farre easier and shorter then an Indian voyage."[25] In *Paradise Lost* when we enter Fancy's chamber at the beginning of Book II Satan appears as an eastern despot on a throne which "far / Outshon the wealth of *Ormus* and of *Ind*" (II.1–2). As Satan approaches the gates of hell, ready to spread the contagion of the *phantastike*, he appears as a fleet "Close sailing from *Bengala* . . . whence Merchants bring / Thir spicie Drugs" (II.638–40). The barren plains of Sericana are the true form of Satan's Indian illusions: the sterility of the plains, "windie Sea of Land," is characterized by the insubstantiality and misjoining of wagons with sails propelled by wind. Thus as the ascent of the vain explodes into a descent, so Satan's flight of fancy here dissolves symbolically into a similar descent. The Paradise of Fools is concerned above all with this, the dissolution of the vain works of fancy:

> All th'unaccomplisht works of Natures hand,
> Abortive, monstrous, or unkindly mixt,
> Dissolvd on earth, fleet hither, and in vain,
> Till final dissolution, wander here.
>
> (III.455–58)

As R. M. Frye suggests, one particular work of vain fancy that Milton may be parodying in the Paradise of Fools episode is the kind of self-glorifying apotheosis represented in illusionistic ceiling paintings, such as the apotheosis of Pope Urban VIII, the founder of St. Peter's, in Pietro da Cortona's *Triumph of Glory*.[26] In this kind of painting the spectator is given "a feeling of being overhung by a whole world of flying figures, that hover and soar in an imaginary palace, or through the open sky."[27] Seen from a set angle the effect is impressive, but there, just as with the ascent of the vain in *Paradise Lost*, by a change of perspective orderly ascent suddenly becomes a chaotic explosion: "a violent cross wind . . . Blows them transverse . . . *then might ye see . . . all these upwhirld aloft*" (my emphasis). Frye's observation appears to be confirmed by the pun on "pontifical" in

---

25. Yale, II, 518.

26. *Milton's Imagery*, pp. 209–17. Smith, "The Source of Milton's Pandemonium," p. 197, suggests that when the devils enter Pandemonium as bees it may be an allusion to Urban VIII's followers who were nicknamed the "bees" after the Pope's personal emblem. The bees are very much in evidence in da Cortona's painting.

27. Germain Bazin quoted in R. M. Frye, *Milton's Imagery*, p. 209.

Book X: Sin and Death are able to enter the world, through the "self same place" (X.315) where Satan first alighted, by means of "wondrous Art / Pontifical" (X.312–13), that is, by means of the bridge-making skill of Death and the visual art of the Popes. That Milton should choose to parody the visual arts in the Paradise of Fools episode is not gratuitous: it explains more than anything else the reason for the anti-Catholic satire, and it establishes the theme of the second and third moments of ascent-into-descent—the downward pull of the purely visual, the sense-bound or carnal imagination in Satan's perception of heaven's gate and the sun.

Although the relationship between heaven's gate and the sun is not immediately obvious, it is clear enough: "the description of the sun functions chiefly as a more concrete image of Heaven. During Satan's flight it shines above all stars 'in splendor likest Heaven.'"[28] The material suggested by the sun's appearance confirms the relationship:

> If mettal, part seemd Gold, part Silver cleer;
> If stone, Carbuncle most or Chrysolite,
> Rubie or Topaz, to the Twelve that shon
> In *Aarons* Brest-plate.
>
> (III.595–98)

Aaron's foursquare breastplate, placed on the ephod of the Aaronic priesthood (Exod. 28:16), is a shadow or type of the foursquare Temple (Ezek. 48:30–35) which in turn is a shadow or type of the foursquare New Jerusalem (Rev. 21:16): the City of God is built out of the precious stones of the Aaronic breastplate. If the appearance of the sun is read symbolically, then the sun is a shadow or type of heaven. On the stairway that ascends to heaven's gate and the City of God, and descends to the world and the sun, Satan chooses to descend. He prefers the shadow to the reality, "*Arons* old wardrope"[29] to the "better reality"[30] it typifies. Like Mammon, whose looks and thoughts even in heaven

> Were always downward bent, admiring more
> The riches of Heav'ns pavement, trod'n Gold,
> Then aught divine or holy else enjoy'd
> In vision beatific,
>
> (I.681–84)

28. Broadbent, *Some Graver Subject*, p. 165.
29. *Of Reformation* (Yale, I, 521).
30. *The Likliest Means to Remove Hirelings* (Columbia, VI, 53).

Satan "looks down with wonder . . . though after Heaven seen"
(III.542, 552). He prefers the creation to its creator, the sight to what
it signifies.

In this Satan reverses Jacob's reaction to heaven's gate. Jacob's reaction is a parable of faith. In much the same way that Adam dreaming
on a shady bank sees Paradise and hears his destiny, and then "wak'd,
and found / Before mine Eyes all real, as the dream / Had lively
shadowd" (VIII.309–11), Jacob "Dreaming by night under the open
Skie" (III.514) sees the gate of heaven and hears his destiny, and then
"waking cri'd, *This is the Gate of Heav'n*" (III.515). Both are confirmed in their belief, but Jacob, unlike the unfallen Adam, still only
has a shadow not the reality. What is important, however, is that he
sees the reality in the shadow, heaven in a stone: "Surely the Lord is
in this place; and I knew it not. . . . How dreadful is this place! This is
none other but the house of God, and this is the gate of heaven. . . .
And this stone, which I have set for a pillar, shall be God's house"
(Gen. 28 : 16–17, 22).[31] This is the true method of ascent and the fundamental meaning of the stairs that are "mysteriously," that is, symbolically, meant—the ability to "lift the eye of the mind above the
corporeal and created,"[32] the ability to see the reality in the shadow,
the invisible in the visible. Thus, those that do ascend the stairway—

> whereon
> Who after came from Earth, sayling arriv'd,
> Wafted by Angels, or flew o're the Lake
> Rapt in a Chariot drawn by fiery Steeds
> (III.519–22)

—do so through faith, the persuasion of things not seen: the ascent
of the faithful is the ideal of which the earlier ascent of the foolish is
a parody. The parody is so distinctly anti-Catholic, because, whereas
Protestantism insists that ascent is by "faith alone," Catholicism,
for Milton, accommodates itself to the visible world and accepts the
validity of the "good works" that precede faith—what for Milton are
"All th'unaccomplisht works of Natures hand": through Catholicism "men came to scan the *Scriptures*, by the Letter, and in the
Covenant of our Redemption, magnifi'd the external signs more
then the quickning power of the *Spirit*."[33] "Rapt in a Chariot" refers

31. Cf. Joseph A. Galdon, *Typology and Seventeenth-Century Literature* (The
Hague: Mouton, 1975), p. 132.
32. Augustine, *Christine Doctrine* III.v (Dods, IX, 86).
33. *Of Reformation* (Yale, I, 522).

to the ascent of Elijah and the point of the story of his ascent is that Elisha inherits Elijah's mantle by inheriting his faith, by his ability to see the invisible:

Ask what I shall do for thee, before I be taken away from thee. . . .
—let a double portion of thy spirit be upon me. . . .
—if thou see me when I am taken from thee, it shall be so. . . .
—there appeared a chariot of fire. . . . And Elisha saw it.

(II Kings 2:9–12)

"Wafted by Angels" refers to Lazarus who was "carried by the angels" (Luke 16:22), and the point of the story of Lazarus takes us a stage further, emphasizing the function of words in seeing the invisible: the persuasion of faith comes through the ear not the eye, by the word not the visual image: "If they hear not Moses and the prophets, neither will they be persuaded, though one rose from the dead" (Luke 16:31). Words make visible what are invisible in images, the Word makes visible what is invisible in the world.

In their dreams what both Adam and Jacob see is modified by a verbal explanation, thus avoiding the danger of the illusion that Calvin sees in figures without an explanation: "from the very beginning of the world, whenever God offered any sign to the holy Patriarchs, it was inseparably attached to doctrine, without which our senses would gaze bewildered on an unmeaning object."[34] The sign that Satan sees here, the ascending stairway and the palace gate, is modified for the reader by reference to the Word, the story of Jacob in Scripture: "The Stairs were such as whereon *Jacob* saw / Angels ascending and descending" (III.510–11). However, the sign is not modified for Satan and what he sees is a purely visual or unmeaning object. It is for this reason that heaven's gate is both associated with and dissociated from the visual arts. The association, the description of the gate as a creation of the visual arts—

as of a Kingly Palace Gate
With Frontispice of Diamond and Gold
Imbellisht, thick with sparkling orient Gemmes
The Portal shon

(III.505–8)

---

34. *Institutes* IV.xiv.4, quoted from John Calvin, *Institutes of the Christian Religion*, trans. Henry Beveridge, 2 vols. (Edinburgh, 1875), II, 493–94. Hereafter cited as Beveridge.

—suggests the "earthly" image that "farr distant" Satan "descries" (III.501). The dissociation, the insistence that such a work as heaven's gate is "inimitable on Earth / By Model, or shading Pencil drawn" (III.508–9) is a warning to the reader not to rest in the image as Satan does. For Satan the frontispiece is "Either a decorated entrance or (more probably) a pediment over the gate,"[35] but for the reader it should be thought of as the title page of a book,[36] the shadow of a much deeper reality. It is clear that Satan knows the work to be heaven's gate: he feels that the stairs are let down to dare him "by easie ascent, or aggravate / His sad exclusion from the dores of Bliss" (III.524–25). But for him, in the prison-house built by his own literal imagination, heaven itself is an object, a physical place not a spiritual state, and as an object it appears no superior to the sun. The precious stones that embesllish heaven's gate are all found in the sun, and there they are more visually magnificent because the physical eye is fully satisfied: "The place he found beyond expression bright, / . . . farr and wide his eye commands, / For sight no obstacle found here" (III.591, 614–15). On the sun Satan achieves the perfect perception of unmeaning objects and dead images. Thus, whereas Jacob sees heaven's gate in a stone, Satan only sees stones in heaven's gate.

In this Satan acts out the descent of those who, as Milton explains in *Of Reformation*, would "bring the inward acts of the *Spirit* to the outward, and customary ey-Service of the body, as if they could make God earthly, and fleshly, because they could not make themselves *heavenly*, and *Spirituall*."[37] By translating the spiritual into the physical and encouraging the mind to rest in the physical object, visual art, although ostensibly religious, has a tendency to reverse the *Phaedrus*-like ascent of the soul:

the Soule by this meanes of over-bodying her selfe, given up justly to fleshly delights, bated her wing apace downeward: and finding the ease she had from her visible, and sensuous collegue the body in performance of *Religious* duties, her pineons now broken, and flagging, shifted off from her selfe, the labour of high soaring any more, forgot her heavenly flight, and left the dull, and droyling carcas to plod on in the old rode, and drudging Trade of outward conformity.[38]

35. Carey and Fowler, p. 391n.
36. See *OED*, 3.
37. Yale, I, 520.
38. Ibid., 522. Cf. *Phaedrus*: "when perfect and fully winged she soars upward, and orders the whole world; whereas the imperfect soul, losing her wings and drooping in her flight at last settles on the solid ground" (246c).

As Satan steps onto "the lower stair / That scal'd by steps of Gold to Heav'n Gate" (III.540–41), through the carnal imagination the possibility of heavenly flight or ascent turns into descent. When Satan sees the world, "then from Pole to Pole / He views in bredth" (III.560–61), his sight answers God's question to Job: "Hast thou perceived the breadth of the earth?" (38:18). But Satan's answer is literal, for he fails to perceive the true significance of what he sees—the glory of God. And betraying his serpent-like nature, he "windes with ease / Through the pure marble Air his oblique way" (III.563–64) to the sun.

The final effect, then, of the sense-bound imagination is to render "the whole faculty of . . . apprehension, carnall"[39] and this Satan continues to exhibit once on the sun. The winged image of the soul's ascent in the *Phaedrus*—"when perfect and fully winged she soars upward, and orders the whole world" (246c)—has a biblical counterpart in the eagle whose strength is renewed in the Lord: "But they that wait upon the Lord shall renew their strength; they shall mount up with wings as eagles" (Isa. 40:31). Because the fourth of those apocalyptic beasts who are "full of eyes" and surround the throne of God is compared to "a flying eagle" (Rev. 4:7), the eagle-soul becomes associated with the spiritual sight of the fourth of the evangelists and the supposed author of Revelation, St. John the Divine. Through him the visionary perception of the eagle-soul becomes associated with the "angel standing in the sun" (Rev. 19:17), the angel Milton calls Uriel, "The same whom *John* saw also in the Sun" (III.623). Through the classical belief in the eagle's ability "to gaze full at the rays of the sun"[40] there emerges the symbol of the ascending soul as an eagle whose spiritual sight enables it to gaze undazzled into the meridian sun. The image is a commonplace: it appears, for instance, in Dante, Chaucer, Giovanni Pico, Spenser, and Sir Thomas Browne.[41] It also appears in the *Areopagitica*: "Methinks I see her [England] as an Eagle muing her mighty youth, and kindling her undazl'd eyes at the full midday beam; purging and unscaling

39. *Of Reformation* (Yale, I, 522).

40. Pliny, *Natural History* X.iii: "The sea eagle only compels its still unfledged chicks by beating them to gaze full at the rays of the sun, and if it notices one blinking and with its eyes watering flings it out of the nest as a bastard and not true to stock, whereas one whose gaze stands firm against the light it rears" (Pliny, *Natural History*, trans. H. Rackham et al., The Loeb Classical Library [London: Heinemann, 1938–63], III, 299).

41. Dante, *Paradiso* i.43–48, xx.31–36; Chaucer, *Parliament of Fowls* 330–31; Pico, *Oration on the Dignity of Man* sect. 20; Spenser, *The Faerie Queene* I.x.47; Browne, *Religio Medici* i.49.

her long abused sight at the fountain it self of heav'nly radiance."⁴²
Like the ascending eagle, Satan arrives on the sun as it appears to
reach its meridian—"as when his Beams at Noon / Culminate from
th'*Aequator*" (III.616–17)—and there "matter new to gaze the Devil
met / Undazl'd" (III.613–14). The irony is of course that, though he
may think he is ascending—"Thither his course he bends / . . . but
up or downe / . . . hard to tell" (III.573–75)—Satan is in fact descending and that all his "sharp'nd . . . visual ray" (III.620) can perceive is "matter," that is, unmeaning objects. The kind of seeing that
Uriel represents is not available to him. Satan is spiritually blind in
much the same way that Milton's adversary, Alexander More, is
thought to be: "But if the choice were necessary, I would, sir, prefer
my blindness to yours; yours is a cloud spread over the mind, which
darkens both the light of reason and of conscience; mine keeps from
my view only the colored surfaces of things, while it leaves me
at liberty to contemplate the beauty and stability of virtue and of
truth."⁴³

The paradox of Satan's sight, that his "sharp'nd . . . visual ray" is
the measure of his spiritual blindness, is apparent in his perception
of the colored surface of the sun. While the precious stones in general suggest heaven, the most important of the stones, the stone
which remains unnamed, mysteriously meant, suggests the way to
heaven. The "stone besides" (III.598) refers to the urim, the addi-
tional object thought to be a precious stone which together with the
thummim was deposited for oracular purposes in the Aaronic breast-
plate.⁴⁴ The vain do what Satan does and apprehend the stone car-
nally so that it becomes the philosophers' stone of alchemy, a physical substance capable of transmuting base metals into gold. Such
literal mindedness leads the alchemists and magicians into delusion—"a stone besides / Imagind rather oft than elsewhere seen"
(III.598–99), to wander endlessly in the maze of their own fancies:

> In vain, though by thir powerful Art they binde
> Volatil *Hermes*, and all up unbound
> In various shapes old *Proteus* from the Sea,
> Draind through a Limbec to his Native forme.
> (III.602–5)

42. Yale, II, 558.
43. *Defensio Secunda*, Robert Fellowes' translation, quoted in *Milton: Poems and Selected Prose*, ed. Marjorie Hope Nicolson (New York: Bantam, 1969), p. 181. Cf. Yale, IV, pt. 1, 589.
44. See I. Mendelsohn, "Urim and Thummim," in *The Interpreter's Dictionary*

Just as the true Hermes is Raphael, who stood like "*Maia's son*" (V.285), the agent of revelation, so the true urim is the word of God. As an oracle the actual urim was made redundant by prophecy and in Milton it is made redundant by the Word. In *Paradise Regained* the Word is Christ himself: "Should Kings and Nations from thy mouth consult," Satan says to Christ, "Thy Counsel would be as the Oracle / *Urim* and *Thummim*, those oraculous gems / On *Aaron's* breast" (III.12–15). In the *Reason of Church-Government* the Word is Christ's gospel: "it were a great folly to seeke for counsell in a hard intricat scruple from a Dunce Prelat, when there might be found a speedier solution from a grave and learned Minister, whom God hath gifted with the judgement of Urim more amply ofttimes then all the Prelates together; and now in the Gospell hath granted the privilege of this oraculous Ephod alike to all his Ministers."[45] The true urim does not transform base metals into gold, but much more important it transforms shadows into reality. Attention to the Word reveals that Satan's ascent to the sun is in fact a promise of his final descent, for his moment on the sun recalls Ezekiel's prophecy against Satan as the king of Tyre:

Thou hast been in Eden the garden of God; every precious stone was thy covering, the sardius, topaz, and the diamond, the beryl, the onyx, and the jasper, the sapphire, the emerald, and the carbuncle, and the gold. . . .

Thou art the anointed cherub that covereth; and I have set thee so: thou wast upon the holy mountain of God; thou hast walked up and down in the midst of the stones of fire.

Thou wast perfect in thy ways from the day that thou was created, till iniquity was found in thee.

. . . therefore I will cast thee as profane out of the mountain of God: and I will destroy thee, O covering cherub, from the midst of the stones of fire.

Thine heart was lifted up because of thy beauty, thou has corrupted thy wisdom by reason of thy brightness: I will cast thee to the ground.

(28:13–17)

---

of the Bible: An Illustrated Encyclopaedia, ed. George A. Buttrick et al., 4 vols. (New York: Abingdon, 1962), IV, 739–40. Cf. also Carey and Fowler, p. 598n; Gunnar Qvarnstrom, *The Enchanted Palace* (Stockholm: Almqvist and Wiksell, 1967), pp. 60–65; Linda Weinhouse, "The Urim and Thummim in *Paradise Lost*," *MiltonQ* 11 (1977): 9–12; and Leib, *Poetics of the Holy*, pp. 54–57.

45. Yale, I, 772. Qvarnstrom refers to the *Reason of Church-Government*, but in his determination to establish the association between urim and "the Chariot which symbolizes God's omnipotence" he distorts the reference: "Milton refers to it in *The Reason of Church-Government* (1642, Book I, Chapter V) in the context of his frequently quoted desire 'to celebrate in glorious and lofty hymns the throne and equipage of God's almightiness, and what he works'" (p. 61). Unfortunately, the quotation

Satan's descent before heaven's gate is the icastic reversal of his fantastic ascent through hellgate (II.926–28). Satan's decision on the stairway is central to the theme of ascent-into-descent: as Alardus Gazaeus explains, "and thus by that ladder by which he should have ascended, turning back, he descended into hell."[46] On Niphates' top, it is clear that he is back in hell and the reader is again offered the wholly consolidated view of evil. Satan who "came down, / . . . To wreck on innocent frail man his loss" is again seen as the apocalyptic monster, "the Dragon" who "Came furious down to be reveng'd on men" (IV.9–11, 3–4). The evil that uncoils itself through the course of Satan's epic dream now recoils upon itself. It is made manifest that Satan's epic design "boiles in his tumultuous brest, / And like a devillish Engine back recoiles / Upon himself" (IV.16–18). It becomes clear that his escape from the reality of hell was imaginary:

> horror and doubt distract
> His troubl'd thoughts, and from the bottom stirr
> The Hell within him, for within him Hell
> He brings, and round about him, nor from Hell
> One step no more then from himself can fly
> By change of place.
>
> (IV.18–23)

The Satanic epic was a narcotic song like Circe's that lulled the sense of hell, but now consciousness, "conscience wakes despair / That slumberd"(IV.23–24).

Most important, the view of things offered by Satan is no longer a divisive alternative, but coincides precisely with the divine view of things. God's affirmation of his justice—"I made him just and right, / Sufficient to have stood, though free to fall" (III.98–99)—is now confirmed by Satan's self-interrogation—"Hadst thou the same free Will and Power to stand? / Thou hadst" (IV.66–67). And as God's justice is transcended by his love, so Satan indicates that the very conception of divine justice is the consequence of the inability to respond to or reciprocate God's love: "whom hast thou then or what to accuse, / But heav'ns free Love dealt equally to all?" (IV.67–68).

---

appears several chapters after the reference to urim in what Milton himself describes as "this digression" (Yale, I, 823).

46. Quoted in George Wesley Whiting, *Milton and This Pendant World* (Austin: University of Texas Press, 1958), p. 66. Cf. also Isabel G. MacCaffrey, "The Theme of *Paradise Lost*, Book III," in *New Essays on* Paradise Lost, ed. Thomas Kranidas (Berkeley: University of California Press, 1969), pp. 58–85.

What is explicit here has been implicit all along: the divine justice that lets down stairs to "aggravate / His sad exclusion from the dores of Bliss" is the creation of alienation, the defensive fantasy of a mind which through its own self-absorption cannot respond to divine love.

THE EMERGENCE OF THE DIVINE EPIC

> [The creations of fancy have] . . . a kind of delightfull libertie in them, wherewith they refresh and doe as it were open and unbind the Thoughts, which otherwise, by a continuall pressure in exacter and more massie reasonings, would easily tyre and despaire.
>
> Reynolds, *Treatise of the Passions and Faculties*, p. 22

The final dissolution of the Satanic epic and the return to the original image of the Devil is the achievement of the icastic imagination, the irradiation of celestial light invoked at the beginning of the poet's hymn. This kind of imagination, imagination as a reflection of the divine mind, is carefully distinguished from its Shakespearean type, imagination as the invention of the human mind, in the opening lines of Book IV—at the moment when the image of the Devil as the apocalyptic dragon reappears. The invocation—

> O for that warning voice, which he who saw
> Th'*Apocalyps*, heard cry in Heaven aloud
> (IV.1–2)

—is so worded that it distinguishes the kind of seeing that *"John saw"* (III.623), the kind of seeing that comes from hearing the Word, from the kind of seeing it recalls, the seeing of autonomously creative fancy, by alluding to the opening lines of *Henry V*:

> O for a Muse of fire, that would ascend
> The brightest heaven of invention.
> (Prologue 1–2)

Not only, however, does the icastic imagination enable us to see the Devil's fantasies from God's perspective, but, much more important, it reveals the substance of God's purpose. Indeed, it is this revelation of God's purpose that gives the symbolic dissolution of Satan's fantasy described above its peculiar force. As it assimilates the Satanic epic into a divine epic, an epic every bit as much like a romance quest as Satan's, the council shows that Satan's spontaneity is merely a part of God's order; the council makes the reader privy to the kind of knowledge that Satan's ungoverned fancy and proud imaginations deny him—the kind of knowledge that makes the argument of the Satanic epic no longer plausible. Not only, then, does the poet's hymn at the beginning of Book III achieve a return to the harmony of reason, but it offers revelation; it directs the mind to the imagination of the divine and in so doing it transcends the brightest heavens of human invention—heavens like those of the divine councils in the opening books of the *Iliad*, the *Odyssey*, and the *Aeneid*.

The key to Milton's council is the dual role of the Son—intercession and interpretation. Intercession is effected through interpretation, and because interpretation involves the activity of the imagination, lifting the eye of the mind above the letter, the Son's intercession, as we shall see, exemplifies the way imagination serves as the instrument of grace. His intercession is best seen first in relation to the council's classical models, and his interpretation in relation to the angels' song with which the council closes.

It is clear that all three classical councils are in Milton's mind. The dramatic point of these councils is intercession. In all three a subordinate deity intercedes with the father of the gods on behalf of the poem's hero: Thetis with Zeus on behalf of Achilles, Athene with Zeus on behalf of Odysseus, and Venus with Jupiter on behalf of Aeneas. The intercession is precipitated by a sense of injustice—that some kind of divine promise has been broken. Implicit in Thetis' complaint to Zeus is the feeling that the promise made to Achilles of a short, but glorious life has been broken: "O would to heaven," she says to Achilles, "that, since / Thy fate is little and not long, thou mightst without offence / And teares performe it" (*Iliad* I.409–11). Explicit in Athene's complaint to Zeus is the feeling that the piety of Odysseus has been betrayed:

> Yet never shall
> Thy lov'd heart be converted on his thrall,
> Austere Olympus. Did not ever he
> In ample Troy thy altars gratifie,
> And Grecians Fleete make in thy offerings swim?
> O Jove, why still then burnes thy wrath to him?
> *Odyssey* I.103–8

And explicit in Venus' complaint to Jupiter is the feeling that the promise of Rome's destiny restoring the loss of Troy has been betrayed:

> certe hinc Romanos olim uoluentibus annis,
> hinc fore ductores, reuocato a sanguine Teucri,
> qui mare, qui terras omnis dicione tenerent,
> pollicitus—quae te, genitor, sententia uertit?
>
> *Aeneid* I.234–37

Yet your promise was of Romans, leaders of men, who should one day with the rolling of the years be their descendants, with Teucer's blood, strong once more, running in their veins; they were to discipline all the sea and all lands under their law. Father, what thought has been changing your will?

The intercession precipitates a course of action, the action of the poem, in which the original injustice is ameliorated. In the case of the more rigorously conceptualized *Aeneid* the intercession precipitates not only divine action but also a revelation of the future effect of that action by which the original injustice is shown to be illusory. Jupiter has not changed his mind and his purpose is triumphantly affirmed:

> 'parce metu, Cytherea, manent immota tuorum
> fata tibi; cernes urbem et promissa Lauini
> moenia, sublimemque feres ad sidera caeli
> magnanimum Aenean; neque me sententia uertit.
> hic tibi (fabor enim, quando haec te cura remordet,
> longius, et uoluens fatorum arcana mouebo).
>
> (I.257–62)

'Spare your fears, Cytherean. You have your people's destiny still, and it shall not be disturbed. You shall see your city, see Lavinium's walls, for I have promised them. And you shall exalt to the stars of Heaven your son Aeneas, the great of heart. There is no thought changing my will. But now, because anxiety for him so pricks you, therefore shall I speak of the more distant future, and, turning the scroll of the Fates, awake their secrets.'

In a much more complex form the same pattern of intercession and revelation of God's purpose is apparent in Milton's council. There, however, the emphasis shifts so that the intercession itself is the essence of the revelation. In the final speech of the debate the Father makes it clear that, unlike the restoration of Troy, the restoration of mankind depends wholly upon the subordinate deity's intercession:

as in Adam "perish all men, so in thee / As from a second root shall be restor'd, / As many as are restor'd, without thee none" (III.287–89). But the Son's intercession in human history and his intercession in the divine council are the same—in as much as the latter is a prefiguration of the former, the intercession of the Son in his first speech is, as we shall see, a prefiguration of the decision in his second speech to intercede physically in human history. Not only, then, is the revelation of God's purpose occasioned by the Son's intercession, but his purpose cannot be effected without that intercession.

The divine council closes with the poet's report of the angels' "sacred Song" (III.369). The importance of the song is that it rehearses the significance of the council—just as the demonic songs after the infernal council echo the false heroism of Satan. Through the medium of the sacred song it becomes apparent that central to the significance of the council is the relationship between the Father and the Son. The relationship is explained, as one might expect with knowledge of God, in terms of seeing. Whereas the Father is invisible, the Son is visible. The Father is celebrated in the paradoxical imagery of the *via negativa*: like Pseudo-Dionysius's "Dark beyond all light,"[47] the Father is "Dark with excessive bright"—so much so that "brightest Seraphim," those angels who most deeply contemplate the mysteries of God, "Approach not, but with both wings veil thir eyes" (III.380–82). His perfection is largely defined by negatives, words which admit the impossibility of definition: he is "Immutable, immortal, infinite . . . invisible . . . inaccessible" (III.373, 375, 377). As Milton explains in the *Christine Doctrine*, "When we talk about knowing God, it must be understood in terms of man's limited powers of comprehension. God as he really is, is far beyond man's imagination, let alone his understanding: I Tim.vi.16: *dwelling in unapproachable light.*"[48] God as he really is is incomprehensible.

As the invisibility of the Father is meant to suggest the incomprehensibility of God, so the visibility of the Son is meant to emphasize the fundamental point that what we can know of God is to be known through the Son. The testimony of St. Paul and the evangelists that the Son "is the image of the invisible God, the firstborn of every creature" (Col. 1 : 15), that "no man hath seen God at any time, the only begotten Son, which is in the bosom of the Father, he hath declared him" (John 1 : 18) is evident in the second part of the angels' song:

47. Quoted from *Varieties of Mystic Experience,* ed. Elmer O'Brien (New York: Holt, Rinehart, and Winston, 1964), p. 83.
48. Yale, VI, 133.

> Thee next they sang of all Creation first,
> Begotten Son, Divine Similitude,
> In whose conspicuous count'nance, without cloud
> Made visible, th'Almighty Father shines,
> Whom else no Creature can behold.
>
> (III.383–87)

The song's point is plain, and as the Son "is the image, as it were, by which God becomes visible, so he is the word by which God is audible."[49] In the council itself we come to see God's purpose through the Son's intercession, and the words of the Father, the words that express his anger and the strife of mercy and justice, only become fully comprehensible through the words of the Son. The angels' song makes it clear that the Son *interprets* the Father:

> No sooner did thy dear and onely Son
> Perceive thee purpos'd not to doom frail Man
> So strictly, but much more to pitie enclin'd,
> He to appease thy wrauth, and end the strife
> Of Mercy and Justice in thy face discern'd,
> Regardless of the Bliss wherein hee sat
> Second to thee, offerd himself to die
> For mans offence. O unexampl'd love.
>
> (III.403–10)

The Son interprets the Father in two complementary senses. First, in as much as he comes to "perceive" or "discern" the Father's purpose before it is formally revealed: "thy dear and onely Son" did "Perceive thee purpos'd not to doom frail Man." Second, in as much as the offer which this perception or act of interpretation precipitates not only makes the Father's purpose possible but it makes his love manifest: that is, the Son's sacrifice, the Father's sacrifice of his "dear and onely Son," not only makes the restoration of mankind possible, but makes the Father's love comprehensible to us. It is this revelation, that the Son is the mediator who interprets the Father, the Word by which we hear God, that explains the triumphal sense of discovery with which the poet's hymn ends:

> Hail Son of God, Saviour of Men, thy Name
> Shall be the copious matter of my Song

---

49. *Christian Doctrine* I.vi (Yale, VI, 297).

Henceforth, and never shall my Harp thy praise
Forget, nor from thy Fathers praise disjoine.
(III.412–15)

The wrath the Son discerns in the Father is concentrated in the Father's opening speech. Both the classical and biblical models for this speech are resonant with anger. In the *Odyssey* Athene's intercession, her sense of an injustice having been done to Odysseus, comes as a response to Zeus' complaint of an injustice having been done to himself:

'O how falsly men
Accuse us Gods as authors of their ill,
When by the bane their owne bad lives instill
They suffer all the miseries of their states.'
(I.50–53)[50]

The same injured tone is immediately apparent in the Father's speech:

So will fall,
Hee and his faithless Progenie: whose fault?
Whose but his own? ingrate, he had of mee
All he could have . . .
. . . nor can justly accuse
Thir maker.
(III.95–98, 112–13)

In the Bible, as a number of critics have suggested,[51] this injured tone, this sense of man's ingratitude, coincides with those moments when Jehovah repents the creation of mankind: "How long will this people provoke me? and how long will it be ere they believe me, for all the signs which I have shewed among them? I will smite them with the pestilence and disinherit them" (Numbers 14:11).[52] It is

50. Zeus' speech is quoted by Milton at the end of his chapter on predestination in the *Christian Doctrine* (I.iv [Yale, VI, 202]). It is noticed by Frye, *Return of Eden*, p. 99, and, following him, Blessington, pp. 47–48, treats it in more detail.

51. See John E. Parish, "Milton and an Anthropomorphic God," *SP* 56 (1959): 619–25; Michael Leib, "*Paradise Lost*, Book III: The Dialogue in Heaven Reconsidered," in *Renaissance Papers 1974*, ed. Dennis G. Donovan and A. Leigh Deneff (Durham, N.C.: Southeastern Renaissance Conference, 1975), pp. 39–50; Kitty Cohen, *The Throne and the Chariot* (The Hague: Mouton, 1975), pp. 103–16. Cf. also Stella Purce Revard, "The Dramatic Function of the Son in *Paradise Lost*: A Commentary on Milton's 'Trinitarianism,'" *JEGP* 66 (1967): 45–58; Arthur E. Barker, "*Paradise Lost*: The Relevance of Regeneration," in Paradise Lost: *A Tercentenary Tribute*, ed. Balachandra Rajan (Toronto: University of Toronto Press, 1969), esp. pp. 67–71.

52. Cf. also Gen. 6:6–7; Exod. 32:7–10.

clear then that the anger of both Zeus and Jehovah is present in the Father's speech. This is where the Father appears as "Th'incensed Deitie" (III.187), where the reader feels the animus of the emotion that the Son has to appease. The Son's offer, "On me, let thine anger fall" (III.237), not only resolves the logical dilemma posed in the Father's second speech, but it allays the emotional state expressed in the first. The desire to root the style of the Father's opening speech in an historical context has obscured its literary context. The desire to demonstrate the presence of the Puritan sermon's supposed plain style and the Royal Society's "mathematical plainness of language"[53] has obscured the emotional quality of the speech, a quality inherited from Homer and the Bible. The propriety of representing an emotional God is confirmed by Milton himself: "It is safest for us to form an image of God in our minds which corresponds to his representation and description of himself in the sacred writings. . . . On the question of what is or what is not suitable for God, let us ask for no more dependable authority than God himself. If *Jehovah repented that he had created man*, Gen. vi.6, *and repented because of their groanings*, Judges ii.18, let us believe that he did repent. . . . let us believe that it is not beneath God to feel what grief he does feel, to be refreshed by what refreshes him, and to fear what he does fear."[54] It is a measure of Milton's achievement that the language of the Father's first speech is both abstract and emotional, that phrases like "faithless Progenie" have both a denotation "as abstract and precise as mathematical notation"[55] and connotations filled with contempt and bitterness, that a word like "ingrate," despite Fish's assertion to

53. For the Puritan plain style, see Broadbent, *Some Graver Subject*, p. 146; for the language of the Royal Society, see Arnold Stein, *Answerable Style* (Minneapolis: University of Minnesota Press, 1953), p. 128. See also Irene Samuel, "The Dialogue in Heaven: A Reconsideration of *Paradise Lost*, III, 1–417," in *Milton: Modern Essays in Criticism*, ed. Arthur E. Barker (New York: Oxford University Press, 1965), pp. 233–45, on the "near tonelessness of his first speech" (p. 235); Fish, *Surprised by Sin*, pp. 57–68, on the nonaffective quality of the Father's language—ingrate "is a term not of reproach, but of definition" (p. 64); Peter Berek, "'Plain' and 'Ornate' Styles and the Structure of *Paradise Lost*," *PMLA* 85 (1970): 237–46, on a language "stripped of emotions, stripped of connotations, and used as though it were as abstract and precise as mathematical notation" (p. 241); Gary D. Hamilton, "Milton's Defensive God: A Reappraisal," *SP* 69 (1972): 87–100, on the "unanthropomorphic voice, passionless, impersonal" (p. 99); Robert Crosman, *Reading* Paradise Lost (Bloomington: Indiana University Press, 1980), on the "impartial, serene, imperturbable, and consistent" tone of the Father (p. 80). For the reaction against the nonaffective quality of the Father's language, see, for instance, Christopher, pp. 114–15.

54. *Christian Doctrine* I.ii (Yale, VI, 133–35). Cf. Leib, "The Dialogue in Heaven," p. 41; Cohen, pp. 104–5.

55. Berek, "'Plain' and 'Ornate' Styles," p. 241.

the contrary, is *both* a definition and a reproach.[56] It would be a mistake to think the emotion accidental: it is deliberate. It may be a source of revulsion—"dismay, disappointment, and a reluctant hostility," according to Fish,[57] "grotesquely bad," according to Frye[58]—but it is also the beginning of wisdom. The speech is not simply the near toneless statement of "what is";[59] it is an expression of anger that is meant to elicit a response—both in the reader and the Son. For the reader it is meant to arouse fear; for the Son a resolution of that fear and an appeasement of the anger. For the Son the Father's anger is a test or provoking object.

The celestial light which plants the eyes of faith at the beginning of the poet's hymn is the light of wisdom.[60] The light of wisdom is the "ofspring of Heav'n first-born" (III.1): the poet's affirmation "Before the Heavens thou wert" (III.9) is a contraction of the testimony of wisdom herself—"The Lord possessed me in the beginning of his way. . . . Before the mountains were settled, before the hills was I brought forth. . . . When he prepared the heavens, I was there" (Prov. 8 : 22, 25, 27). Wisdom, however, begins with the fear of God: "The fear of the Lord is the beginning of wisdom" (Prov. 9 : 10).[61] The historical efficacy of the fear of God is explained by Michael. When mankind is restored after the Flood it prospers through fear of God:

> This second sours of Men, while yet but few;
> And while the dread of judgement past remains
> Fresh in thir mindes, fearing the Deitie,
> With some regard to what is just and right
> Shall lead thir lives, and multiplie apace.
>
> (XII.13–17)

The "dread of judgement past" is precisely the result of the anger of those moments when Jehovah *"repented that he had created man"* (Gen. 6 : 6). What that dread effects is "some regard to what is just and right," and this is the purpose of the anger the Father shows in his opening speech: "Fear not," says Moses, "for God is come to prove you, and that his fear may be before your faces, that ye sin not" (Exod. 20 : 20). The relationship between fear and wisdom, the psychology of Michael's historical example, is expanded by Calvin:

56. See Fish, *Surprised by Sin*, p. 64.
57. Ibid., p. 81.
58. Quoted in ibid., p. 80.
59. Samuel, "The Dialogue in Heaven," p. 235.
60. See pp. 76–77.
61. Cf. Job 28 : 28; Ps. 111 : 10; Prov. 1 : 7; Ecclus. 19 : 20.

being aroused by fear [we] may learn humility. For as there exists in man something like a world of misery, and ever since we were stript of the divine attire our naked shame discloses an immense series of disgraceful properties, every man, being stung by the consciousness of his own unhappiness, in this way necessarily obtains at least some knowledge of God. Thus, our feeling of ignorance, vanity, want, weakness, in short, depravity and corruption, remind us . . . that in the Lord, and none but He, dwell the true light of wisdom, solid virtue, exuberant goodness.[62]

Fear arises out of the divine anger that makes us conscious of our fallen state and that consciousness is the first step towards knowing God and the heavenly grace of faith—which is another way of describing wisdom. This is exactly the process as it is explained by the Father in his second speech:

> The rest shall hear me call, and oft be warnd
> Thir sinful state, and to appease betimes
> Th'incensed Deitie, while offerd grace
> Invites; for I will cleer thir senses dark,
> What may suffice, and soft'n stonie hearts
> To pray, repent, and bring obedience due.
>
>   (III.185–90)

The process is similar to the one in which Prospero uses fear to clear the senses of Alonso. Alonso's guilt is brought to consciousness and the illusions of "strong imagination" ultimately responsible for that guilt are dispelled by the dreadful judgment of Ariel masquerading as a furious harpy.[63] So in Milton the reader's guilt is brought to consciousness and the Satanic illusions ultimately responsible for that guilt are dispelled by the dreadful judgment of God appearing as Jehovah. As Fish suggests, the reader's "complacence does not survive the inexorability of 'and shall pervert, / For Man will heark'n to his glozing lies, / And easily transgress the sole Command, / Sole pledge of his obedience' (92–95)."[64] But most important, the moral process outlined above by the Father (III.185–90) is re-created mimetically by the dramatic impact of the opening speech: the fear that precipitates the desire for grace is re-created

---

62. *Institutes* I.i.1 (Beveridge, I, 37–38).

63. Alonso's complicity in the usurpation of Prospero's dukedom, no less than Sebastian's attempted usurpation of Alonso's kingdom, is, according to Prospero, the result of the persuasive power of Antonio's "strong imagination": "This King of Naples, being an enemy / To me inveterate, hearkens my brother's suit" (I.ii.121–22).

64. Fish, *Surprised by Sin*, p. 81.

mimetically in the reader's "visceral reaction" to the Father, a reaction that longs for an intercessor.

The light of wisdom, the celestial light that plants the eyes of faith, is also of course the Son himself. He is the "ofspring of Heav'n firstborn": he is "the first born of every creature" (Col. 1:15), "of all Creation first, / Begotten Son" (III.383–84). When the poet reflects "since God is light" (III.3) he is thinking of the Son—"the true Light, which lighteth every man that cometh into the world" (John 1:9). The light of wisdom intensifies with the Son's intercession, with his resolution of the reader's fear and appeasement of the Father's anger. The Son's intercession takes the form of an interpretation of the Father, a re-sounding that allays the perturbations of the reader's mind and begins to set the apparent affections of the Father in right tune. In much the same way that Alonso's restoration to the harmony of reason is prefigured by the way in which the harpy's discursive but dread sentence is apprehended as music—"The winds did sing it to me" (III.iii.97)[65]—so the possibility of our redemption is prefigured by the way in which the Father's discursive but dread voice is echoed by the Son but with the emphasis on its harmony—on the gracious note of its mercy. The final note of the Father's speech, "Man therefore shall find grace" (III.131), which comes almost as a surprise, an embellishment, an ornamental addition, a "grace-note," is resounded as the first note of the Son's speech: "O Father, gracious was that word which clos'd / Thy sovran sentence, that Man should find grace" (III.144–45). But this note is so amplified that the Son, like Echo, gives "*resounding grace to all Heav'ns harmonies*" (*Mask* 242). In other words, by amplifying the grace-note of mercy the Son provides the divine response to the reader's embryonic faith, the desire for grace that grows out of the awareness of our sinful state. His response provides the evidence of faith, an assurance of things hoped for. As mercy allays the reader's fear, so the love it will arouse appeases the Father's anger. Unlike Zeus in the *Odyssey* the Father's anger proceeds not simply from the false accusation of injustice, but from the failure of man to reciprocate his love. The desire for man's love is implicit in the Father's account of the necessity of free will:

> Not free, what proof could they have givn sincere
> Of true allegiance, constant Faith or Love,
> Where onely what they needs must do, appeard,
> Not what they would? what praise could they receive?

65. See pp. 24–25.

> What pleasure I from such obedience paid,
> When Will and Reason (Reason also is choice),
> Useless and vain, of freedom both despoild,
> Made passive both, had servd necessitie,
> Not mee.
> (III.103–11)

What is implicit here becomes explicit in the Son's restatement of the Father's feeling for man—"Man / Thy creature late so lov'd, thy youngest Son" (III.150–51). The emotive phrase "thy youngest Son" identifies the Father's feelings with the intense love of the Patriarchs for their youngest sons, for example, "Now Israel loved Joseph more than all his children, because he was the son of his old age" (Gen. 37:3). The Son's restatement also suggests a memory of Lear's love for Cordelia. Although the wording is too common to enable us to be sure, Fowler thinks the Father's reference to man, "nor Man the least / Though last created" (III.277–78), might be a memory of Lear's reference to Cordelia as "our joy, / Although the last, not least" (*Lear* I.i.82–83 in the quartos).[66] When Lear feels that Cordelia fails to reciprocate his love, unlike the Father, he offers no grace and his anger remains unappeased by an intercessor:

> Peace, Kent!
> Come not between the dragon and his wrath.
> I loved her most, and thought to set my rest
> On her kind nursery.—Hence and avoid my sight!
> (I.i.121–24)

Lear's angry insistence on distributive justice—"Nothing will come of nothing. . . . The bow is bent and drawn; make from the shaft" (I.i.90, 143)—precipitates the tragedy. Whereas Lear is unbending, the Father is gracious and his offer of resounding grace means that God's love will be reciprocated: it means, as the Son's loving response both explains and enacts, that "th'innumerable sound / Of Hymns and sacred Songs . . . shall resound thee ever blest" (III.147–49). The reciprocity of love between God and man is symbolized in the reciprocity of musical harmonies, a reciprocity itself imitated in the echoing of "sound" and "resound."

The dual nature of the Son's role, the simultaneity of his intercession on behalf of man and interpretation on behalf of God, is very clearly demonstrated in the second half of the speech. There the in-

66. See Carey and Fowler, p. 576n.

tercession is concentrated in the connotations, and the interpretation in the denotation. While the classical connotations of the second half of the speech are those of the subordinate deity interceding with the father of the gods, the biblical connotations are those of the Patriarchs interceding with Jehovah at those moments when he repents the creation of mankind.[67] Abraham's intercession is very consciously alluded to with the wording of "that be from thee farr, / That farr be from thee, Father, who art Judg / Of all things made, and judgest onely right" (III.153–55): "That be far from thee to do after this manner, to slay the righteous with the wicked: and that the righteous should be as the wicked, that be far from thee: Shall not the Judge of all the earth do right?" (Gen. 18:25). Moses' intercession is equally consciously alluded to in the argument. The Son makes three points which appear to question the fearful implications of the Father's anger: first, "should Man finally be lost?" (III.150–53); second, "shall the Adversarie thus obtain / His end, and frustrate thine?" (III.156–62); and third, "wilt thou thy self / Abolish thy Creation?" (III.162–64). The questions amount to an argument which is clearly related to the one Moses puts to Jehovah when he threatens to destroy the faithless Israelites—that the Egyptians should thus obtain their end and frustrate his:

> Lord, why doth thy wrath wax hot against thy people, which thou hast brought forth out of the land of Egypt with great power, and with a mighty hand?
> Wherefore should the Egyptians speak, and say, For mischief did he bring them out, to slay them in the mountains, and to consume them from the face of the earth? Turn from thy fierce wrath, and repent this evil against thy people.
> Remember Abraham, Isaac, and Israel, thy servants, to thom thou swarest by thine own self, and saidst unto them, I will multiply your seed as the stars of heaven, and all this land that I have spoken of will I give unto your seed, and they shall inherit it for ever.
>
> (Exod. 32:11–13)

Moses' final point that destroying Israel means breaking the covenant is both the biblical antitype of the classical intercessor's sense of a divine promise having been broken (especially Jupiter's promise

67. Cf. Parish, "Milton and an Anthropomorphic God"; Leib, "The Dialogue in Heaven"; Cohen, pp. 103–16. The allusions are familiar and have been recorded since Bishop Newton, but, as Leib says, "error has arisen as the result of our not having placed enough emphasis upon the importance of the Abrahamic and Mosaic episodes to the Son's dialogue with the Father in Book III" (p. 40).

to exalt Aeneas to "the stars of heaven"), and the Old Testament type of the Son's final point: "or wilt thou thy self / Abolish thy Creation, and unmake, / For him [Satan], what for thy glorie thou hast made?" (III.162–64). The Son as intercessor makes it clear that if man should be finally lost through the Fall it would be impossible to justify the ways of God to men: "So should thy goodness and thy greatness both / Be questiond and blaspheam'd without defence" (III.165–66).[68] The Son makes it clear that justice without mercy is not really justice, that there is a contradiction between man being finally lost through the Fall and the justice of him who "judgest only right" (III.155). A similar point is made in the *Christian Doctrine*: "So, too, where God explains in distinct terms the justice of his ways [Ezek. 18:25–27, 31–32; 33:11, 14, 15]. . . . he considers all worthy of sufficient grace, and the cause is his justice. . . . he must also wish that no one should lack sufficient grace for salvation. Otherwise it is not clear how he can demonstrate his truthfulness to mankind."[69] As Milton's proof-texts from Ezekiel establish, God's justice in the fullest sense involves mercy. As Una explains to Redcross, "Where iustice growes, there grows eke greater grace" (*FQ* I.ix.53). Distributive justice, justice without mercy, is a falliable human formulation. Justice without mercy is the wrath of God and it is only for the damned, like Sin, that justice and wrath appear as the final equation: "his wrath, which he calls Justice" (II.733).

Thus, when the intercessional aspect of the Son's speech is stressed, his response answers the reader's deepest longings for a defender. It answers Job's longing for a mediator: "O that one might plead for a man with God, as a man pleadeth for his neighbour!" (16:21). The Son's response is intended to make a faith like Job's possible: in the Son's response, Job's faith, "I know that my redeemer liveth" (19:25), becomes through the agency of the poet's icastic imagination a fact.

The Son's intercession as a dramatic challenge to the Father is, however, an accommodation—the Son's mediation seen from a purely human perspective: the intercessional aspect of the Son's speech alludes to what his perfect mediation supersedes, the imperfect mediation of the Son's classical and biblical types. To characterize his response as "the undeniable challenge of one figure to another," as an "indictment,"[70] is to insist upon a half-truth. For in the Son's re-

---

68. For God to abolish his creation is the aim of the demonic strategy as outlined by Beelzebub—"that thir God / May prove thir foe, and with repenting hand / Abolish his own works" (II.368–70).

69. I.iv (Yale, VI, 191, 193).

70. Leib, "The Dialogue in Heaven," p. 43.

sponse, the intercessor has been assimilated into the interpreter. The syntax of the speech transforms the connotations of challenge into the denotation of explanation. The Son's first point is not really a question, but a conditional clause—"For should Man finally be lost"—modifying a main clause—"that be from thee farr, / That farr be from thee." The main clause insists that the fearful implication of the Father's anger contained in the conditional clause is a wild misinterpretation: the wildness is expressed in the rearrangement of Abraham's words so that "farr" is placed for emphasis at the end of one line and the beginning of the next. This insistence on misinterpretation applies by ellipsis to the other two points: "or shall the Adversarie thus obtain / His end" (that be from thee farr); "or wilt thou thy self / Abolish thy creation" (that be from thee farr). The Son is not challenging the Father, but explaining him. What the Father and Son offer are not alternatives but incremental repetitions in the movement of God's progressive self-revelation. In as much as the Father and Son "speak and act as one,"[71] their debate is a fiction—much like the one Sir Thomas Browne describes: God "holds no Councell, but that mysticall one of the Trinity, wherein though there be three persons, there is but one minde that decrees, without contradiction."[72] The coincidence of their views reaffirms the critical point that God can only be known through the Son. The Son's interpretation of the Father's anger is the fulfilment of Moses' mediation as described by Michael:

> But the voice of God
> To mortal eare is dreadful; they beseech
> That *Moses* might report to them his will,
> And terror cease; he grants what they besaught
> Instructed that to God is no access
> Without Mediator, whose high Office now
> *Moses* in figure beares, to introduce
> One greater, of whose day he shall foretell.
> (XII.235–42)

The poet senses this before the Son speaks, and the Father confirms it once he has finished. Just as the face of Moses, the interpreter of God's will, shines with a divine radiance (Exod. 34:29–35), so in the Son the Father shines, he becomes visible, comprehensible: in the Son, the poet imagines, "all his Father shon / Substantially express'd,

71. *Christian Doctrine* I.v (Yale, VI, 220).
72. *Religio Medici* i.13 (Martin, p. 13).

and in his face / Divine compassion visibly appeered, / Love without end, and without measure Grace" (III.139–42). As far as the Father himself is concerned, the Son's response proves him to be "My word, my wisdom, and effectual might, / All hast thou spok'n as my thoughts are" (III.170–71).

In fact, the Father greets the Son's resounding of his wrath with delight:

> O Son, in whom my Soul hath chief delight,
> Son of my bosom, Son who art alone
> My word, my wisdom, and effectual might
> All hast thou spok'n as my thoughts are, all
> As my Eternal purpose hath decreed.
>
> (III.168–72)

And the Father's delight suggests the work of both faith and its mental agency, the imagination. Leib's comment that the Father "even suggests in His omniscience that He has known all along what the Son was going to say,"[73] though accurate enough in its substance, belies the emotional quality of the Father's declaration; it is not an admission forced like Jehovah's repentance in Exodus (32:14), but a spontaneous expression of pleasure in an act of comprehension—a divine and much more exuberant version of Michael's response to Adam: "Dextrously thou aim'st" (XI.844). The Father's response, which goes on to continue the resounding of heaven's harmonies by amplifying the process of grace, suggests that the Son's understanding proceeds not as in Browne's Trinity from omniscience, but from a trust in the Father's goodness, that is, from faith and love, "the interpreter and guide of our faith."[74] What pleasure could the Father receive from an understanding that proceeded from the necessity of omniscience? It is precisely because the Son's knowledge originates in faith that the words that transform his intercession into an interpretation, the decisive main clause "that be from thee farr," are the words with which Abraham expresses his faith in God's justice. The echoing of Abraham at this point is very deliberate because Abraham's chief function in Scripture is, as Michael, following Hebrews, sees, to act as an example of faith: "he straight obeys, / Not knowing to what Land, yet firm believes: / I see him, but thou canst not, with

---

73. Leib, "The Dialogue in Heaven," p. 44.
74. *The Doctrine and Discipline of Divorce* I, Preface (Yale, II, 236). Cf. Revard, "The Dramatic Function of the Son," and for a different view, C. A. Patrides, "The Godhead in *Paradise Lost*: Dogma or Drama," *JEGP* 64 (1965): 29–34.

what Faith / He leaves his Gods" (XII.126–29). Abraham's faith, says Calvin, "is set before us as the best model of believing."[75] Thus the Son's mediation, his intercession and interpretation, is an act of faith, the correct response, the response that originates in love, to the test of faith implicit in the Father's wrath. This is the central point of the debate. As Adam discovers, "So willingly doth God remit his Ire" once his grace "shall one just Man find" (XI.885, 890); so here the Father's affections begin to be set in right tune once his love finds and is reciprocated by the Son.

The heavy emphasis on the Father's "delight" with what the Son says suggests that the understanding that proceeds from faith proceeds through the imagination. In the invocation to Book I, as we have seen,[76] the feeling that "*Sion* hill / . . . and *Siloa*'s brook that flow'd / Fast by the Oracle of God" may "Delight thee more" (I.10–12) assumes that delight is the characteristic response to the gospel and to the most poetic and imaginative parts of revelation generally, the revelation that provides the evidence of faith. In Milton's mind, delight is firmly associated with the effect of art. The Lady's song effects "such a sacred, and home-felt delight" (*Mask* 261). The works of God are "Pleasant to know, and worthiest to be all / Had in remembrance alwayes with delight" (*PL* III.703–4). Eve, whose birth is such a powerful affirmation of human art, the human imagination reflecting the design of God,[77] is "Heav'ns last best gift, my ever new delight" (V.19): "in her looks [she] summs all Delight" (IX.454). Delight as the characteristic effect of art derives not only from the traditional explanation of poetry as teaching by delight, but from the etymological meaning of Eden, the art of God to which human art aspires, being "well known in the seventeenth century to be 'pleasure, delight.'"[78] Thus, when Satan views Eden, he "saw undelighted all delight" (IV.286).

What the Father's delight suggests is confirmed by the repeated use of the metaphor of reflected light to express the Son's understanding. His understanding is the visible reflection of the Father's excessive brightness—"in him all his Father shon / Substantially express'd" in his

> conspicuous count'nance, without cloud
> Made visible, th'Almighty Father shines,

75. *Institutes* II.x.ii (Beveridge, I, 375).
76. See pp. 78–79.
77. See pp. 119–20.
78. Carey and Fowler, p. 609n.

Whom else no Creature can behold: on thee
Impresst the effulgence of his Glorie abides,
Transfus'd on thee his ample Spirit rests.
(III.385–88)

The spirit that rests on the Son is of course the Holy Spirit, but in this context the Holy Spirit, according to the *Christian Doctrine*, means the light of wisdom—"the light with which God illuminates Christ himself. Isa. xi.2: *the spirit of Jehovah shall rest upon him, the spirit of wisdom and understanding.*"[79] Because the spirit of the Father rests on the Son, the Father considers him "my wisdom" (III.169). Now the light of wisdom is, as we have seen, the celestial light that must shine inward to plant the eyes of faith, the eyes with which the poet may behold reflected in his imagination things invisible to mortal sight. In other words, the Son sees in much the same way as the poet hopes to see—through the light of wisdom and the instrument of wisdom, the icastic imagination. In as much as both provide reflections of the divine, the effects of wisdom and the imagination coincide. The poet's reference to wisdom as the "Bright effluence of bright essence increate" (III.6) calls attention to the reflective nature of wisdom: she is "a pure influence flowing from the glory of the Almighty . . . she is the brightness of everlasting light, the unspotted mirror of the power of God, and the image of his goodness" (Wisdom 7:25–26). It is because Milton wishes to associate the icastic imagination with the light of wisdom that in the invocation to Book VII the poet makes his muse the sister of wisdom:

Heav'nlie-borne,
Before the Hills appeered, or Fountain flow'd,
Thou with Eternal wisdom didst converse,
Wisdom thy Sister, and with her didst play
In presence of th'Almightie Father, pleas'd
With thy Celestial Song.
(VII.7–12)

The difference between the Son and the poet is that whereas the Son reflects the light of wisdom directly from the Father, the poet hopes to reflect it from the Son. The Holy Spirit whom the poet invokes to move over the face of his imagination—the Spirit of creativity who "from the first / Wast present, and with mighty wings outspread / Dove-like satst brooding on the vast Abyss / And mad'st it pregnant"

79. I.vi (Yale, VI, 283).

(I.19–22)—is the light of the Son—"that passage in Gen. i.2: *the spirit of God brooded*. . . . we should here interpret . . . as a reference to the Son, through whom, as we are constantly told, the Father created all things."[80]

As the debate continues, the true magic, the transforming power of the Son's imagination re-created in the imagination of the poet, becomes increasingly apparent.

The wrath the Son has to appease is concentrated in the Father's first speech; the strife of justice and mercy he has to resolve is concentrated in the Father's second speech. After amplifying the theme of mercy by explaining the workings of grace, the Father returns to the demands of distributive justice: "But yet all is not don" (III.203–16). He restates the Son's test of faith, but this time the language is different. He reformulates the demands of distributive justice in a language where the vocabulary of logical discourse has given way to that of "those lofty Fables and Romances, which recount in solemne canto's the deeds of Knighthood."[81] In the first formulation the Father's language presents the Fall as a logical necessity, a necessary consequence of free will:

> I formd them free, and free they must remain,
> Till they enthrall themselves: I else must change
> Thir nature, and revoke the high Decree
> Unchangeable, Eternal, which ordain'd
> Thir freedom, they themselves ordain'd thir fall.
> (III.124–28)

The force of the logic, so carefully heightened by the repetition of a limited number of words as though they were mathematical symbols, appears to render the Father helpless. The argument, "almost mathematically demonstrative,"[82] is, however, an impasse which arises out of the weak mightiness of man's reasoning. The effect, as Broadbent describes it, one of being led "into a corridor of verbal mirrors in which unbodied concepts are defined by their antitheses,"[83] recalls the labyrinthine impasse of the devils' discursive reasoning:

80. Ibid. (Yale, VI, 282).
81. *An Apology* (Yale, I, 891). For Milton's attitude towards romance, see Barbara K. Lewalski, "Milton: Revaluations of Romance," in *Four Essays on Romance*, ed. Herschel Baker (Cambridge, Mass.: Harvard University Press, 1971), pp. 56–70.
82. *Areopagitica* (Yale, II, 513).
83. *Some Graver Subject*, p. 147.

In discourse more sweet

. . . .

Others apart sat on a Hill retir'd,
In thoughts more elevate, and reason'd high
Of Providence, Foreknowledge, Will and Fate,
Fixt Fate, free will, foreknowledge absolute,
And found no end, in wandring mazes lost.

(II.556–61)[84]

Without the "grace-note" at the end of the Father's discourse, we would be equally lost. The formulation is fallible and human: such knowledge, the Fall as a corollary of free will, is accessible to natural reason—as Boethius puts it, when men "lose possession of their reason," they "are, as it were, the captives of their own freedom."[85] To take the Father's first formulation at face value is for reason to abandon hope, to deny faith and surrender, as Redcross almost does, to despair. In fact Milton's initial presentation of the Father clearly owes something to Despair's view of God:

Is not he iust, that all this doth behold
From highest heauen, and beares an equall eye?
Shall he thy sins vp in his knowledge fold,
And guiltie be of thine impietie?
Is not his law, Let euery sinner die:
Die shall all flesh? What then must needs be donne,
Is it not better to doe willinglie,
Then linger, till the glasse be all out ronne?
Death is the end of woes: die soone, O faeries sonne.

(*FQ* I.ix.47)

As Northrop Frye explains, "Despair's argument in Spenser is based on the logic of law without gospel":[86] once Despair has finished his argument, "nought but death before his eyes he saw, / And euer burning wrath before him laid, / By righteous sentence of th'Almighties law" (*FQ* I.ix.50). The Father's apparent helplessness reflects the inability of both discursive reason and the law on its own to redeem mankind.

84. Cf. Crosman, p. 79: "Trying to follow the logic of the Father's words we are, like the fallen angels of Book II, 'in wand'ring mazes lost' (II, 561)."
85. *Consolation of Philosophy* V.2, quoted from Boethius, *The Consolation of Philosophy*, trans. Richard Green, The Library of Liberal Arts (New York: Bobbs-Merrill, 1962), p. 104.
86. *Return of Eden*, p. 125.

In the second formulation the logical necessity has been replaced by a feudal penalty. The substitution has been effected by means of a metaphor: the latinate, abstract terms for man's first disobedience, "transgress" and "trespass," have been replaced by "Disloyal [man] breaks his fealtie" (III.94, 122, 204). The metaphor transforms man into a feudal tenant or vassal and God into his king or lord, fealty being, according to Bacon, "an oath upon a book that hee will bee a faithfull Tenant to the King."[87] The particular act which breaks the bond of fealty is the vassal's attempt to usurp his lord's place—man is guilty of "Affecting God-head" (III.206). This is the act of "Treason" (III.207) that condemns him to death. His punishment is expressed in a development of the fealty metaphor—man is now "to destruction sacred and devote" (III.208). The image suggests that by breaking fealty with his rightful lord man's allegiance has been captured by a new lord, the personified figure of destruction. It also suggests the romance theme of St. George, a theme to be distinguished from the "sweet *rapsodies* of Heathenism and Knighterrantry"[88] by the fact that its imagery is so firmly rooted in the structure of the Bible.[89] The image implies that man's punishment means playing the role of the king's daughter, a sacrificial offering dedicated to destruction—the "mighty sailewing'd monster that menaces to swallow up the Land, unlesse her bottomlesse gorge may be satisfi'd with blood of the Kings daughter the Church."[90] The importance of the second formulation, the fealty metaphor and its romance development, is that it makes it possible to imagine a solution to the logical impasse of the first speech. The radical shift from abstraction to metaphor makes it possible to imagine God's mercy, and by imagining it, to believe in it, and by believing in it, to bring it about. For whereas it is difficult to understand how God man renew man's freedom without impairing the reality of his original freedom, his freedom to fall, it is not difficult to imagine a traitor being pardoned, a captured vassal being ransomed, or the king's daughter being rescued. It is the possibility of these solutions, explicitly ransom and rescue, that the Father's speech invites: "Dye hee or Justice must; unless for him / Som other able, and as willing, pay / The rigid satisfaction, death for death. / Say, Heav'nly powers, where shall we find such a love"

---

87. Quoted in *OED*, s.v. Fealty. "Fealty" is not a word that occurs in the Bible and by using it Milton, it seems to me, is deliberately, albeit very subtly, heightening the romance quality of mankind's situation.

88. *Eikonoklastes* I (Yale, III, 367).

89. For a brief synopsis of the evidence, see Frye, *Return of Eden*, pp. 118–20.

90. *Reason of Church-Government* II, Conclusion (Yale, I, 857).

(III.210–13). But the ransom and the rescue are in fact a pardon because it is the king's own son who will rescue man and, as the biblical source of the romance theme makes clear, it is the king's own love that will redeem him: it is Jehovah himself who promises, "I will ransom them from the power of the grave; I will redeem them from death: O death, I will be thy plagues; O grave, I will be thy destruction" (Hosea 13:14).[91] Fallen man's inability to act and God's inability to act without impairing man's freedom is resolved by God's becoming man, and this wonder is made comprehensible by a metaphor.

The shift from abstraction to metaphor indicates another tradition that Milton's divine council has assimilated. In the traditional debate between the four daughters of God over justice and mercy,[92] the reasoning of Truth and Righteousness is superseded by the poetry of Mercy and Peace. The immediate reason for the supersession of discourse by poetry is probably that the reconciliation of justice and mercy, the reconciliation from which the debate derives, occurs in the Psalms and the Psalms are of course "the poetical part of the Scripture":[93] "Mercy and Truth that long were missed / Now joyfully are met / Sweet Peace and Righteousness have kissed / And hand in hand are set" (85:10 in Milton's translation). Thus, in what Milton calls "*the vision and Creed of Pierce plowman*,"[94] Truth and Righteousness ridicule the redemptive metaphors of Mercy and Peace:

> 'What, rauestow?' quod Rightwisnesse, 'or þow art right dronke?
> Leuestow þat yond light vnlouke myȝte helle
> And saue mannes soule? suster, wene it neuere.
> (B.XVIII.188–90)[95]

In Giles Fletcher's *Christs Victorie in Heaven*, Justice argues like the Father in his opening speech—

> His soule thy Image: what could he enuie?
> Himself most happie: if he so would bide:

91. Significantly, these are the words with which Faith in *Piers Plowman* prophesies the victory of the Christ-knight (B.XVIII.35).

92. Cf. Cohen, pp. 109–10.

93. Sidney, *Apology*, p. 102.

94. *An Apology* (Yale, I, 916).

95. *Piers Plowman* is quoted from *Piers Plowman: The B Version: Will's Visions of Piers Plowman, Do-Well, Do-Better, and Do-Best*, ed. George Kane and E. Talbot Donaldson (London: Athlone Press, 1975).

Now grow'n most wretched, who can remedie?
He slew himselfe, himselfe the enemie
(st. 18)[96]

—while Mercy's "persuasive power" is identified with poetry:

As melting hony, dropping from the combe,
So still the words, that spring between thy lipps,
Thy lippes, whear smiling sweetnesse keepes her home,
And heav'nly Eloquence pure manna sipps,
He that his pen but in that fountaine dipps,
   How nimbly will the golden phrases flie,
   And shed forth streames of choycest rhetorie,
Willing celestiall torrents out of poësie?
(st. 48)

Fletcher's lines probably owe something to Portia's response to Shylock's insistence on the logic of distributive justice, mercy characteristically expressed in a metaphor:

The quality of mercy is not strained;
It droppeth as the gentle rain from heaven
Upon the place beneath.
(*Merchant of Venice* IV.i.182–84)

The inadequacy of the law so apparent from the Father's moment of helplessness in the first speech (and from the tradition that culminates in Shylock's discomfiture) is implicit in the Father's second formulation of the demands of distributive justice. Whereas in the first speech the abstractions make the rhetoric sound logical, in the second speech the metaphors make the logic, the logic of the law, sound rhetorical. Justice is no longer a principle, but a personification competing with man for life: "Dye hee or Justice must." And the more rhetorical its logic sounds, the more cruel or "severe" (III.224) its demands seem. Justice itself appears deathlike: the satisfaction it demands the Father calls "rigid," and the "death for death" it demands draws attention to its sterility by inverting the positive terms of the Mosaic principle of restitution—"life for life" (Exod. 21:23).[97] Above all, the inadequacy of distributive justice and its manifestation in

96. Fletcher is quoted from *Giles and Phineas Fletcher: Poetical Works*, ed. Frederick S. Boas, 2 vols. (Cambridge: Cambridge University Press, 1908).
97. The Son returns the terms to "life for life" (III.236) in order perhaps to emphasize the idea that he comes not to destroy but to fulfil the law (Matt. 5:17).

the Mosaic law is emphasized by the Father's ability to imagine a love that can supersede it and that love begins to reveal itself in his ability to imagine a way it may fulfil the demands of justice. Just as the Son re-sounds the Father's wrath by amplifying the Father's "grace-note" of mercy, so now he resolves the strife of justice and mercy by exploiting the Father's romance metaphor. The Father's reformulation is thus not only a test of faith, but a guide. It is no accident that the redemptive metaphor should be drawn from romance, and that the divine epic should have such a strong romance quality. As we discovered with *The Tempest*, romance, because it provides an assurance of things hoped for, is closely related to faith: romance is the creation of the imagination which moves the imagination of others to believe that the deepest desires will be fulfilled: in Puck's terms, all shall be well—as he applies the magical antidote to deluding fancy, he promises:

> Jack shall have Jill,
> Naught shall go ill,
> The man shall have his mare again, and all shall be well.
> (*MND* III.ii.461–63)

In *The Winter's Tale*, a romance in which the king's wife is killed by weak-hinged fancy (II.iii.118) and only brought back to life once the king has awakened his faith (V.iii.95) by contemplating a work of art, the happy ending is repeatedly described as something from "an old tale." The phrase refers to those old stories that arouse a sense of wonder because they make the marvelous plausible and the incredible credible. They are often interpenetrated with magic because magic symbolizes the way the imagination dislocates the logic of everyday experience in order to re-create the actual world in the image of human desire. At one point in Shakespeare's play an example is given of such an old tale: we are told that the king and his counsellor "looked as they had heard of a world ransomed" and as a result "A notable passion of wonder appeared in them" (V.ii.14–16). The story of a world ransomed, and as far as Shakespeare is concerned the original story of a world ransomed, is precisely the old tale that the Son now proceeds to tell.

The Son's story is the climax of the divine council's revelation to the reader. This is why the moment before the Son begins to speak "all the Heav'nly Quire stood mute, / And silence was in Heav'n" (III.217–18). The second line associates this moment with the "silence in heaven" before the opening of the seventh seal of Revelation

(8 : 1), while the first line suggests that the Son's climactic offer be compared to Satan's—"but all sate mute" (II.420). It suggests that the divine romance outlined in the Son's offer is the true form of which the epic undertaking outlined in Satan's offer is merely a parody. The Son's story is the kind of song that proceeds from the icastic imagination and provides certainty of waking bliss, while the Devil's proceeds from deluded fancy and will only lull the sense. The silence of the angels before the Son speaks is itself a device one associates with romance; here the pause serves to heighten the suspense before both the Father's challenge is accepted and man's rescue effected. The reaction of the angels after the Son has spoken, their passion of wonder, suggests that both the Son's act of mediation and the events it prefigures are the stuff of romance: "Admiration seis'd / All heav'n" (III.271 – 72).

Just as "amazement seis'd / All th'Host of Heav'n" (II.758 – 59) at the birth of Sin—the great work of Satan's imagination, the symbol of his epic, so "Admiration seis'd / All heav'n" after the Son has told his story—the great work of his imagination, the outline of the divine romance. The difference between "amazement" and "admiration" is the difference between the *phantastike* and the *eikastike*: the parallel again suggests that the climactic point of the Son's mediation, his interpretation of the Father's will, requires the activity of the imagination.

The Son renews "His dearest mediation" by continuing to echo the Father's key refrain, "Man therefore shall find grace": "Father, thy word is past, man shall find grace" (III.226, 131, 227). He then personifies grace as "The speediest of thy winged messengers" (III.229) and by so doing he makes it clear that all Milton's winged messengers, the Attendant Spirit, Raphael, Michael, personify the operation of grace.[98] They are all storytellers who move the imagination to be-

98. The Attendant Spirit and Raphael are both associated with Hermes, not only because his "Pype resembleth Eloquence, which refresheth the mynde, as Harmony doth the eares" (Stephen Batman, *The Golden Booke of the Leaden Gods* [London, 1577; rpt. New York: Garland, 1976], p. 5), but because he "reveales the pleasure of God unto man"; he is a storyteller whose messenger-function signifies "that divine knowledge infused from above, which is the rule and direction of our sober actions" (Sandys, p. 123). Compare his role as the divine mystagogue in Botticelli's *Primavera* (Wind, pp. 113–27). Michael, on the other hand, is associated with Iris, first because the immediate purpose of his task is the expulsion of Adam and Eve, and "when the gods themselves had intended to afflict mortals with pestilences, wars, or some other all ruinating mischeefes, then was Iris commonly imployed in these fatall messages" (*Fountaine of Ancient Fiction*, s.v. Mercurie), and second because the underlying purpose of his task is the story that offers the promise of things hoped for.

lieve: Michael, for instance, tells Adam the story of mankind so "that thou mayst beleeve, and be confirmd" (XI.355). Grace precedes will: as the Father somewhat paradoxically explains, "Man shall not be quite lost, but sav'd who will, / Yet not of will in him, but grace in me / Freely voutsaft" (III.173–75). And the heavenly grace of faith precedes will through the persuasive power of the imagination: "work my flatter'd fancy to belief" ("The Passion" 31) is the radical purpose of all Milton's poetry. In his *Apology against a Pamphlet* he explains from his own experience the efficacy of stories as agents of grace: "those lofty Fables and Romances, which recount in solemne canto's the deeds of Knighthood. . . . prov'd to me so many incitements as you have heard, to the love and stedfast observation of that vertue which abhorres the society of Bordello's."[99] But, of course, the chief model for this effect, the chief romance, is the story of Christ, the story of the Bible. Thus the Son as he recounts his divine romance makes himself the archetype of all those winged messengers: the Word is quite literally the source of grace. According to Calvin, through grace God "both corrects, or rather destroys, our depraved will, and also substitutes a good will from himself."[100] So here, as far as the reader is concerned, the purpose of the divine council is to correct or destroy the depraved will caught from the Satanic story and replace it with the good will inspired by the divine romance. The purpose of the divine council is grace.

The romance itself falls into three parts,[101] each amplifying one of the three romance elements apparent in the Father's reformulation of justice's demands: first, the death-ordeal by which the Son pays the ransom for man—"now to Death I yield, and am his due" (III.245); second, the battle with death by which he rescues man—"I shall rise Victorious, and subdue / My vanquisher, spoild of his vanted spoile" (III.250–51); and third, the triumph by which the Father makes his pardon manifest—"Then with the multitude of my redeemd, / [I] Shall enter Heaven . . . / Father, to see thy face, wherein no cloud / Of anger shall remain" (III.260–63). Here, God's wrath is finally appeased and the strife between mercy and justice finally resolved. All three parts of the Son's story recall romance analogues. When the Son promises redemption and rescue, the language the poet imagines him using recalls Hal's messianic promise to his father:

99. Yale, I, 891.
100. *Institutes* II.iii.7 (Beveridge, I, 256).
101. This is similar to, though not exactly the same as, Northrop Frye's familiar division of romance into three stages—"the *agon* or conflict, the *pathos* or death-struggle, and the *anagnorisis* or discovery, the recognition of the hero, who has clearly

I will redeem all this on Percy's head
And, in the closing of some glorious day,
Be bold to tell you that I am your son,
When I will wear a garment all of blood,
And stain my favors in a bloody mask,
Which, washed away, shall scour my shame with it.

(*1H4* III.ii.132–37)

When he foresees the final reconciliation between God and man, his language recalls the mood, if not the exact sense, of Camillo's prophetic outpouring of hope:

Methinks I see
Leontes opening his free arms and weeping
His welcomes forth; asks thee the son forgiveness,
As 'twere i'th'father's person; kisses the hands
Of your fresh princess; o'er and o'er divides him
'Twixt his unkindness and his kindness; th'one
He chides to hell and bids the other grow
Faster than thought or time.

(*WT* IV.iv.540–46)

There are, however, no specific allusions to secular romance; all the allusions are very consciously biblical—as if to emphasize the conviction that the one true romance is the story of Christ, and that all those desires we seek to fulfil in romance are most truly fulfilled in Scripture.[102] It is in Scripture that the origin of the desire we feel for Hal to redeem himself and for Leontes and his family to be reconciled is truly fulfilled.[103]

The arrangement of the biblical allusions is complex. The three parts of the Son's story each echoes a passage from the New Testament itself triumphantly echoing an Old Testament act of faith. In the death-ordeal, the Son's belief that

---

proved himself to be a hero even if he does not survive the conflict" (*Anatomy of Criticism: Four Essays* [Princeton: Princeton University Press, 1957], p. 187).

102. Cf. Lewalski, "Milton: Revaluations of Romance," p. 68.

103. As the invocation to Book IX makes clear, the reality of romance, the point at its core, is not the tedious havoc of fabled knights but the better fortitude of patience and heroic martyrdom, not the secular stories but their true original, the story of Christ, the Bible. For the story of Milton's attitudes to the romance tradition, see Annabel M. Patterson, "*Paradise Regained*: A Last Chance at True Romance," *MiltonS* 17 (1983): 187–208.

> Thou wilt not leave me in the loathsom grave
> His prey, nor suffer my unspotted Soule
> For ever with corruption there to dwell
>   (III.247–49)

echoes St. Peter's announcement that David's faith—

> For thou wilt not leave my soul in hell; neither wilt thou suffer thine Holy
> One to see corruption
>   (Ps. 16:10)

—is realized in Christ:

> For David speaketh concerning him. . . . thou wilt not leave my soul in
> hell, neither wilt thou suffer thine Holy One to see corruption. . . . [David]
> spake of the resurrection of Christ, that his soul was not left in hell, neither
> his flesh did see corruption.
>   (Acts 2:25, 27, 31)

In the battle with death, the Son's confidence that death will be disarmed of his mortal sting (III.253) echoes St. Paul's declaration that
Isaiah's faith—

> He will swallow up death in victory; and the Lord will wipe away tears from
> all faces
>   (Isa. 25:8)

—is fulfilled in Christ:

> then shall be brought to pass the saying that is written, Death is swallowed
> up in victory. O death, where is thy sting? O grave; where is thy victory? . . .
> thanks be to God which giveth us the victory through our Lord Jesus Christ.
>   (I Cor. 15:54–55, 57)

Finally, the Son's triumph ("I through the ample Air in Triumph
high / Shall lead Hell Captive maugre Hell"; III.254–55) echoes St.
Paul's explanation that David's faith—

> Thou hast ascended on high, thou hast led captivity captive: Thou hast re-
> ceived gifts for men
>   (Ps. 68:18)

—refers to the transmission of grace through Christ:

But unto every one of us is given grace according to the measure of the gift of Christ.

Wherefore he saith, When he ascended up on high, he led captivity captive, and gave gifts unto men.

(Eph. 4:7–8)

This pattern of allusion reinforces the impression that the Son is both making an act of faith and at the same time fulfilling it. The Son's romance fulfils the faith of the prophets, but because he identifies the faith of the prophets with his own motivation, his romance fulfils his own faith—the paradox symbolizes the mystery of the Son's joining "Manhood to Godhead" (XII.389). Because his romance fulfils faith, it provides the ground of faith for mankind. This is how the Son gives us grace; and just as grace found means through his faith, so it will through ours. This is the importance of the allusions to the testimony of Christ's disciples. St. Peter justifies himself, that is, demonstrates the descent of grace, by retelling the story of Christ. This is the essence of what speaking "with other tongues, as the Spirit gave them utterance" (Acts 2:4) means. Out of his own faith, Peter provides the ground of faith for others: "Now when they heard this, they were pricked in their heart, and said unto Peter and the rest of the apostles, Men and brethren, what shall we do?" (Acts 2:37). Thus, the poet, after the darkness of the Satanic poem, in his hymn to Holy Light is justifying himself or demonstrating the descent of grace by re-creating the Word, by retelling the story of Christ—like Peter. Out of his own faith, he provides the ground of faith for the reader.

With the Son's romance, the revelation of the essence of the Father's purpose is complete: through the Son's mediation man is saved and God's love made manifest. The Father's final speech confirms the Son's act of faith and recapitulates the progress of the debate. It then becomes apparent that the debate has re-created the course of the Bible from the Fall to the Apocalypse. Most important, the tone of the Father's last speech is radically different from that of the first. In terms of style, although the sustained play on the logic of free-fall—"An extraordinary pattern of alliteration, prosonamasia and traductio on the words free-freely-all-fall-fault-failed-fell"[104]—is answered almost in passing by the play on the paradox of dying-rise

104. Broadbent, *Some Graver Subject*, p. 146.

(III.294–301), abstract symmetries have given way to the great visionary metaphors of the Bible:

> The World shall burn, and from her ashes spring
> New Heav'n and Earth, wherein the just shall dwell,
> And after all thir tribulations long
> See golden days, fruitful of golden deeds,
> With Joy and Love triumphing, and fair Truth.
> Then thou thy regal Scepter shalt lay by,
> For regal Scepter then no more shall need,
> God shall be All in All.
>
> (III.334–41)

The poetic imitation of prose has given way to poetry. In terms of its classical models, the angry self-defence of Zeus in the *Odyssey* has given way to the beneficent vision of Jupiter in the *Aeneid*:

> Olli subridens hominum sator atque deorum
> uultu, quo caelum tempestatesque serenat,
> oscula libauit natae, dehinc talia fatur:
>
> . . . .
>
> 'aspera tum positis mitescent saecula bellis:
> cana Fides et Vesta, Remo cum fratre Quirinus
> iura dabunt; dirae ferro et compagibus artis
> claudentur Belli portae; Furor impius intus
> saeua sedens super arma et centum uinctus aënis
> post tergum nodis fremet horridus ore cruento.'
>
> (I.254–96)

The creator of the gods and of human kind smiled on her, with the smile which he wears when he calms the storms and clears the sky. Lightly he kissed his daughter, and then spoke. . . . 'Then shall our furious centuries lay down their warring arms, and shall grow kind. Silver-haired Fidelity, Vesta, and Quirine Romulus, with his brother Remus at his side shall make the laws. And the terrible iron-constricted Gates of War shall shut; and safe within them shall stay the godless and ghastly Lust of Blood, propped on his pitiless piled armoury, and still roaring from gory mouth, but held fast by a hundred chains of bronze knotted behind his back.'

In terms of Scripture, the wrath of Jehovah has given way to the beneficent vision of God in the Apocalypse:

> And I heard a great voice out of heaven saying, Behold, the tabernacle of God is with men, and he will dwell with them, and they shall be his people, and God himself shall be with them, and be their God.

And God shall wipe away all tears from their eyes; and there shall be no
more death, neither sorrow nor crying, neither shall there be any more pain:
for the former things are passed away.

(Rev. 21:3–4)

Calvin explains what has happened: through the Son's faith, which
is the ground of our faith, God has become "instead of a judge, an
indulgent Father."[105] Without faith, without the Son's mediation,
God will always appear, as he does for Satan, as the incensed deity.
The root cause of Satan's damnation is that he cannot believe, because he cannot *imagine* God as anything other than "my punisher"
(IV.103).

The metaphor at the center of the Father's final speech is that
of the tree of life. The tree of life is one of those metaphors that form
the spine of the Bible. Scripture opens with its loss and closes with
its recovery: on either side of the river proceeding out of the throne
of God "was there the tree of life" (Rev. 22:2). The means by which
the tree is recovered is Christ, because Christ through his redemptive
sacrifice recovers the possibility of eternal life. For the same reason
Christ himself is identified with the tree of life: "I am the vine, ye
are the branches: He that abideth in me, and I in him, the same
bringeth forth much fruit: for without me ye can do nothing" (John
15:5). Thus, the Father identifies the mediation of the Son, explicitly in history but implicitly in the debate, with the growth of the
tree of life: his "wondrous birth" will be "of Virgin Seed" (III.285,
284); he will replace Adam as mankind's "second root" (III.288); he
will be the tree upon which mankind will be grafted—man will "live
in thee transplanted" (III.293); he will recover the "God-like fruit-
ion" which he gave up in becoming man, and in so doing he will
enable mankind to recover the "immortal fruits of joy and love"—
through him the just shall "See golden days, fruitful of golden deeds"
(III.307, 67, 337). Now mankind will live in him transplanted through
faith: "Thou wilt say then," St. Paul explains, "The branches were
broken off, that I might be graffed in. Well; because of unbelief they
were broken off, and thou standest by faith" (Rom. 11:19–20). This
means that the eternal life made possible by Christ may be realized
simply by believing that he did make it possible. But that belief, the
ability to believe, depends on the Word dwelling in us: it depends
upon the story of Christ moving our imagination so that a "FIRM

105. *Institutes* III.xi.1 (Beveridge, II, 37). Cf. Christopher, p. 115: "the changing
faces of God in *Paradise Lost* gauge the faith of the narrator and the putative reader."

PERSUASION" is "IMPLANTED IN US."[106] That persuasion is the tree of faith—the real tree of life, the tree at the center of the garden within, the tree that flowers in heaven. It is the tree that grows in the parable of the sower and seed: "But he that received seed into the good ground is he that heareth the word, and understandeth it; which also beareth fruit, and bringeth forth, some an hundredfold, some sixty, some thirty" (Matt. 13:23). It is, as we have seen,[107] the tree of "pure-ey'd Faith" (*Mask* 212) that "lives and spreds aloft by those pure eyes, / And perfet witnes of all judging *Jove*" (*Lycidas* 81–82). Before the debate the poet prays for its plantation—"thou Celestial light / Shine inward, and the mind through all her powers / Irradiate, there plant eyes" (III.51–53). During the debate it grows and finally blooms as amaranthus, a flower meaning "everlasting" and providing a sensible image of all the joys of eternal life:

> Immortal Amarant, a Flour which once
> In Paradise, fast by the Tree of Life
> Began to bloom, but soon for mans offence
> To Heav'n remov'd where first it grew, there grows,
> And flours aloft shading the Fount of life,
> And where the river of Bliss through midst of Heavn
> Rowls o're *Elisian* Flours her Amber stream.
>   (III.353–59)

The very deliberate Virgilian sensuousness of the image suggests that the tree of faith grows in the rich soil of the human imagination, and that the desires evident in Book VI of the *Aeneid* are fulfilled in the Word. Through the course of the debate faith grows in the Son by the light of the Father's wisdom; it grows in the Poet by the light of the Son; it grows in the reader by the light of the Poet's imagination.

Literally, the divine council is a debate between God the Father and God the Son in which, as in the *Aeneid*, intercession leads to revelation—in this case the revelation that the hero of the poem, mankind, will be saved and all will be well. Figuratively, however, this simple movement conceals and, on analysis, reveals a complex range of significance. Allegorically,[108] the council re-creates the complete movement of God's progressive self-revelation through the

---

106. *Christian Doctrine* I.xx (Yale, VI, 471).
107. See pp. 76–77.
108. I use the Fourfold Method simply as a convenient way of organizing my own observations.

course of the Bible. When Milton says, "It is safest for us to form an image of God in our minds which corresponds to his representation and description of himself in the sacred writings,"[109] it is this total image he means, not just the Old Testament Jehovah at his most anthropomorphic. To characterize Milton's God as the incensed deity of the Father's opening speech, which Frye seems to do through the influence of Blake and Empson through that of Orwell, is to credit Milton with Satan's lack of imagination. The developing image of God which culminates in the imperative identification of the Father with the Son—"Adore the Son, and honour him as mee" (III.343)— springs out of the developing relationship between Man and God. The council re-creates that relationship, the biblical progress from distributive to transforming justice, a progress made possible by the Son's faith and the guide and interpreter of our faith, his love. The progress is explained by Milton in his Circumcision ode: "O more exceeding love or law more just? / Just law indeed, but more exceeding love!" (15–16). Morally, the council re-creates the operation of grace in the individual soul, the operation described by the Father in his second speech. Through faith man echoes God's call: as God calls man "To pray, repent, and bring repentence due," so "To prayer, repentence, and obedience due" (III.190–91) God is attentive. The accuracy of man's response is determined by "My Umpire *Conscience*" (III.195), that is, consciousness or reason in the service of faith. If conscience is heard man will grow in faith—"Light after light well us'd they shall attain, / And to the end persisting, safe arrive" (III.196–97). Thus, the Son grows in faith by analyzing and interpreting the Father, the poet by analyzing and interpreting Scripture, the reader by analyzing and interpreting the debate. Analogically, the council justifies the ways of God to men by re-creating the central Protestant idea of justification by faith. The council re-creates and by so doing hopes to realize St. Paul's belief that

before faith came, we were confined under the law, kept under restraint until faith should be revealed. So that the law was our custodian until Christ came, that we might be justified by faith. But now that faith has come, we are no longer under a custodian; for in Christ Jesus you are all sons of God, through faith.

(Gal. 3:23–26)[110]

---

109. *Christian Doctrine* I.ii (Yale, VI, 133).
110. Revised Standard Version.

For this reason the authoritarian metaphor of monarchy for God is finally abandoned: "Then thou thy regal Scepter shalt lay by, / For regal Scepter then no more shall need, / God shall be All in All" (III.339–41).

Ultimately, the point of the divine council is very simple. According to Calvin, "man's only resource for escaping the curse of the law, and recovering salvation lies in faith."[111] The Son's intercession and interpretation exemplifies the way faith works. We are released from the bondage of the law by an act of faith, and that act of faith turns out to be an act of imagination. We are released from the impasse of the Father's discursive logic by the Son's raising the eye of the mind above the letter and exploiting the romance metaphor emebedded in the words of the Father. In this, the council demonstrates the way that in matters of faith and religion we need, as Bacon puts it, to raise our imagination above our reason. The same pattern is apparent in the regeneration of Adam and Eve, but first we must look at the Fall.

111. *Institutes* III.xi.1 (Beveridge, II, 37).

PART THREE

Imagination and Adam and Eve in *Paradise Lost*

CHAPTER FIVE

Phantastike Imagination and the Fall

THE WILL-OF-THE-WISP

The reason why, notwithstanding all our acute reasons and subtile disputes, truth prevails no more in the world, is, we so often disjoin truth and true goodness, which in themselves can never be disunited. . . . All the light and knowledge that may seem sometimes to rise up in unhallowed minds, is but like those fuliginous flames that rise up from our culinary fire, that are soon quenched in their own smoke; or like those foolish fires that fetch their birth from terrene exudations, that do but hop up and down, and flit to and fro upon the surface of this earth, where they were first brought forth; and serve not so much to enlighten, as to delude us; not to direct the wandering traveller into his way, but to lead him farther out of it.

Smith, *The True Way or Method of Attaining Divine Knowledge* (*Select Discourses*, pp. 4–5)

At one of the climactic moments in the seduction of Eve, as Satan guides her to the tree of knowledge, their journey is compared in a long simile to that of a night-wanderer losing his way by following a will-of-the-wisp or *ignis fatuus*:

> as when a wandring Fire,
> Compact of unctuous vapor, which the Night
> Condenses, and the cold invirons round,
> Kindl'd through agitation to a Flame,
> Which oft, they say, some evil Spirit attends
> Hovering and blazing with delusive Light,
> Misleads th'amaz'd Night-wanderer from his way
> To Boggs and Mires, and oft through Pond or Poole,
> There swallow'd up and lost, from succour farr.

So glister'd the dire Snake, and into fraud
Led *Eve* our credulous Mother, to the Tree
Of prohibition, root of all our woe.

(IX.634–45)

As we discovered in the *Mask*,[1] in *A Midsummer Night's Dream*, and *The Tempest*, the *ignis fatuus* is a commonplace for the delusions of fancy ungoverned by reason. Just as unrestrained fancy's personification, Puck, misleads "night-wanderers, laughing at their harm" (*MND* II.i.39), so Ariel's spirits mislead the fancy-ruled mind of Caliban—"like a firebrand, in the dark / Out of my way" (*Tmp.* II. ii.6–7). In "L'Allegro," a poem whose central character, Mirth, is resonant with the memory of Puck, lack of judgment renders those who tell stories over "the Spicy Nut-brown Ale" (100) likely to be misled "by the Friars Lanthorn" (104), while in the *Mask* the Lady's chastity, the fruit of a harmonious relationship between her fancy and her judgment, renders her invulnerable to any "evil thing that walks by night / In fog, or fire, by lake, or moorish fen," any "Goblin, or swart Faery" (431–32, 435).[2] We saw in John Swan's *Speculum Mundi* that the *ignis fatuus* is an image of beguiling fancy because it is a classic example of how those whose judgment is weak allow themselves to be deluded by their fancy. Through fancy, the credulous transform the natural phenomenon of marsh lights into evil spirits:

the much terrified, ignorant, and superstitious people may see their own errours in that they have deemed these lights to be walking spirits. . . .
They are no spirits, and yet leade out of the way, because those who

1. See p. 23.
2. Cf. John Fletcher's *Faithful Shepherdess* I.i.111–20:

> Yet I have heard (my mother told it me)
> And now I do believe it, if I keepe
> My virgin flower uncropt, pure, chaste, and faire,
> No Goblin, wood-god, Faiery, Elfe, or Fiend,
> Satyr, or other power that haunts the groaves,
> Shall hurt my body, or by vaine illusion,
> Draw me to wander after idle fiers,
> Or voices calling me in dead of night,
> To make me followe, and so tole me on,
> Through mire and standing pools.

Quoted from *The Dramatic Works in the Beaumont and Fletcher Canon*, gen. ed. Fredson Bowers, 5 vols. (Cambridge: Cambridge University Press, 1966–82).

see them are amazed, and look so earnestly after them that they forget their way . . . sometimes to waters, pits, and other dangerous places; whereupon the next day they will undoubtedly tell you strange tales (as one saith) how they were led up and down by a light, which (in their judgement) was nothing else but some devil or spirit in the likenesse of fire which fain would have hurt them. (pp. 94–95)

In the anonymous *Mad Pranks of Robin Goodfellow* the will-of-the-wisp is explicitly identified with Puck—"some call him Robin Goodfellow . . . some againe doe tearme him oft by name of Will the Wispe";[3] and in his *Epithalamion* Spenser makes it clear that Pucks exist only in the imagination:

> Let no deluding dreames, nor dreadful sights
> Make sudden sad affrights;
> Ne let housefyres, nor lightnings helplesse harmes,
> Ne let the Pouke, nor other euill sprights,
> Ne let mischiuous witches with theyr charmes,
> Ne let hob Goblins, names whose sence we see not,
> Fray vs with things that be not.
>
> (338–44)

In *Paradise Lost* the will-of-the-wisp simile makes it equally clear that, although the evil spirit exists, his power over Eve exists only in the susceptibility of her imagination. The simile makes it clear that Eve loses her way in much the same manner as the reader does at the beginning of the poem—through the *phantastike*, through the uninformed operation of fancy. Just as the will-of-the-wisp amazes night-wanderers out of their way, so Ariel by infecting reason with the fantasy of a tempest "flamed amazement" (*Tmp.* I.ii.198) among the King of Naples' followers, so Satan by conceiving Sin in his proud imagination "flames . . . amazement" (II.754, 758) among his followers, and so the serpent by creating fantastic shapes, visual and mental, kindles "agitation to a Flame" (IX.637) in Eve's amazed imagination. Her increasing amazement, a word which literally means being put out of one's wits or losing rational control, is the measure of her delusion: she hears the serpent "Not unamaz'd" (IX.552), "Yet more amaz'd" (IX.614), until she is finally misled like an "amaz'd Night-wanderer from his way" (IX.640).

---

3. Quoted in *OED*, s.v. Will-of-the-Wisp.

FANCY'S WANTON GROWTH

> to reform
> Yon flourie Arbors, yonder Allies green,
> Our walk at noon, with branches overgrown,
> That mock our scant manuring, and require
> More hands then ours to lop thir wanton growth:
> Those Blossoms also, and those dropping Gumms,
> That lie bestrowne unsightly and unsmooth,
> Ask riddance, if we mean to tread with ease.
>
> *Paradise Lost* IV.625–32

The principal activity of the unfallen Adam and Eve is gardening. The first time gardening is mentioned by Adam—"following our delightful task / To prune these growing Plants, and tend these Flours" (IV.437–38)—it is somewhat ambiguously identified with abstaining from the tree of knowledge. The location of the phrase "our delightful task" at the end of the line allows a pause which separates it from its true referent, "To prune these growing Plants, and tend these Flours," and encourages the reader to think it refers back to the foregoing preoccupation of the speech: "This one, this easie charge, of all the Trees / In Paradise that bear delicious fruit / So various, not to taste that onely Tree / Of knowledge" (IV.421–24). As the poem proceeds it becomes apparent that the ambiguity is not accidental, and that Fowler's caution over the moral significance of the gardening—"the gardening should probably be regarded as an emblem of moral or even of political activity"—is unnecessary.[4] The reality

4. Carey and Fowler, p. 633n. Fowler's caution arises out of Broadbent's confusion of innocence with effortlessness: "Adam and Eve's sweet gardening labour . . . taken emblematically . . . is a model of order in the commonwealth like the gardening in *Richard II*. . . . This is an anachronism, like Milton's psychology, because neither the garden nor the microcosm and macrocosm it represents should need pruning and weeding in innocence" (*Some Graver Subject*, p. 177). Both the *activity* of innocence and the way that that activity is symbolized by gardening is treated in detail in J. M. Evans, Paradise Lost *and the Genesis Tradition* (Oxford: Clarendon Press, 1968), pp. 242–71: "Adam and Eve's physical relationship to the garden is in fact an image of their psychological relationship both to their own passions and to each other" (p. 250). Following Evans and Barbara Lewalski ("Innocence and Experience in Milton's Eden," in *New Essays on* Paradise Lost, ed. Thomas Kranidas [Berkeley: University of California Press, 1969], pp. 86–117), Louis Martz (*Poet of Exile* [New Haven: Yale University Press, 1980]) goes on to make the connection between the garden's wanton growth and fancy: "things unconfined and unrestrained tend to become 'luxurious,' tend to run beyond the rule and art of reason. Man's duty is to bring these 'Virgin Fancies' of nature under the control of reason, for fancy, we recall, can make 'wilde work'" (p. 130).

of Paradise is the garden within and mankind's gardening symbolizes the cultivation of that inner state. The image is a commonplace: Iago, albeit with a perverse emphasis on the independence of the will, articulates it thus:

'Tis in ourselves that we are thus or thus. Our bodies are our gardens, to the which our wills are gardeners; so that if we will plant nettles or sow lettuce, set hyssop and weed up thyme, supply it with one gender of herbs or distract it with many—either to have it sterile with idleness or manured with industry—why, the power and corrigible authority of this lies in our wills. If the balance of our lives had not one scale of reason to poise another of sensuality, the blood and baseness of our natures would conduct us to most preposterous conclusions. But we have reason to cool our raging motions, our carnal stings, our unbitted lusts.

(Othello I.iii.319–30)

In Milton's Eden the purpose of mankind's gardening is to control "wanton growth" (IV.629, IX.211). This growth occurs at night: "what we by day / Lop overgrown, or prune, or prop, or bind, / One night or two with wanton growth derides / Tending to wilde" (IX.209–12). Wanton growth is the work of Nature's fancy: "for Nature here / Wantond as in her prime, and plaid at will / Her Virgin Fancies, pouring forth more sweet, / Wilde above Rule or Art; enormous bliss" (V.294–97). It is Puck-like in that it derides and mocks "our scant manuring" (IV.628) and although it is essentially innocent, for mankind it is dangerous: for in the garden without there is always the threat that fancy's wanton growth will transform the "Wilderness of sweets" (V.294) into a real wilderness, "a steep wilderness . . . overgrown, grottesque[5] and wilde," a "steep savage Hill" where "the undergrowth / Of shrubs and tangling bushes" would have "perplext / All path of Man or Beast that past that way" (IV.135–36, 172, 175–77; cf. IX.244–45),[6] while in the garden within there is always the threat that fancy's wanton growth, the "perplexing thoughts" that

5. Fowler's definition of grotesque makes the same connection between fancy and wanton growth: "Originally used with reference to an antique style of ornament consisting of fantastically interwoven foliage. It often took the form of extravagant, excessive, or even monstrous and diabolic forms" (Carey and Fowler, p. 616n).

6. Lewalski, "Innocence and Experience," p. 91, explains the tendency towards degeneration in these terms: "As the materials of chaos are the substratum of everything made, everything has a tendency to regress to the chaotic state unless continually acted upon by a creative force akin to the divine creative power that first brought order out of chaos. The highly cultivated Garden which yet tends to 'wild' manifests this tension and so defines the responsibility of Adam and Eve as gardeners."

characterize the tendency of "the Mind or Fancie . . . to roave / Uncheckt" (VIII.183, 188–89), will subvert reason and provide the means
by which upstart passion may catch the government. Our first night
in Paradise is dominated by the wanton growth of fancy in the mind
of Eve.

From the first Eve is immediately and emphatically associated with
the wanton growth that gradually emerges as an image of unrestrained
fancy. Her hair, unlike Adam's (his "Hyacinthin Locks" [IV.301] with
all its associations of rational control),[7] suggests her inner susceptibility: "Shee. . . / Her unadorned golden tresses wore / Dissheveld,
but in wanton ringlets wav'd / As the Vine curles her tendrils"
(IV.304–7). Her coming to consciousness reveals the same susceptibility. Unlike Adam, the activity which characterizes her awakening is not the accurate operation of discursive reason, the harmonious interaction of imagination and judgment that enables Adam to
move unerringly from perusing the book of nature to the conception
of "some great Maker then, / In goodness and in power praeemi-
nent" (VIII.278–79), but "unexperienc't thought" (IV.457), that is,
the kind of thinking where the evidence of the senses is unrestrained
by the distinctions of judgment. Since "thought," according to Aristotelian psychology, "is held to comprise imagination and judgement,"[8] thought without judgment, what Eve calls "unexperienc't
thought," means uninformed imagination. In this state Eve is at
the mercy of appearances. Like Bottom she cannot distinguish the
painted lion from the real one, the image from the actual. Like
Narcissus, she mistakes her own image for a real person: "As I bent
down to looke, just opposite, / A Shape within the watry gleam
appeerd / Bending to look on me" (IV.460–62). As with Narcissus,
her error releases passion and engenders vain desires:

---

7. The classical references, for instance, firmly associate Adam's beauty with divinely inspired reason. The primary allusion is to Athene's restoration of Odysseus'
beauty, an act which suggests the inspiration of her wisdom: "His locks (clensd) curld
the more, and matcht (in power / To please an eye) the Hyacinthin flower. . . . So
Pallas wrought in him a grace as great / From head to shoulders" (*Odyssey* VI.364–65,
374–75). Adam's description also alludes to the Hyacinthine beauty that attracts
Apollo: "the God of wit, of learning, and the Muses" is attracted to Hyacinthus, according to Sandys, because "the naturall understanding, when innocent and uncor-
rupted, resembles a boy; that is, wanting wisdome, yet repleat with beauty, in that it
exciteth the mind to a selfe contemplation: whereby at length putting off the affections and fervor of youth, by his owne vigour it produceth the flower of knowledge and
wisdome, sweetly smelling with the fragrant odours of Vertue" (p. 482).
8. Aristotle, *De Anima* III.iii (p. 157).

I started back,
It started back, but pleas'd I soon returnd,
Pleas'd it returnd as soon with answering looks
Of sympathie and love; there I had fixt
Mine eyes till now, and pin'd with vain desire,
Had not a voice thus warnd me.
(IV.462–67)

Eve's weakness is carefully associated with the error of Narcissus because his story illustrates the operation of the sense-bound imagination: his story externalizes the operation in which images that appear in the glass of one's own fancy are confused with objective realities. This is the meaning of Satan's narcissism.[9] Sin is an image of the conspiracy against God born in Satan's imagination: Sin is born in "Heav'n . . . at th'Assembly, and in sight / Of all the Seraphim with thee combin'd / In bold conspiracy against Heav'ns King" (II.749–51). While Satan is hatching his conspiracy, he is giving birth to Sin. She is merely an image of his own desire, but once she appears Satan treats her as an external reality: "Thy self in me thy perfect image viewing / Becam'st enamour'd" (II.764–65). The result is Death. To a large extent the story of how Eve loses her way is a particular example of the phenomenon allegorized by the birth of Sin. There is, however, a radical difference between the narcissism of Satan and that of Eve. Satan is much more truly narcissistic: whereas his delusion proceeds from self-love, Eve's does not. With Satan desire engenders delusion;[10] with Eve delusion engenders desire. In terms of the psychology what this means is that whereas Satan through inordinate desire has long since subverted the rational power that would enable him to understand the images in his fancy, Eve has not yet developed that power. She is not, as Patrides asserts, "partly fallen before she actually ate the forbidden fruit,"[11] and because her error is innocent she is rescued. The word of God makes the distinctions which allow her to penetrate the illusion: "What thou seest, / What there thou seest fair Creature is thy self, / With thee it came and goes" (IV.467–69). The divine voice leads her to Adam with whom she will continue to cultivate reason. Indeed, his words, as Burden points out,[12] allow her to make her first rational

9. See pp. 118–19.
10. Cf. Narcissus' final admission: "Ah, He is I! now, now I plainly see: / Nor is't my shaddow that bewitcheth me. / Love of myselfe me burnes" (*Met.* III.458–60).
11. C. A. Patrides, *Milton and the Christian Tradition* (Oxford: Clarendon Press, 1966), p. 105.
12. Burden, pp. 84–85.

choice: though Adam is "less faire, / Less winning soft, less ami-
ablie milde" (IV.478–79), she prefers him to her own image, realizing
that "beauty is excelld by manly grace / And wisdom, which alone
is truly fair" (IV.490–91).

Nothing epitomizes the difference between the *phantastike* and
the *eikastike* so clearly as the difference between Eve's awakening
and that of Adam. She awakens and is almost immediately beguiled
by the failure of reason to order her imagination. He awakens and after
doing what discursive reason can receives a vision of God through his
imagination because its glass has been cleared by its harmonious
interaction with reason.[13] However, although Adam's inward wits are
superior to Eve's—she is "th'inferiour, in the mind / And inward
Faculties" (VIII.541–42)—he is, as we shall see later, far from being
free from the danger of narcissism or the threat of fancy's wanton
growth.

THE RELATIONSHIP BETWEEN THE DREAM AND THE
VERBAL TEMPTATION OF EVE

> there he slept,
> And dream'd, as appetite is wont to dream,
> Of meats and drinks, Natures refreshment sweet.
> *Paradise Regained* II.263–65

> See here be all the pleasures
> That fancy can beget on youthfull thoughts.
> *Mask* 667–68

Eve's account of her own weakness is the second of the first two
speeches, the "new utterance" (IV.410), that Satan overhears in Paradise. The first, Adam's opening speech, provides him with knowledge of the external means, the object, with which to provoke mankind, the second, Eve's, with the internal means, the psychology
with which to make that object provoking. It is quite clear that Satan
feels he has learnt something from both their speeches: "Yet let me
not forget what I have gain'd / From *thir own* mouths" (IV.512–13,
my emphasis). His response to Adam's speech is explicit, to Eve's im-

---

13. See pp. 65–69. Cf. Harvey, *The Inward Wits*, p. 50: "True dreams come to men
who are accustomed to true imaginations, because their senses are used to serving
reason."

plicit. Indeed, his understanding of Eve's speech—that it is through fancy when separated from judgment that desire may most easily be excited and that it is Eve's fancy that may most easily be exploited— only becomes apparent as he begins the process of temptation:

> him there they found
> Squat like a Toad, close at the eare of *Eve*;
> Assaying by his Devilish art to reach
> The Organs of her Fancie, and with them forge
> Illusions as he list, Phantasms and Dreams,
> Or if, inspiring venom, he might taint
> Th'animal Spirits that from pure blood arise
> Like gentle breaths from Rivers pure, thence raise
> At least distemperd, discontented thoughts,
> Vaine hopes, vaine aimes, inordinate desires
> Blown up with high conceits ingendering pride.
> (IV.799–809)

The process of temptation begins at the only obvious time that fancy will be separated from reason, and Eve from Adam—at night in sleep when fancy may wanton and grow wild.

The importance of Eve's demonic dream is central. It is, according to Patrides, the only aspect in Milton's presentation of the seduction of Eve that is not a part of Christian tradition.[14] However, its importance is not in itself, but in its relation to the verbal temptation of Eve in Book IX. The idea that the dream constitutes a separate, unsuccessful temptation, that it "marks the first attempt of Satan directed at man" is misleading.[15] Mankind could not be seduced solely in a dream, because, as Burden (following Adam's account of Aristotle's view) points out, sleep "divests the mind of moral responsibility":[16] "Evil into the mind of God or Man / May come and go, so unapprov'd, and leave / No spot or blame behind" (V.117–19). The dream does all that the dream is intended to do, but still Eve remains unfallen. The success of its ultimate design in engendering pride cannot be gauged until Eve makes the moral choice, the unsleeping decision to eat the forbidden fruit, because "pride," unlike "thoughts," "hopes," "aimes," "desires," or "conceits," by definition indicates a moral transgression. Even so as far as its more immediate aims are

---

14. *Milton and the Christian Tradition*, p. 105.

15. William B. Hunter, Jr., "Eve's Demonic Dream," *ELH* 13 (1946): 255. The idea is implicit throughout Fish's discussion of the dream, *Surprised by Sin*, pp. 216–32.

16. Burden, p. 129.

concerned, the dream is obviously successful: illusions are forged in her fancy and by means of those illusions inordinate desire is raised:

> he drew nigh, and to me held,
> Even to my mouth of that same fruit held part
> Which he had pluckt; the pleasant savourie smell
> So quick'nd appetite, that I, methought,
> Could not but taste.
>
> (V.82–86)

Although, as Fish points out, the act of eating the forbidden fruit itself is very carefully elided over,[17] Eve does taste something of the pleasures that Satan associates with the fruit: his exhortation, "Taste this, and be henceforth among the Gods," "Ascend to Heav'n" (V.77, 80), is realized in Eve's flight of fancy—"Forthwith up to the Clouds / With him I flew" (V.86–87). It is clear for Adam, if not for Fish, that in the dream Eve is made to go through all the motions of the fall: he hopes "that what in sleep thou didst abhorr to dream, / Waking thou never wilt consent to do" (V.120–21). But the point is that they are only the motions and in a dream that is all they can be. Fish's preoccupation with whether or not Eve gives her consent in the dream is unnecessary. Even if she had given her consent, and it is by no means certain that she does not,[18] as long as it took place in a dream the evil necessarily remains "unapprov'd." Thus, however much she dreams of falling, her innocence remains unimpaired. As in the *Mask*, no matter how much Comus waves his wand and forges illusions, he cannot touch the freedom of the Lady's mind (662). As in the opening canto of *The Faerie Queene*, no matter how much Redcross is made to dream "of loues and lustfull play," no matter how much he is "Bathed in wanton blis and wicked ioy" (I.i.47), he remains unfallen because when he wakes he refuses the verbal temptation that would consummate the dream.

Like the relationship between dream and verbal temptation in *The Faerie Queene*, the relationship between dream and verbal temptation in *Paradise Lost* is both analogous and actual. It is analogous in as much as the dream provides an image of the psychological nature of Satan's verbal temptation.[19] In both cases the mind is ruled by fancy's wanton growth. However, in the first, this state is involun-

---

17. *Surprised by Sin*, p. 222.
18. Cf. Burden, p. 129.
19. Cf. ibid., pp. 130, 132: "Eve's dream is an exercise of the fancy and the appetite uninfluenced by judgement. . . . The dream was a useful invention because it enabled Milton to show the decisive role that judgement plays in the moral life."

tary, while in the second at the moment of eating, it is chosen: reason is not just asleep, but it is "perplexed," it has been subverted. The relationship is actual in as much as the dream comes to contribute, though, as we shall see, it need not have done, to the effectiveness of Satan's verbal temptation.

The Dream as an Analogy of the Verbal Temptation

> my discourse. . . . This only is the witchcraft I have
> used.
>
> *Othello* I.iii.150, 169

Although the influence of Redcross's dream on that of Eve is fairly obvious—for instance, Satan tries "to reach / The Organs of her Fancie, and with them forge / Illusions as he list, Phantasms and Dreams" just as Archimago tries "to forge true-seeming lyes" and "with false shewes abuse his fantasy" (I.i.38, 46]—even more so is the influence of *A Midsummer Night's Dream*. We have already noticed how the immediate cause of Eve's dream, what Adam calls "mimic Fansie" (V.110), is a memory of Puck,[20] and how the fantastic nature of Satan's epic, which in its airy nothingness is so like Eve's dream, is suggested by the warning allusion to *A Midsummer Night's Dream* at the end of Book I.[21] As the last example indicates, the play's most important influence is on the analogous relationship between dream and verbal temptation: the play's commanding influence arises out of its emphasis on love-language as the verbal manifestation of dream-logic, on amorous rhetoric as the verbal manifestation of fancy uninformed by reason.

Just as Titania sleeps in a "close and consecrated bower" (III.ii.7) forbidden to all creatures but her—

> You spotted snakes with double tongue,
> Thorny hedgehogs, be not seen;
> Newts and blindworms, do no wrong,
> Come not near our Fairy Queen . . .
>
> Weaving spiders, come not here;
> Hence, you long-legged spinners, hence!
> Beetles black, approach not near;
> Worm nor snail, do no offense
>   (II.ii.9–12, 20–23)

20. See p. 15.
21. See pp. 83–90.

—so Eve sleeps in a "shadie Bower . . . sacred and sequesterd" (IV.705–6) forbidden to all creatures but her and Adam: "other Creature here / Beast, Bird, Insect, or Worm durst enter none" (IV.703–4). In their respective bowers just as Titania is filled with "hateful fantasies" (II.i.258) by Oberon through the agency of his magic "liquor" (II.i.178) and Puck's "mimic" (III.ii.19)—the nocturnal misjoining of Bottom's body to an ass's head—so Eve is filled with illusions, phantasms, and dreams by Satan through the agency of "mimic Fansie." Satan enters the bower as a toad. Oberon enters as himself, but just before he enters the bower, before he repeats his intention of beguiling Titania, he refers to the presence in her bower of one of those snakes specifically banished by the fairies' song, "spotted snakes with double tongue":

> There sleeps Titania . . .
>
> . . . .
> And there the snake throws her enamelled skin,
> Weed wide enough to wrap a fairy in.
> And with the juice of this I'll streak her eyes
> And make her full of hateful fantasies.
>
> (II.i.253–58)

The intrusion of a double-tongued snake (at first sight so innocuous and then its "enamelled skin, / Weed wide enough to wrap a fairy in" so ambiguously sinister, vaguely reminiscent of the means by which Comus would "charm my judgement, as mine eyes / Obtruding false rules pranckt in reasons garb" [*Mask* 757–81]), suggests that the real means of enabling fancy to overcome reason is not magic or dreams in their literal sense, but words—the kind of language symbolized by magic and dreams. The juxtaposition of the intention to forge hateful fantasies with the intrusion of the snake makes the connection between dream-logic and false rhetoric, most specifically because snakes and serpents in the play are consistently associated with love-language when seen from the unbeguiled perspective of its victim. Hermia, for instance, considers Demetrius's representation of himself as courtly lover—"Pierced through the heart with your stern cruelty" (III.ii.59)[22]—serpentlike hypocrisy: "with doubler tongue / Than thine (thou serpent!) never adder stung" (III.ii.72–73).

---

22. Brooks, p. 65n, draws attention to the similarity between this line and Palamon's exclamation on first seeing Emelye: "And therewithal he bleynte, and cride, 'A!' / As though he stongen were unto the herte" (*Knight's Tale* 1078–79). Demetrius's sentiment is, however, surely a commonplace of "courtly love" rhetoric.

She pictures him as one of the creatures banished from Titania's bower, creeping up on Lysander to slay him while asleep:

> O, once tell true: tell true, even for my sake.
> Durst thou have looked upon him, being awake?
> And hast thou killed him sleeping? O brave touch!
> Could not a worm, an adder, do so much?
> An adder did it; for with doubler tongue
> Than thine (thou serpent!) never adder stung.

Even more to the point, the words of Lysander's rationalization of his fancy-sick love for Helena translate themselves in Hermia's dreaming mind into another image of the intruding snake. The implications of this are complex. Lysander is awake and appears to be reasoning:

> Not Hermia, but Helena I love.
> Who will not change a raven for a dove?
> The will of man is by his reason swayed,
> And reason says you are the worthier maid.
> Things growing are not ripe until their season:
> So I, being young, till now ripe not to reason.
> And touching now the point of human skill,
> Reason becomes the marshal to my will,
> And leads me to your eyes.
>   (II.ii.113–21)

But the speech is ironic because it indicates the opposite of what it says, and in so doing it reveals the extent to which Lysander's reason has been subverted by desire through fancy. Hermia is asleep and her mind appears to be ruled by fancy:

> Help me, Lysander, help me! Do thy best
> To pluck this crawling serpent from my breast.
> Ay me, for pity. What a dream was here!
> Lysander, look how I do quake with fear.
> Methought a serpent eat my heart away,
> And you sat smiling at his cruel prey.
>   (II.ii.145–50)

The dream is accurate, however, because it indicates the falseness of Lysander's words, and in so doing it reveals the perceptiveness of an imagination habitually exercised by reason—a perceptiveness which Eve has not yet had the opportunity to develop. Thus, as the snake image indicates, Oberon's beguiling of Titania suggests the power of language in separating fancy from reason. When Egeus accuses Lysander of bewitching Hermia, it is course no accident that the emphasis should fall on his words as the chief of his magical devices:

> Thou hast by moonlight at her window sung
> With feigning voice verses of feigning love,
> And stol'n the impression of her fantasy.
> (I.i.30–33)

Similarly, in *Othello*, the "chains of magic" that Othello uses to enchant Desdemona, the "foul charms," the "drugs or minerals / That weaken motion" (I.ii.64, 73, 74–75), that is, the magic potions that subvert her reason, all turn out to be words—"my discourse. . . . This only is the witchcraft I have used" (I.iii.150, 169).

When we return to Eve's dream, the same feeling that the magic which forges illusions, phantasms, or dreams is only a figure for those words that excite desire at the expense of reason through fancy's wanton growth is even stronger. Just as Oberon's intrusion into Titania's bower is marked by the juxtaposition of the snake with its enameled skin and the magical juice with its power to forge hateful fantasies, so Satan's intrusion is marked by a similar juxtaposition of images which suggest false words and magic. This time, however, the syntax clearly identifies the one with the other: "Squat like a Toad, close at the eare of Eve" is in apposition to "Assaying by his Devilish art to reach / The Organs of her Fancie." As the opening words of Eve's account of the dream confirm, Satan's devilish art, his magic,[23] is essentially his skill with words: "Close at mine ear one call'd me forth to walk / With gentle voice" (V.36–37). The dream itself is made up of three movements in each of which a visual illusion is preceded by a Satanic speech: the illusion is forged, that is, both shaped and counterfeited, by words.

In the first movement, for instance, the visual illusion (V.48–57) confronts Eve with images of the tree of knowledge and an angelic figure. The tree now seems "Much fairer to my Fancie then by day" (V.53) because in the preceding speech there is the suggestive observation—"now reignes / Full Orb'd the Moon, and with more pleasing light / Shadowie sets off the face of things" (V.41–43). The power

---

23. Cf. Archimago's "diuelish arts" (*FQ* I.ii.9), the magic with which he separates Redcross from truth—"his guests / He saw diuided into double parts." Cf. also Quilligan, pp. 48–49.

of the word over what is seen here exemplifies what Coleridge calls poetry's power "of giving the interest of novelty by the modifying colors of imagination." His analogy, which he says he draws from "the poetry of nature," ironically emphasizes his point because it is actually drawn not from nature but from Milton's poetry, as its wording suggests—"The sudden charm, which accidents of light and shade, which moon-light or sun-set diffused over a known and familiar landscape"[24]—is an unconscious memory of what Satan says and Eve sees above. The angelic figure that confronts Eve has an intensely sensual appearance. In fact, the image she sees—"his dewie locks distill'd / *Ambrosia*" (V.56–57)—is that of the bride's lover from the Song of Solomon:

> I sleep, but my heart waketh: it is the voice of my beloved that knocketh, saying, Open to me, my sister, my love, my dove, my undefiled: for my head is filled with dew, and my locks with the drops of the night.
>
> (5:2)[25]

The sensual appearance of the angel is determined by the preceding speech: it is a visualization of the amorous voice that calls Eve, the voice she initially mistakes for Adam's. For the voice imitates the love-language of Solomon. Satan's "Serenate" (IV.769)—

24. *Biographia Literaria* XIV, quoted from S. T. Coleridge, *Biographia Literaria*, ed. J. Shawcross (1907; rpt. London: Oxford University Press, 1962), II, 5.

25. For a number of reasons the image, "his dewie locks distill'd / *Ambrosia*," is also meant to recall the loveliness of Venus—"Dixit et auertens rosea ceruice refulsit, / ambrosiaeque comae diuinum uertice odorem / spirauere" (*Aen.* I.402–4; "So Venus spoke, and as she turned away her loveliness shone, a tint of rose glowed on her neck and a scent of Heaven breathed from the divine hair of her head"). In *Christabel* the sensuality of the angel is captured and amplified in the appearance of the sinister Geraldine: like Eve Christabel awakes in the middle of the night, passes through a moonlit landscape, and arrives at a tree beneath which she discovers

> a damsel bright,
> Drest in silken robe of white,
> That shadowy in the moonlight shone:
> The neck that made the white robe wan,
> Her stately neck, and arms were bare;
> Her blue-veined feet unsandal'd were,
> And wildly glittered here and there
> The gems entangled in her hair.
>
> (58–65)

Quoted from *The Complete Poetical Works of Samuel Taylor Coleridge*, ed. E. H. Coleridge, 2 vols. (1912; rpt. Oxford: Clarendon Press, 1975).

Why sleepst thou *Eve?* now is the pleasant time,
The cool, the silent, save where silence yields
To the night-warbling Bird, that now awake
Tunes sweetest his love-labor'd song

(V.37–40)

—is a parody of Solomon's Song—"Rise up, my love, my fair one, and
come away" (2 : 10–13)—and a distortion of Adam's genuine version
of the Song: "Awake / My fairest, my espous'd" (V.17–25). A similar
relationship between speech and illusion is apparent in the other two
movements. In the second, the angel's emphasis on the idea of tasting—"taste thy sweet . . . what reserve forbids to taste?" (V.59, 61)—
materializes in the image of his own tasting—"He pluckt, he tasted"
(V.65). In the third, his promise of heavenly ascent materializes in the
illusion of Eve's flight.

The bitter irony is of course that the shaping power of Satan's language is directed against the very nature of language. When true to
its original nature language is both the symbol and faithful vehicle of
reason, "the outward manifestation of the inner Paradise."[26] In Eden
there is a direct relationship between language and truth: "to speak I
tri'd, and forthwith spake, / My Tongue obey'd and readily could
name / What e're I saw" (VIII.271–73).[27] Even in the fallen world language retains its fundamental association with reason, an association captured in the dual meaning of *logos*, the word and reason:
"the word," according to Descartes, "is the sole sign and only certain
mark of the presence of thought hidden and wrapped up in the
body."[28] Language because it is the outward show of reason exhibits
most clearly the difference between man and the animals: "now all
men, the most stupid and the most foolish, those even who are de-
prived of the organs of speech, make use of signs, whereas the brutes
never do anything of the kind; which may be taken for the true distinction between man and brute."[29] As Satan's words forge their images, so the association between language and reason begins to disin-

26. Fish, *Surprised by Sin*, p. 118.
27. Cf. ibid., pp. 107–30.
28. Quoted in Noam Chomsky, *Cartesian Linguistics* (New York: Harper and Row,
1966), p. 6. Cf. Milton's *Art of Logic* on the divine origin of language in both the fallen
and unfallen worlds: "But languages, both that first one which Adam spoke in Eden,
and those varied ones also possibly derived from the first, which the builders of the
tower of Babel suddenly received, are without doubt divinely given" (I.xxiv [Co-
lumbia, XI, 221]).
29. Quoted in Chomsky, p. 6.

tegrate. As the growth of wanton fancy is made to accelerate in Eve's mind, so truth is dismembered and evil begins to uncoil itself in precisely the same way that it did at the beginning of *The Faerie Queene* and in the opening books of *Paradise Lost*. In Spenser the unity of truth is shattered by Archimago's "diuelish arts" (I.ii.9), his forging of Duessa, a counterfeit Una or Truth, in Redcross's imagination. The allegory represents the creation of opinion,[30] opinion being another name for reason subverted by desire through fancy:

a vaine, light, crude and imperfect iudgement of things drawen from the outward senses, and common report, setling and holding it selfe to be good in the imagination, and never arriving at the vnderstanding, there to be examined, sifted, and laboured; and to be made reason, which is a true, perfect and solide iudgement of things.[31]

In the opening books of *Paradise Lost*, the unity of truth is shattered in much the same way: Satan's divisive language, symbolized by his identification with Typhon who in his Egyptian form "took the Virgin Truth, hewd her lovely form into a thousand peeces and scatterd them to the four winds,"[32] creates opinion in the imagination of the reader, that is, it creates an alternative view of things to that revealed by Scripture. So here in Eve's imagination, Satan's "Devilish art," the shaping power of his words, creates an alternative view of things to that revealed by God through Adam.

In Satan's first speech, the dependence of Eve's uninformed fancy on appearances, a dependence from which she is so carefully weaned while awake by the rational voice first of God and then of Adam, is now, in sleep, revived. The close of Satan's Circean speech answers the question at the close of Eve's "sacred and home-felt" love-lyric to Adam: Satan's explanation that the moon shines

in vain,
If none regard; Heav'n wakes with all his eyes,
Whom to behold but thee, Natures desire,
In whose sight all things joy, with ravishment
Attracted by thy beauty still to gaze
(V.43–47)

---

30. Cf. Fowler, *Spenser and the Numbers of Time*, p. 8, and Quilligan, pp. 48–49.
31. Charron, *Of Wisdome*, p. 67.
32. *Areopagitica* (Yale, II, 549).

answers Eve's question:

> But wherfore all night long shine these, for whom
> This glorious sight, when sleep hath shut all eyes?
> (IV.657–58)

Satan's answer, given in a counterfeit of Adam's voice, provides an alternative to Adam's answer, the true answer. Eve's assumption that the heavens shine for our sake, an assumption based on appearances interpreted only by desire, that is, the "voluntary appetite" or innate desire for one's own physical good,[33] is so qualified by Adam that the emphasis falls on the reverse:

> These then, though unbeheld in deep of night,
> Shine not in vain, nor think, though men were none,
> That heav'n would want spectators, God want praise.
> (IV.674–76)

Satan's alternative answer not only revives Eve's untutored assumption, but intensifies it by suggesting that the heavens do shine for her sake in terms that revive the memory of her very first dependence on appearances at the pool: that the heavens shine in order to behold her, because she is "Natures desire," because in her sight "all things joy, with ravishment / Attracted by thy beauty still to gaze," is meant to restore her confidence in her original, misguided perception of her own beauty, a perception based on appearances interpreted only by desire—"there I had fixt / Mine eyes till now, and pin'd with vain desire" (IV.465–66).

In his second speech, Satan, this time simulating not Adam but an angel, another counterfeit agent of revelation, provides Eve with an alternative to Adam's explanation of the tree of knowledge (IV.420–32). Here Satan again demonstrates that the sense-bound imagination he seeks to exploit in Eve is very much his own. The alternative view he offers—

> O fair Plant . . . with fruit surcharg'd,
> Deigns none to ease thy load and taste thy sweet,
> Nor God, nor Man; is Knowledge so despis'd?
> Or envie, or what reserve forbids to taste?
> Forbid who will, none shall from me withhold
> Longer thy offerd good, why else set here?
> (V.58–63)

---

33. Cf. Bamborough, *The Little World of Man*, pp. 41–42.

—substantially reproduces his own misunderstanding of Adam's explanation:

> One fatal Tree there stands of Knowledge call'd,
> Forbidden them to taste: Knowledge forbidd'n?
> Suspicious, reasonless. Why should thir Lord
> Envie them that? can it be sin to know,
> Can it be death? and do they onely stand
> By ignorance, is that thir happie state,
> The proof of thir obedience and thir faith?
>
> (IV.514–20)

This is a misunderstanding, an impoverishment of Adam's meaning, because the heavy emphasis Adam places on the symbolic value of the tree—"The only sign of our obedience left / Among so many signes of power and rule" (IV.428–29)—is lost in a maze of literal-minded questions, questions that betray Satan's assumption of a literal relationship between the tree and knowledge, questions that betray the same state of mind that leads Satan, poised on the stairway to heaven's gate, to choose the sun before the reality it symbolizes. In this, as in so many other things, in his powers of comprehension, Satan shows himself to be the antithesis of God the Son. The accuracy of the Son's interpretation of the Father's words arises out of faith, the imagination moved by the love of God. The inaccuracy of Satan's interpretation of Adam's words arises out of that kind of reasoning which is merely a manifestation of the sense-bound imagination, the imagination dominated by the appearances it registers. As Sibbes explains, revelation, the effect of true interpretation, turns on faith—"There must be a double light. So there must be a Spirit in me, as there is a Spirit in Scripture before I can see anything."[34] That is, unless the eyes of faith are planted in the soul, things invisible to mortal sight cannot be seen; "Unless you believe, you shall not understand;" unless words are interpreted according to the spirit as opposed to the letter—that is, both the figurative as opposed to the literal and the intention as opposed to the form—then they cannot be understood. It is for this reason that Satan's analysis of Adam's speech sounds so much like Empson's criticism of *Paradise Lost*. Because the symbolic value of the tree is not accessible to the weak mightiness of Satan's reasoning, faith is identified with ignorance— an identification Empson accepts without a second thought: Satan

---

34. Quoted in Nuttall, p. 23.

"seems genuinely indignant (520) at hearing the conditions of igno-rance which God has imposed upon them."[35] Thus, by insisting on the literal at the expense of the symbolic, the rhetorical question with which the Satanic angel's speech closes—"Forbid who will, none shall from me withhold / Longer thy offerd good, why else set here?"—creates opinion; by implying the exclusive reality of ap-pearances it suggests the illusoriness of mankind's faith. Even the sound of those words with which Adam defines the significance of the sign have been slurred into a verbal imitation of the tree's volup-tuousness, its "offerd good": "this *easie charge* . . . not to *taste* that onely Tree" (IV.421–23) degenerates into "O fair Plant . . . with fruit sur*charg'd*, / Deigns none to *ease* thy load and *taste*" (my emphasis).

Satan's third speech, unlike the first two, does not offer misjoined versions of Adam and Eve's earlier conversations, but a speculation based on those versions, a speculation intended to excite Eve's mind "With more desire to know" (IV.523). The change suggests the move-ment we noticed in the opening books of the poem from the fantastic landscape of hell to the spacious hall of Pandemonium—a develop-ment from unrestrained fancy to proud imaginations.[36] Building on the first two speeches, the third offers a conjecture that completes Satan's Babel-like mental construct. By stressing the literal or magi-cal relationship between the fruit and knowledge, he suggests the possibility of an ascent to heaven independent of God:

> Taste this, and be henceforth among the Gods
> Thy self a Goddess, not to Earth confind,
> But somtimes in the Air, as wee, somtimes
> Ascend to Heav'n, by merit thine, and see
> What life the Gods live there, and such live thou.
> (V.77–81)

This Satanic alternative is of course a parody of the ascent later out-lined by Raphael (V.469–505); it is also related to the ascent of the soul in the *Phaedrus*, an ascent which enables the soul to contem-plate the festival of the gods and to "see many blessed sights in the inner heaven" (247). As we suggested,[37] in as much as the classics comprise an alternative to Christian revelation, the ideas of the *Phaedrus* are the same as the illusions Satan seeks to forge in Eve's

35. Empson, p. 69. Cf. Carey and Fowler, p. 643n.
36. See pp. 103–7.
37. See pp. 109–10.

mind—parodies of the truth, "false, or little else but dreams, / Conjectures, fancies, built on nothing firm" (*PR* IV.291–92). In as much as the classics comprise a shadowy type of Christian revelation, the ideas of the *Phaedrus* provide an image of mankind's divinely implanted desire to ascend to knowledge of God. This is how the *Phaedrus* is used in the "Vacation Exercise": [38]

> Yet I had rather, if I were to chuse,
> Thy service in some graver subject use,
> Such as may make thee search thy coffers round,
> Before thou cloath my fancy in fit sound:
> Such where the deep transported mind may soare
> Above the wheeling poles, and at Heav'ns dore
> Look in, and see each blissful Deitie
> How he before the thunderous throne doth lie.
>
> (29–36)

In Eve's dream, Satan uses the *Phaedrus* as an alternative to Christian revelation and at the same time he parodies it as a type of Christian revelation. He parodies it in that whereas Plato, like Raphael, makes it clear that ascent depends upon controlling appetite (253d–54), the Satanic angel suggests that it depends upon the reverse, upon satisfying appetite—"Taste this, and be henceforth among the Gods." In this, for the reader at least, the *Phaedrus* as a type of revelation provides a commentary on the process of the dream. Failure to control appetite, according to Plato, leads to the creation of opinion: uncontrolled souls "are lamed or have their wings broken through the ill-driving of the charioteers; and all of them after a fruitless toil, not having attained to the mysteries of true being, go away, and feed upon opinion [or appearance]" (248b). Here Satan's uncontrolled appetite, his insatiable desire, creates opinion in Eve's mind so that her appetite in turn may become uncontrolled. And as the *Phaedrus* imagery of *Of Reformation* confirms, he does this through the sense-bound imagination: as we have seen before,[39] through the carnal imagination, the imagination that would bring "the inward acts of the *Spirit* to the outward, and customary ey-Service of the body" the soul "bated her wing apace downeward: and finding the ease she had from her visible, and sensuous collegue the body in performance of *Religious* duties, her pineons now bro-

38. See pp. 53–55.
39. See pp. 101–3.

ken, and flagging, shifted off from her selfe, the labour of high soaring any more, forgot her heavenly flight."⁴⁰ Thus, Eve's heavenly flight, the ascent promised by the Satanic angel, is in fact a descent. The inflation and deflation she experiences—"Forthwith up to the Clouds / With him I flew," "suddenly / My Guide was gon, and I, me thought, sunk down" (V.86–91)—is the same as that experienced by Satan himself through the course of his epic reverie and its dissolution, and by the inhabitants of the Paradise of Fools.

In this, in the dismemberment of truth and the creation of opinion, above all in the way the dream-state symbolizes the power of language in separating fancy from reason, Eve's dream provides the most accurate analogy of the actual process of seduction in Book IX. To return to the gardening metaphor, the dream demonstrates how the walks and bowers of Eden, fancy regulated by reason to create understanding, are later obliterated by fancy's wanton growth.

The Verbal Temptation as a Renewal of the Dream

> *Antonio*: And yet methinks I see it in thy face,
>   What thou shouldst be. Th'occasion speaks thee, and
>   My strong imagination sees a crown
>   Dropping upon thy head.
> *Sebastian*:   What? Art thou waking?
> *Antonio*: Do you not hear me speak?
> *Sebastian*:   I do; and surely
>   It is a sleepy language, and thou speak'st
>   Out of thy sleep. What is it thou didst say?
>   This is a strange repose, to be asleep
>   With eyes wide open; standing, speaking, moving,
>   And yet so fast asleep.
>   *The Tempest* II.i.200–11

Towards the end of *A Midsummer Night's Dream* Theseus explains the experience of the lovers in the familiar terms of unrestrained fancy—"antic fables," "fairy toys," "shaping fantasies" (V.i.3, 5). Hippolyta, however, perceives something more than "fancy's images" (V.i.25) in their story, "something of great constancy" (V.i.26) in the operation of their imaginations. That constancy is consistently referred to by the lovers themselves as "faith." When Demetrius, for

40. Yale, I, 520, 522.

instance, wakes from his "dream," he explains the morning's dissolution of fantasy as a renewal of "faith":

> But, my good lord, I wot not by what power
> (But by some power it is) my love to Hermia,
> Melted as the snow, seems to me now
> As the remembrance of an idle gaud
> Which in my childhood I did dote upon;
> And all the faith, the virtue of my heart,
> The object and pleasure of mine eye,
> Is only Helena.
>
> (IV.i.163–70)

This transition from unrestrained fancy to "faith" is remembered, among other places, in the transition from "L'Allegro" to "Il Penseroso." Demetrius's fantasy which now seems to him like "an idle gaud" is remembered in the "fancies fond with *gaudy* shapes" that possess "some *idle* brain" ("Il Penseroso" 6, 5; my emphasis), fancies that are superseded by the educated imagination's search for "something like Prophetic strain" (174). The fancy-sick Demetrius is returned to "faith" by Oberon, but Oberon dissolves Demetrius's fantasies by the same means that he creates Titania's—by Cupid's flower. This apparent contradiction suggests that constancy is not magical; it does not depend on some inherent property of the flower, but on how the flower is used, that is, it depends on how the passions fancy arouses are directed. Just as faith in its full sense depends on the intelligence with which the imagination, and the emotions of love the imagination arouses, are governed. In other words, fancy needs to be tempered by reason or, as Bottom observes, "reason and love keep little company together nowadays. The more the pity that some honest neighbors will not make them friends" (III.i.130–33). For ultimately, as Milton explains, the passions "rightly temper'd are the very ingredients of vertu,"[41] and virtue "united to the heavenly grace of faith makes up the highest perfection."[42] Oberon creates fantasies in Titania's mind only to exorcise those that are already there[43]—just as Prospero does in the minds of the shipwrecked passengers in *The Tempest*,[44] and Milton himself does in the reader's mind at the beginning of *Paradise Lost*.[45] Titania, who made Theseus "with fair Aegles break his faith, / With Ariadne, and Antiopa"

41. *Areopagitica* (Yale, II, 527).
42. *Of Education* (Yale, II, 367).
43. See pp. 85–87.
44. See pp. 22–25.
45. See pp. 90–103.

(II.i.79–80), is beguiled so that she will give up the lovely boy and be released from her dotage: "ere I take this charm from off her sight . . . I'll make her render up her page to me" (II.i.183, 185). And since, as we have suggested,[46] the Indian boy is a personification of fancy, this, the mainspring of the plot of *A Midsummer Night's Dream*, the transference of the boy from Titania to Oberon, is concerned with the ordering of fancy and the renewal of "faith." The same is true of Eve's dream. There *is* an actual relationship between Eve's dream and her fall in Book IX, the one does contribute to the other, but as the analogy of *A Midsummer Night's Dream* suggests and the presence of the play in the verbal texture of our first parents' response to Eve's dream confirms, there need not have been.

The immediate response of unfallen mankind to Eve's dream illustrates the process of reason ordering fancy, a process which climaxes in a hymn like the poet's hymn to heavenly light at the beginning of Book III, or the Lady's song to Echo in the *Mask*. It is a process which prompts the influx of the heavenly grace of faith. Grace, "The speediest of thy winged messengers" (III.229), takes the form here of Raphael whose storytelling is the substance of grace in that it moves the imagination to believe in and so see the unity of truth, the divine perspective fragmented by opinion in the dream. Reason's ordering of fancy begins with Eve herself and continues with Adam. The hateful fantasies of the dream are initially checked by Eve's waking consciousness of their "offence and trouble" (V.34). The fantasies are then disarmed of much of their potency as Adam, echoing Theseus, explains the mechanism of dreams. Theseus's dismissal of the creative imagination in terms of unrestrained fancy—

> And as *imagination* bodies forth
> The *forms* of things unknown, the poet's pen
> Turns them to *shapes*, and gives to *airy* nothing
> A local habitation and a name
> (V.i.14–17; my emphasis)

—is remembered and condensed in Adam's explanation of fancy's operation before it has been ordered by reason—"She forms Imaginations, Aerie shapes" (V.105).[47] His explanation of its operation after

46. See p. 86.
47. Guillory's analysis of the relationship between these passages is inaccurate. First, Theseus' speech is only the "most aggrandizing text on imagination" (p. 17) once it has been placed in the context of Hippolyta's response. As it stands, it derogates imagination by identifying the creative activities of poets with imagination uninformed by reason. Theseus attributes the work of Oberon to an unrestrained Puck. Second, the

fancy has separated itself from reason is, as we have seen, a memory of Puck. Once he has established the emptiness and illusoriness of the dream, he recognizes that it is best to treat it as a "providential warning": [48] since "Evil into the mind of God or Man / May come and go, so unapprov'd, and leave / No spot or blame behind," he hopes "That what in sleep thou didst abhorr to dream, / Waking thou never wilt consent to do" (V.117–21). In so doing, Adam makes it clear how Satan's evil intentions may be turned to good and how the dream may be used as an opportunity to develop the power of Eve's rational faculty. It may become, like the reader's own delusion at the beginning of the poem, the experience that will steel the will by making reason less susceptible to fancy's illusions.

However, as the echoing of Theseus is perhaps meant to suggest, cool reason is inadequate; it can only go so far. Adam's unaided reason cannot comprehend the demonic coherence of the dream, the "addition strange":

> nor can I like
> This uncouth dream, of evil sprung I fear;
> Yet evil whence? in thee can harbour none,
> Created pure.
>
> (V.97–100)

Eve's fantasy is finally exorcised, the source of evil explained, only after Adam and Eve make their morning orisons, an act of faith in which the "rational fancy" arouses and directs the emotions of love to God. The prayer is poetry at its highest potential: "for neither various style / Nor holy rapture wanted they to praise / Thir Maker" (V.146–48). The prayer's final note, an appeal for the dissolution of illusion—

> Hail universal Lord, be bounteous still
> To give us onely good; and if the night
> Have gathered aught of evil or conceald,
> Disperse it, as now light dispels the dark
> (V.205–8)

---

absence of the word "nothing" in Milton is explained not by Milton's rejection of creation *ex nihilo*, but because Adam is explaining the way imagination represents actual objects whereas Theseus is explaining the way poets create fictions. Adam echoes Theseus because unless the airy shapes the imagination forms of actual objects are ordered by reason, then they will remain as insubstantial as the wildest fictions, the wildest work of Puck.

48. Burden, p. 129.

—is answered by an outpouring of grace, the dispatch of Raphael and his story whose appeal to the icastic imagination, *alta fantasia* or our "high-raised fantasy," enables Adam and Eve to apprehend more than cool reason can comprehend, that is, the genesis of evil and God's re-creation of the good. Raphael does what he appears to suggest is impossible:

> for who, though with the tongue
> Of Angels, can relate, or to what things
> Liken on Earth conspicuous, that may lift
> Human imagination to such highth
> Of Godlike Power.
>
> (VI.297–301)

He does raise the imagination because there is an answer to his rhetorical question and that answer, as the allusion to St. Paul suggests, is love, the guide and interpreter of faith: "Though I speak with the tongues of men and of angels, and have not charity, I am become as sounding brass, or a tinkling symbal" (I. Cor. 13:1). In other words, Raphael's story completes what mankind's hymn begins; through the agency of the rationally exercised imagination Raphael's love—"from among / Thousand Celestial Ardours, where he stood" (V.248–49)—arouses and directs mankind's love to knowledge of God. Thus, Raphael who "shook his Plumes, that Heav'nly fragrance filld / The circuit wide" (V.286–87) is the true Christian antitype of Virgil's Venus whose hair breathed the scent of heaven; his story is the true antitype of her revelation to Aeneas (*Aeneid* I.335–401). The Satanic angel whose "dewie locks distill'd / Ambrosia" (V.56–57) is a demonic parody of Raphael and his dream a distortion of the winged messenger's appeal to the imagination.

The whole process of fancy being ordered and faith renewed is symbolized by mankind's return to its gardening tasks and God's response to that return. In Shakespeare, Oberon finally decides to exorcise illusion after seeing Titania and Bottom locked in a fruitless embrace:

> So doth the woodbine the sweet honeysuckle
> Gently entwist; the female ivy so
> Enrings the barky fingers of the elm.
> (IV.i.41–43)

The embrace is fruitless because Titania's simile is a dreamlike distortion of what Spenser calls the "vine-prop Elm" emblem (*FQ* I.i.8).

The traditional significance of this emblem, according to Fowler, is the "mutual dependence and complementary gifts" of marriage, the elm standing for masculine strength and the vine for feminine fruitfulness.[49] In Ovid, for instance, Vertumnus woos Pomona by referring to "an Elme" which "with purple clusters shin'd":

> if this Elme should grow alone,
> Except for shade, it would be priz'd by none:
> And so this Vine, in amorous foldings wound,
> If but dis-joyn'd, would creepe upon the ground.
> 　　　　　　　　　　　　　　(*Met.* XIV. 662, 664–67)

The emblem also appears as an image of true marriage in *The Comedy of Errors*:

> Come, I will fasten on this sleeve of thine:
> Thou art an elm, my husband, I a vine,
> Whose weakness married to thy stronger state
> Makes me with thy strength communicate.
> If aught possess thee from me, it is dross,
> Usurping ivy, brier, or idle moss;
> Who all for want of pruning, with intrusion
> Infect thy sap and live on thy confusion.
> 　　　　　　　　　　　　　　(II.ii.172–79)

Titania's use of the image is a dreamlike distortion because the vine has been replaced by ivy;[50] the misjoining of the elm with "usurping ivy" not only suggests fruitlessness, but also fancy's wanton growth—for want of pruning, the ivy lives on confusion and infects the life-giving sap.[51] In Milton, the image appears in its proper form: as the mind returns to its "wonted calm," so Adam and Eve haste "to thir mornings rural work":

49. Carey and Fowler, p. 687n. Sibbes, *The Brvised Reede, and Smoaking Flax* (London, 1630; rpt. Menston, Yorks.: Scolar Press, 1973), uses the image as an emblem of the relationship between Christ and his Church: "The Vine stayeth it selfe upon the Elme. . . . The consciousnesse of the churches weaknesse makes her willing to leane on her beloved, and to hide her selfe under his wing" (pp. 29–30).

50. Cf. Brooks, p. 89n: "Does Shakespeare deliberately substitute the ivy for the vine (the wife) because Titania's embrace, like that of the ivy in *Err.* (1.178), is not marital?"

51. Ivy is not only barren but, as Vaughan indicates, poisonous: "The poisonous Ivie here no more / His false twists on the Oke shall score, / Only the Woodbine here may twine, / As th'Embleme of her Love, and mine" ("Upon the Priorie Grove" 11–14).

where any row
Of Fruit-trees overwoodie reachd too farr
Thir pamperd boughes, and needed hands to check
Fruitless imbraces: or they led the Vine
To wed her Elm; she spous'd about him twines
Her mariageable arms, and with her brings
Her dowr th'adopted Clusters, to adorn
His barren leaves.

(V.210, 211, 212–19)

The image signifies not only the reunion of Adam and Eve, but of reason and fancy, reason tempering fancy and, perhaps more important, fancy adorning reason's barren leaves with fruit. And just as the distorted image—qualified by Titania's newfound awareness of her beguiled state—moves Oberon to pity and grace in the sense of forgiveness and release from illusion; so the true image moves God to pity and grace in its full sense. Just as Oberon is moved—

Seest thou this sweet sight?
Her dotage now I do begin to pity.

(IV.i.45–46)

—so is God—

Them thus imploid beheld
With pittie Heav'ns high King, and to him call'd
Raphael.

(V.219–21)

Despite the exorcism of the dream, when we turn to the Fall itself the *actual* nature of the relationship between the dream and the verbal temptation is unmistakable. The illusions by which Eve falls are essentially the same as those first forged in the dream. Despite the pruning of fancy's wanton growth, despite fancy's being led to wed the elm of reason and so bear the fruits of revelation, its tendency to grow wild is a constant: as Eve herself acknowledges, "what we by day / Lop overgrown, or prune, or prop, or bind, / One night or two with wanton growth derides / Tending to wilde" (IX.209–12). Mankind's gardening task and the psychological reality it signifies is a permanent part of being human. As long as reason rules fancy, as long as Eve remains conscious of the dream, then the experience of the dream reinforces the efficacy of reason's rule. But as soon as fancy is separated from reason, as soon as the memory of the dream slips from Eve's consciousness, then the desires engendered in the dream may so renew themselves in the fancy that they will usurp reason's rule. This is, of course, what Satan's final temptation seeks to do; it seeks to separate fancy from reason by re-creating the conditions and perceptions of the dream in the waking mind of Eve, and it seeks to do so through his devilish art, the magic of his suasive rhetoric, a form of language which like the serpentine love-language of *A Midsummer Night's Dream* would steal "the impression of her fantasy" (I.i.32), or like the narcotic songs of Circe would in pleasing slumber lull the sense, and in sweet madness rob it of itself (*Mask* 259–60).

Satan's re-creation of the conditions of the dream is prefigured by his second entry into Paradise. His method of entry indicates something much more precise than Fowler's suggestion "that evil enters life at its very origin."[52] Satan enters Paradise by means of the river of life:

> There was a place,
> Now not, though Sin, not Time, first wrought the change,
> Where *Tigris* at the foot of Paradise
> Into a Gulf shot under ground, till part
> Rose up a Fountain by the Tree of Life;
> In with the River sunk, and with it rose
> Satan involv'd in rising, Mist, then sought
> Where to lie hid.
>
> (IX.69–76)

The river of life in Paradise is the macrocosm of the rivers of life in the body, the blood. It is for this reason that the fountain of life which fertilizes Paradise is said to rise "through veins / Of porous Earth with kindly thirst up drawn" (IV.227–28). Thus, the rising mist, which literally suggests simply the concealment necessary for a successfully covert entry,[53] suggests physiologically the "animal Spirits that from pure blood arise / Like gentle breaths from Rivers pure" (IV.805–6), breaths or vapours which Satan at the ear of Eve attempts to taint. Because the animal spirits carry the images of objects from the outward senses to the imagination[54]—in the dream

---

52. Carey and Fowler, p. 860n.
53. The rising mist also enables Milton to account for the Authorized Version's translation of the fountain as "a mist from the earth" (Gen. 2:6).
54. Cf. Carey and Fowler, pp. 661–62n; Bamborough, *The Little World of Man,* pp. 54–57; Harvey, *The Inward Wits,* pp. 49–50.

the sense-data of the previous night's conversations—tainting the animal spirits means manipulating the fancy. Thus, Satan entering Paradise involved in rising mist symbolizes the impending dream-like manipulation of fancy in the paradise within.

The separation of fancy from reason which Satan's temptation eventually effects is prefigured by the separation of Eve from Adam. The separation enacts what it prefigures, because the separation of the characters is precipitated by an act of the sense-bound imagination. Eve takes the gardening too seriously—"Yet not so strictly hath our Lord impos'd / Labour" (IX.235–36). From our perspective, Eve, because she is so impressed by appearances, takes the gardening metaphor literally. What she sees as the chief obstacle to gardening in its literal sense is the point of gardening in its true, or metaphoric sense. The interruptions that arise out of their mutual love—"Looks intervene and smiles, or object new / Casual discourse draw on, which intermits / Our dayes work brought to little" (IX.222–24)—are, as Adam explains in a gentle understatement, manifestations of reason, which with the love it engenders is both the end and means of cultivating the true garden, the garden within: "for smiles from Reason flow, / To brute deni'd, and are of Love the food, / Love not the lowest end of human life" (IX.239–41). Against the evidence of the outward senses, the demands of the physical garden, Adam opposes a trust in God's providence: God made us "not to irksom toile but to delight / . . . and delight to Reason joyn'd. / These paths & Bowers doubt not but our joynt hands / Will keep from Wilderness with ease" (IX.242–45). This opposition between the zeal that arises out of a literal understanding of the garden and the trust that arises out of a metaphoric understanding reveals the core of Milton's story of the Fall as an opposition between the weak mightiness of man's reasoning and the mighty weakness of faith.[55] For Satan—whose "entire argument," according to Fish, "is contained in two phrases: Look on me (687) do not beleeve (684)"[56]—is bent on reversing Adam's opposition. Satan confronts Eve with the same choice that he himself faced on the stairway to heaven. Satan's temptation insists on the evidence of things seen, *sight*, against the evidence of things not seen, *faith*. And in matters of faith "sight," because it places reason in the service of appearances, reveals itself as the creature of unrestrained fancy.

55. Fish, *Surprised by Sin*, pp. 245–54, makes the central point that Eve's error is that of "substituting the law of reason and the evidence of things seen for the law of God" (p. 254).

56. Ibid., p. 249.

Thus, Eve's first step away from faith towards "sight" is firmly associated with the liberation of fancy from reason. As she leaves Adam she is compared to Pomona—"To *Pales*, or *Pomona* thus adornd, / Likeliest she seemd, *Pomona* when she fled / *Vertumnus*" (IX.393–95).[57] As Pomona's proposed union with Vertumnus is expressed in terms of the vine-prop elm image, so her flight signifies the disjoining of the vine: fancy is set free to "creepe upon the ground." The sterility of the separation and the fruitlessness of Titania's "fancy-sick" embrace is perhaps remembered in Eve's unconscious substitution of ivy for the vine in her exhortation to Adam to work alone, to "direct / The clasping Ivie where to climb" (IX.216–17).

The seduction of Eve falls into two parts. In much the same way that the seduction of the reader at the beginning of the poem reveals a movement from hell where fancy is separated from reason to Pandemonium where reason builds on the foundation of unrestrained fancy, in much the same way that the temptation in the dream moves from misjoined conversations to rationally constructed speculations, so here the temptation moves from a direct appeal to the imagination to a display of ratiocination built on that appeal. This movement from poetry to discourse reverses the movement of the speeches in the divine council, the fundamental paradigm for the process of faith, and, as we shall see, there is a curious similarity in style between God the Father's first speech and the tempter's last speech. The appeal to the imagination with which the temptation begins comprises an apostrophe to Eve's beauty and a parable which explains the serpent's ability to appreciate that beauty. Here the contribution of the dream is immediately apparent.

As Redcross loses his way once he fails to recognize Duessa as a counterfeit imitation sprung from his own fancy, and the reader loses his way once he fails to recognize hell as a fantasy sprung from Satan's very human mind,[58] so Eve loses her way once she fails to recognize the serpent's information as a projection of her own fancies. They are her own fancies not because she is corrupt, but because they are the desires first engendered or given shape in the dream. She fails to recognize the fantasies of the tempter's first speech because her attention is distracted by the appearance of the snake—the "specious

---

57. Cf. Martz, *Poet of Exile*, pp. 136–37, on Ovid's Pomona as a "true original for Milton's Eve."
58. See pp. 90–103.

object," the "faire appeering good" (IX.361, 354) of which Adam warned her.[59] While she marvels at the phenomenon of a talking snake, "Into the Heart of *Eve* his words made way" (IX.550)—that is, while Eve is conscious only of the sound not the significance of the words, precisely because she is not conscious, the significance of the words reawakens the illusions of the dream in her imagination, and they in turn touch her heart, the seat of her passions. Not only does the snake's appearance distract literally, but it symbolizes the tempter's verbal mode of distraction. Just as the fancifulness of the love-language in *A Midsummer Night's Dream* is symbolized by the snake's "enamelled skin" (II.i.255), so the appeal to unrestrained fancy in Satan's verbal temptation is symbolized by the snake's "sleek enamel'd Neck" and "Serpent Tongue / Organic" (IX.525, 529–30). Both the actual appearance of the snake and the kind of language it symbolizes revive Eve's dependence on appearances. The fair appearing good of the serpent's language in his opening apostrophe—

> Fairest resemblance of thy Maker faire,
> Thee all things living gaze on, all things thine
> By gift, and thy Celestial Beautie adore
> With ravishment beheld
>
> (IX.538–41)

—revives the narcissistic illusion of the opening dream-speech:

> Heav'n wakes with all his eyes,
> Whom to behold but thee, Natures desire,
> In whose sight all things joy, with ravishment
> Attracted by thy beauty still to gaze.
>
> (V.44–47)

And this illusion, as we have seen, is meant to release the voluntary appetite (that is, to engender desire) chiefly by restoring Eve's confidence in her original mode of apprehension—a mode based purely on objects as they appear in the imagination before they can be ordered by the voice of reason.

The serpent's apostrophe condenses the whole range of the dream temptation. Eve's original self-regarding desire, renewed in the first dream-speech, is now rendered inordinate by being carefully misjoined to the ratiocinative speculation of the last dream-speech on her divinity. The serpent's opinion, you "shouldst be seen / A God-

---

59. Cf. Frye, *Return of Eden*, pp. 77–78.

dess among Gods" (IX.546–47), is meant to revive all the force of the Satanic angel's critical imperative—"Taste this, and be henceforth among the Gods / Thy self a Goddess" (V.77–78). At the same time that the fair seeming good of his words uncoil the fantasies of the dream in Eve's unconscious mind, so the fair seeming good of the serpent's appearance leads her to doubt revelation in favor of appearances. The talking snake provides the evidence of sight which contradicts the evidence of revelation that animals do not talk: "The first at lest of these [human language] I thought deni'd / To Beasts, whom God on thir Creation-Day / Created mute to all articulat sound" (IX.555–57). Instead of her belief in revelation leading her to suspect the specious object before her eyes, the reverse occurs: the past tense "thought" indicates her trust in this point of revelation is passing or already past. The talking snake also renews an older doubt based on appearances, a doubt which rejects Raphael's assurance that other creatures are not "endu'd / With Sanctitie of Reason" (VII.507–8):[60] "The latter [that animals may express human sense] I demurre [hesitate about], for in thir looks / Much reason, and in thir actions oft appeers" (IX.558–59). Here Eve takes the next step after separating from Adam away from faith towards "sight."

Eve's renewed dependence on appearances is reinforced by the serpent's parable of apprehension. His account of coming to consciousness is a parody of Eve's account of her own awakening. Both the serpent and Eve explain the present state of their understanding by relating the events of a particular day. But what happens to the serpent who "apprehended nothing high: / Till on a day roaving the field" (IX.574–75) reverses what happened to Eve on "That day" which "I oft remember" (IV.449). The moral of Eve's experiences at the pool indicates that understanding depends on appearances, the images of external things shaped in the fancy, being framed by rea-

---

60. When God says that the beasts "reason not contemptibly" (VIII.374), he is testing Adam's faith, just as the talking snake tests Eve's. Adam passes this part of the test by pointing out that the essential difference between man and beast is the animals' inability to participate in "All rational delight" (VIII.391). In making this distinction, he actually exhibits the nature of the difference between human and brute reason. And that is of course self-knowledge or consciousness:

> Thus farr to try thee, *Adam*, I was pleas'd,
> And finde thee knowing not of Beasts alone,
> Which thou hast rightly nam'd, but of thy self,
> Expressing well the spirit within thee free,
> My Image, not imparted to the Brute.
> (VIII.437–41)

son, and the desires provoked by appearances being redirected by reason, the umpire placed within us whose voice echoes the voice of God. The moral of the serpent's experiences before the tree, however, indicates that understanding depends upon appearances being left unmodified, and the desires provoked by naked appearances being immediately satisfied. Both stories exemplify what they teach. Eve's story is the work of the *eikastike*: it re-creates desire in order to educate it. The serpent's story is the work of the *phantastike*: it re-creates desire in order to satisfy it. The serpent's story is meant to affect Eve in much the same way that the fruit affects the serpent. The serpent's story transforms the fruit into a provoking object.[61] The imagined fruit is meant to arouse Eve's appetite in much the same way that the fruit itself arouses the serpent's. The serpent's verbal re-creation of his sharp desire—"hunger and thirst at once, / Powerful perswaders, quick'nd at the scent / Of that alluring fruit" (IX.586–88)—is meant to renew the desire Eve experienced in her dream—"the pleasant savourie smell / So quick'nd appetite, that I, methought, / Could not but taste" (V.84–86)—and so color her reaction to the fruit itself. It is a measure of the sense-bound degree to which Eve's imagination has returned that she, unlike the Lady in the *Mask*, apprehends the serpent's words not as words, verbal echoes of her own words which might arouse suspicion and the conscious memory of the dream, but merely as images, sensations which arouse appetite and the unconscious desire of the dream. Although Eve's immediate response to the serpent's flattery is an instinctive flicker of irony, the best evidence of the still latent power of her critical intelligence, a response which almost absentmindedly ("unwarie") undermines the point of the serpent's parable—"Serpent, thy overpraising leaves in doubt / The vertue of that Fruit, in thee first prov'd" (IX.615–16)—she still allows her desire free rein: "But say, where grows the Tree, from hence how far?" (IX.617).

Clearly then, the suasive power of the parable of "sight," the mightiness of man's reasoning, rests not on the force of its logic but on the desire it arouses. In this it mirrors the true nature of "sight." The substance of reason divorced from its divine source, reason the servant of appearances, reason as exemplified by Satan's account of his own origin—

>   rememberst thou
> Thy making, while the Maker gave thee being?

61. Cf. Burden, pp. 124–49, on the way that imagination unchecked by judgment amplifies the attractiveness of the fruit.

> We know no time when we were not as now;
> Know none before us, self-begot, self-rais'd
> By our own quick'ning power
> (V.857–61)

—or by the serpent's doubt that all things proceed from the "Gods": "this fair Earth I see, / Warm'd by the Sun, producing every kind, / Them nothing" (IX.720–22)—turns out to be nothing but a meandering maze of unrestrained fancy. The kind of understanding that the serpent arrives at by depending on appearances—

> Thenceforth to Speculations high or deep
> I turnd my thoughts, and with capacious mind
> Considerd all things visible in Heav'n,
> Or Earth, or Middle, all things fair and good
> (IX.602–5)

—is precisely the kind condemned by Raphael in those who "build, unbuild, contrive / To save appeerances" and recognized by Adam as the result of the aptness of "the Mind or Fancie . . . to roave / Uncheckt" (VIII.81–82, 188–89). "Sight" is the mode of apprehension which once reestablished in Eve's mind, in practice by the apostrophe and in principle by the parable, enables the serpent's display of ratiocination to appear incontrovertible. As Broadbent, a passionate advocate of "sight," puts it, "Satan's argument, granted its fundamental lie that the snake has eaten the fruit, is intellectually unanswerable."[62] Eve's last defense, her memory of the tree's symbolic value, is easily overturned by the serpent's appeal to its observed or literal virtue: "doe not believe . . . look on me, / Mee who have touch'd and tasted" (IX.684, 687–88). Adam's word that the tree is the "only sign of our obedience" (IV.428) is the echo of God's "sole Command, / Sole pledge" (III.94–95) of man's obedience— "The Pledge of thy Obedience and thy Faith" (VIII.325). This echo is the "Sole Daughter of his voice" (IX.653), that is, the *filia vocis* or kind of revelation "made to one . . . that was no way prepared for prophecy."[63] The ear that would hear this voice, the echoes of Adam's warning or the echoes of her own dream in the serpent's temptation, the ear that enables the Lady in the *Mask* and the reader at the beginning of the poem to penetrate the illusions of fancy, is finally closed by "sight." Eve finally chooses reason before revelation, but

---

62. *Some Graver Subject*, p. 258.
63. Smith, *Of Prophecy* (*Select Discourses*, p. 268).

because reason in opposition to revelation is merely the work of the *phantastike*, she chooses unrestrained fancy. The rationcinative style of the serpent at the end of the temptation is not unlike that of God the Father at the beginning of the divine council. Both apprehend things according to "sight" in that they both, to adapt Fish's phrase,[64] acquiesce in the appearance of remedilessness. The Father deliberately limits himself within the bounds of human reason—"Dye hee or Justice must" (III.210)—while the serpent, albeit rather dubiously, limits God within the same bounds—"God therefore cannot hurt ye, and be just; / Not just, not God" (IX.700–701). Whereas the Father's ratiocinative style, a style which indicates what Arthur Barker calls "the Father's ironic adoption of a Satanically conceived role,"[65] is meant to provoke the Son's great act of faith, the serpent's style is meant to provoke mankind's collapse of faith. Both are successful. Whereas the Son because of his icastic imagination is able to interpret the Father's words, Eve because of her sense-bound imagination is condemned to parrot the serpent's.

ADAM'S NARCISSISM

> [He] changed the truth of God into a
> lie, and worshipped and served the
> creature more than the Creator.
>
> Romans 1 : 25

It remains to emphasize that Adam falls no less a victim of the *phantastike* than Eve. For Eve the provoking object, the fair appearing good, is ultimately the fruit; for Adam it is Eve herself. Adam remains undeceived by the fruit, but not by Eve. As the narrator explains: "he scrupl'd not to eat / Against his better knowledge, not deceav'd, / But fondly overcome with Femal charm" (IX.997–99). It is for this reason that the Father can refer to the *whole* of mankind as being "deceiv'd / By the other first" (III.130–31). Both Adam and Eve are deceived by Satan's magic: Eve because the serpent's words transform the fruit as it appears in her imagination into a provoking object; Adam because Eve's words, which persuade him of nothing but her deception by Satan, transform what was the fairest object of good

---

64. Fish, *Surprised by Sin*, p. 264.
65. "*Paradise Lost*: The Relevance of Regeneration," p. 69.

conceived in his imagination, that is, herself, into an equally provoking object. In Eve's case, through the agency of unrestrained fancy
Satan establishes an opposition between the sight of the fruit and
the revelation of its significance; in Adam's case, through the same
agency he establishes an opposition between the sight of Eve and the
revelation of what her seduction must mean. Adam falls *"through
vehemence of love"* (IX.Argument). What vehemence, "lacking in
mind," means is that the image of Eve, and the passion aroused by
that image, is so strong that it resists the efforts of reason to inform
it with new significance. Although reason tells Adam that Eve is
now "Defac't, deflourd, and . . . to Death devote" (IX.901), it is the
original significance of her image as the epitome of life[66]—an image
that has not changed from when she first appeared

> so lovly faire,
> That what seemd fair in all the World, seemd now
> Mean, or in her summd up, in her containd
> And in her looks
> (VIII.471–74)

—that determines his choice:

> O fairest of Creation, last and best
> Of all Gods works, Creature in whom excell'd
> *Whatever can to sight or thought be formd,*
> Holy, divine, good, amiable, or sweet!
> . . . .
> How can I live without thee.
> (IX.896–99, 908; my emphasis)

In this, Adam, like Eve, chooses sight before revelation. They both
make their understanding independent of God; they transfer their
fealty from the Creator to an aspect of his creation and in so doing
render themselves idolators. Eve literally does reverence to the tree
and Adam figuratively to Eve.

Because Eve is so carefully associated with fancy and Adam with
reason, his seduction by her may be seen as an allegorical projection
of reason's subversion by fancy, but if it is, it is an allegory of something which actually occurs in Adam and for which he is wholly re-

---

66. Cf. Revard, *The War in Heaven*, p. 284: "Eve, accepting the fruit of pride and
tempting Adam, no longer is the emanation of God and man, but the emanation
of Satan."

sponsible. The danger to Adam of fancy's wanton growth is every bit as great as it is to Eve. Just as the danger of unrestrained fancy is first apparent in Eve as she gazes at her own image, so it is in Adam as *he* gazes at her image. As he explains to Raphael, he feels weak only "Against the charm of Beauties powerful glance" (VIII.533). In Eve's case, the image of herself in her fancy arouses "vain desire" (IV.466), because it is uninformed by reason; in Adam's case, the image of Eve in his fancy arouses such passion, such "Commotion strange" (VIII.531), that it consistently overcomes the informing power of reason:

> All higher knowledge in her presence falls
> Degraded, Wisdom in discourse with her
> Losses discount'nanc't, and like folly shewes.
> (VIII.551–53)

Reason becomes the servant of appearances:

> Authority and Reason on her waite,
> As one intended first, not after made
> Occasionally.
> (VIII.554–56)

For Eve at the pool, delusion precedes the control of reason; for Adam, it overcomes that control. In this, and once we remember that Eve is the creation of Adam's imagination, then Adam, like Satan, is much more truly narcissistic than Eve. As we have seen,[67] both Eve and Sin are creations of the imagination: Eve of Adam's—"My Author and Disposer, what thou bidst / Unargu'd I obey" (IV.635–36)— and Sin of Satan's—"my Father . . . my Author," "whom should I obey / But thee" (II.864–66). Whereas Sin is both the image and issue of false creativity, Satan's fantastic imagination, Eve is the image and issue of true creativity, Adam's icastic imagination. When Satan becomes infatuated with Sin, the creation of his own imagination— "Thy self in me thy perfect image viewing / Becam'st enamour'd" (II.764–65)—it explains the narcissistic nature of Sin; it exemplifies the way Sin was first conceived. When Adam becomes infatuated with Eve, the creation of his imagination, he repeats Satan's act of sin; he reverses the way Eve was first conceived. For whereas Satan's imagination of Sin is an act of invention independent of God's creativity, Adam's imagination of Eve is a perception or reflection of

67. See pp. 117–20.

God's creativity. By preferring the love of his creation to the love of God, the final source of that creation, Adam renders himself a maker independent of God, transforms Eve into Sin, and the *eikastike* into the *phantastike.*

The seduction of Adam reveals the familiar movement from unrestrained fancy to proud imaginations, from fantasy to ratiocination. The display of ratiocination with which Adam, now "in calm mood" (IX.920), follows his passionate refusal to see Eve as anything other than a symbol of life, as one in whose "look summs all Delight" (IX.454), reveals itself on analysis as a dreamlike pastiche of misjoined fragments, embedded in the heart of which is an unconscious parody of the divine council.[68] Just as God the Father represents himself bound by the limits of human reason—

> I form'd them free, and free they must remain,
> . . . I else must change
> Thir nature, and revoke the high Decree
> Unchangeable, Eternal which ordain'd
> Thir freedom
>
> (III.126–28)

—so Adam represents God, wildly misjoined to fate, bound by the same limits: "But past who can recall, or don undoe? / Not God Omnipotent, nor Fate" (IX.926–27). In the divine council, the Son meets the Father's trial of faith and breaks the impasse of human reason echoing Abraham's argument of faith: "For should Man finally be lost" "that be from thee farr" (III.150, 153). In Adam's display of ratiocination, Adam breaks the impasse echoing Eve's (originally the serpent's) argument of "sight": "yet so / Perhaps thou shalt not Die" "Nor yet on him [was the fruit] found deadly, he yet lives" (IX.927–28, 932). Whereas the Son's response reveals his trust in the Father's mercy, Adam's response reveals no such trust, only the ambition that helps animate his rationalization: the serpent

> yet lives,
> Lives, as thou saidst, and gaines to live as Man
> Higher degree of Life, inducement strong
> To us, as likely tasting to attaine
> Proportional ascent, which cannot be
> But to be Gods, or Angels Demi-Gods.
>
> (IX.932–37)

68. Cf. Revard, *The War in Heaven,* pp. 284–85.

What remains of Adam's faith is placed in the service of "sight." The Mosaic argument which the Son uses to demonstrate his faith— "Or shall the Adversarie thus obtain / His end, and frustrate thine" (III.156–57)—Adam uses to supplement the evidence of his, or rather Eve's, senses ("as thou saidst"): "Nor can I think that God, Creator wise, / Though threatning, will in earnest so destroy / Us," he "would be loath / Us to abolish, least the Adversary / Triumph" (IX.938–40, 946–48). The faith that the Son demonstrates with the Mosaic argument enables him to sacrifice himself for mankind. The complacency or self-delusion that Adam demonstrates with the same argument enables him to sacrifice himself for Eve. But whereas the Son's sacrifice is a heroic act of imagination, Adam's is a fantastic act of self-dramatization. The Son's faith enables him to confront the reality of death and know—that is, see in his imagination and believe—that through the Father he will overcome it:

> thou hast givn me to possess
> Life in my self for ever, by thee I live,
> Though now to Death I yield, and am his due
> All that of me can die, yet that debt paid,
> Thou wilt not leave me in the loathsom grave.
> (III.243–47)

Adam's complacency, on the other hand, merely denies the reality of death and so renders his act of "faithful Love unequald" (IX.983) an empty boast: "if Death / Consort with thee, Death is to mee as Life" (IX.953–54). Adam's inversion of life and death echoes Satan's inversion of good and evil—"Evil be thou my Good" (IV.110)—the final act of a mind ruled by fancy. In both cases, the destruction of meaning indicates the triumph of the *phantastike*.

CHAPTER SIX

Eikastike Imagination and Regeneration

ESCAPE FROM DESPAIR

> Now now Sir knight, shew what ye bee,
> Add faith vnto your force, and be not faint.
>
> *The Faerie Queene* I.i.19

The formal subject of the last three books of the poem is Genesis 3:8–24, the judgment and expulsion of Adam and Eve from the Garden of Eden. The real subject is their regeneration.[1] They descend to the subjected plain only after they have ascended in the visions of God. The story of their regeneration, the restoration of their faith, gives the closing movement of "what Milton believed to be the archetypal myth of tragedy" a romance quality.[2] The story, which focuses on Adam's regeneration, clearly bears the influence of the story of Redcross's regeneration in the last cantos of *The Faerie Queene*, Book I, that book being a re-creation of the Bible story in

---

1. Cf. John E. Parish, "Milton and God's Curse on the Serpent," *JEGP* 58 (1959): 241: "After the account of the Fall in Book IX, the remainder of the epic might well be entitled separately *Paradise Regained*." This is something of an overstatement, but has to be read in the context of the effort to rehabilitate the last books, especially XI and XII. A discussion of the more influential criticism in this effort to 1972 is contained in Raymond B. Waddington, "The Death of Adam: Vision and Voice in Books XI and XII of *Paradise Lost*," *MP* 70 (1972): 9–12. See also the more recent work of Robert L. Entzminger, "Michael's Options and Milton's Poetry: *Paradise Lost* XI and XII," *ELR* 8 (1978): 197–211; George Miller, "Archetype and History: Narrative Technique in *Paradise Lost*, Books XI and XII," *MLS* 10 (1980): 12–21; Lee W. Patterson, "'Rapt with Pleasaunce': Vision and Narration in the Epic," *ELH* 48 (1981): 455–75; Christopher, pp. 175–98.

2. Frye, *Anatomy*, p. 211. I do not suggest that *Paradise Lost* is a romance, but that the divine epic, the story of Christ, which animates the very careful preparation of Adam and Eve for "the battle of the wilderness" (Christopher, p. 193) fulfils all those desires we seek to fulfil in romance. And to the extent that Adam and Eve *believe* in Christ's story they take part in it.

the form of a chivalric romance.[3] Milton's Book X and Spenser's Canto ix both end with the hero's escape from despair; Book XI begins and Canto x ends with the hero's ascent of a visionary mountain; and Book XII and Canto xi both end with victory over the great dragon of the Apocalypse. In *The Faerie Queene* the victory is the hero's—it expresses his imitation of Christ. In *Paradise Lost* the victory is Christ's—it is only heard of by the hero. The difference is of considerable importance because it suggests that in Adam's acquisition of the ability to witness, that is, to hear and believe in Christ's victory, lies the true nature of *imitatio Christi*. In other words, what mankind needs to imitate above all is Christ's faith: the benefits of his supreme act of faith, his redemptive sacrifice, are imputed to man by faith—"his obedience / Imputed becomes theirs by Faith" (XII.408–9)—and the psychological mechanism which facilitates faith, the power to believe, is the icastic imagination.

Thus, it is no accident that the climax of Adam's regeneration, the confirmation of his faith, should take the form of him listening, and listening to what sounds like something out of an old romance. His listening draws attention to the external sense by which we come to faith, the ear, and his listening to an old romance draws attention to the internal sense by which we come to faith, the imagination.

We come to faith by the ear because, as we have seen,[4] it is by the ear that we hear the word of God: the spirit that moves us to believe is the word—"the sword of the Spirit . . . is the word of God" (Eph. 6:17)—and the word is heard, not seen ("Our Regeneration," says Donne, echoing Romans 10:17, "is by the Word: that is, by faith, which comes by hearing"[5]). It is for this reason that in Vaughan's poem, "Regeneration," the climax is an act of listening and hearing.

In Vaughan's poem, the pilgrim ascends a purgatorial mountain at the top of which, like Dante, he discovers the Garden of Eden—"Full East, a faire, fresh field" (27).[6] There he is amazed by what he sees, but seeing soon gives way to hearing: "Thus fed my Eyes / But all the Eare lay hush. / Only a little Fountain lent / Some use for Eares" (47–50). His listening intensifies until "I heard / A rushing wind" (69–70). This is the "rushing mighty wind" of the Holy Spirit (Acts

3. Cf. Frye, *Anatomy*, p. 194: "We may take the first book of *The Faerie Queene* as representing perhaps the closest following of the Biblical quest-romance theme in English literature."
4. See pp. 69–70.
5. *Sermons*, VI, 216.
6. Cf. *Purgatorio* xxviii.

2:2), the pentecostal inspiration that enables Peter to speak the Word, that is, to retell the story of Christ (Acts 2:22–36). The pilgrim tries in vain to see the wind, but then

> while I listning sought
> My mind to ease
> By knowing, where 'twas, or where not,
> It whisper'd; *where I please.*
> (77–80)

The wind's still small voice thus identifies itself with the Spirit of God: "The wind bloweth where it listeth, and thou hearest the sound thereof, but canst not tell whence it cometh, and whither it goeth: so is every one that is born of the Spirit" (John 3:8). Because in identifying itself with the Spirit—the wind echoes Christ's words to the pharisee Nicodemus—it also reminds us that the Spirit of God is his word. And because the wind is both the Spirit and the Word, Christ's speech acts out what it relates: the wind blowing is an image of Christ speaking, either directly as in the gospel story or indirectly through the Bible as in the poem.

In the gospel Nicodemus fails to hear the wind because he cannot understand what Christ is saying. To Christ's injunction, "Except a man be born again, he cannot see the kingdom of God," Nicodemus replies, "How can a man be born when he is old? can he enter the second time into his mother's womb, and be born?" (3:3–4). To Christ's even more cryptic identification of the wind and the Spirit,[7] he answers in bewilderment, "How can these things be?" (3:9). Nicodemus' inability to hear the wind is the result of a literal-minded inability to interpret, to understand the spiritual sense of words—he denies himself regeneration because, like Satan, his imagination is sense-bound. He exemplifies Augustine's explanation of the way the letter kills:

For when what is said figuratively is taken as if it were said literally, it is understood in a carnal manner. And nothing is more fittingly called the death of the soul than when that in it which raises it above the brutes, the intelligence namely, is put in subjection to the flesh by a blind adherence to the letter. For he who follows the letter takes figurative words as if they were proper, and does not carry out what is indicated by a proper word into its secondary signification.[8]

7. In the Greek original "spirit" is not distinguished from "wind" by different words—*pneuma* is used for both.
8. *Christian Doctrine* III.v (Dods, IX, 86).

Unlike Nicodemus, in the poem the pilgrim does hear the wind precisely because he is capable of understanding the secondary signification of the otherwise mysterious phrase, *"where I please"*: that is, through his familiarity with Scripture, he recognizes the allusion: he recognizes that the rushing wind is Christ speaking— "Lord, then said I" (81). And because in the story alluded to Christ makes it clear that hearing the wind means believing in him ("That whosoever believeth in him should not perish, but have eternal life"; 3:15), the pilgrim recognizes that regeneration is not the effect of the Law and its works—the scales and the "late paines" weighed against "smoake, and pleasures" (20–24)—but of faith, the act of believing that opens the soul to the quickening power of the Spirit. The pilgrim's response to the wind's whisper—

> Lord, then said I, *On me one breath,*
> *And let me dye before my death!*
> (81–82)

—acts out the understanding it reveals. The prayer is its own answer. Because the wind is the Spirit, and the Spirit is the breath of God,[9] the rushing wind, first experienced as hostile "surly winds" (6), is the vital *"one breath"* prayed for, and the prayer, the pilgrim's response to that *"one breath,"* is the first breath of regeneration. The paradoxical, *"let me dye before my death,"* is literally a breathing out of God's breath in as much as it is a re-creation of Scripture (Romans 6), a re-creation that declares the pilgrim's faith that dying with Christ means everlasting life.

It is this paradigm of regeneration, hearing leading to breathing, that explains why Adam's critical act of repentance (X.1013–96), an act which depends upon his ability to understand the secondary signification of the curse on the serpent, is described as "sighs now breath'd / Unutterable" (XI.5–6); and why his response to Michael's words, a response which by re-creating Gabriel's words to Mary at the Annunciation declares his faith, is also described in terms of breathing—"words, which . . . he breathd" (XII.374).[10]

What this paradigm of regeneration suggests above all is the activity of understanding: breathing out God's breath comes down to interpreting, that is, re-creating God's word. The outward sign of re-

9. Cf. Hobbes, *Leviathan* III.xxxiv (p. 428): "*Wind, or Breath, or* (because the same are called in the Latine *Spiritus*) *Spirits."*
10. Cf. Christopher, pp. 163–74.

generation is uttering the Word: "My spirit," God says to Isaiah, "is upon thee, and my words . . . I have put in thy mouth" (Isa. 59:21). This is what happens to Adam and to Vaughan's pilgrim, to Peter and the other disciples at Pentecost: "And they were all filled with the Holy Ghost, and began to speak with other tongues, as the Spirit gave them utterance" (Acts 2:4). And this is what the poet, identifying himself with the bride of Christ (Song 4:16), prays for at the end of Vaughan's poem: "*Arise O North, and come thou South-wind, and blow upon my garden, that the spices thereof may flow out.*" Just as Adam's "sighs now breath'd / Unutterable . . . clad / With incense" (XI.5–6, 17–18) describes his prayer, or the "soft and solemn breathing sound" that "Rose like a stream of rich distill'd perfumes" (*Mask* 554–55) describes the Lady's song to Echo, so the flowing out of the spices, the fructifying of the garden, describes the making of Vaughan's poem. As the breathing metaphor indicates, the idea that poetry is the human response to the movement of the divine Spirit is at the heart of Sidney's theory of poetry:

give right honour to the heavenly Maker of that maker, who having made man to His own likeness, set him beyond and over all the works of that second nature: which in nothing he showeth so much as in Poetry, when with the force of a divine breath he bringeth forth far surpassing her doings.[11]

The same idea is at the heart of Milton's understanding of poetry: the spirit he imagines animating the poet "in the high region of his fancies" is grace, the spirit of prophecy, the wind that blows where it pleases—"that eternall Spirit who can enrich with all utterance and knowledge, and sends out his Seraphim with the hallow'd fire of his Altar to touch and purify the lips of whom he pleases."[12] In *Paradise Lost* we see Milton setting about his own regeneration, breathing out God's breath.

Imagination is the internal sense by which we come to faith because it is only by imagination that we can see the evidence of things not seen—that we can understand what the ear hears. What Vaughan's pilgrim hears is an allusion to a story of Christ, a story whose marvelous meaning has to be expressed in a figure because it is not accessible to "sight" or discursive reason: "If I have told you earthly things, and ye believe not," Christ asks Nicodemus, "how shall ye believe, if I tell you of heavenly things?" (John 3:12). What Adam

11. *Apology*, p. 101.
12. *Reason of Church-Government* II, Introduction (Yale, I, 808, 820–21).

hears is the total story of Christ, that is, the Bible from the re-creation of mankind after the flood to the Apocalypse. It is a story whose marvelous meaning is emphasized by recurrent reference to the romance theme of dragon-slaying, a theme which evolves out of the figurative interpretation of God's word. God's curse on the serpent, "Her Seed shall bruse thy head" (X.181), is revealed, immediately to the reader, but only gradually to Adam, as a figure of the Son's deliverance of mankind. The curse conceals its marvelous meaning, the Son's conquest of Sin and Death, within its "mysterious terms" (X.173) and only when it is understood imaginatively does the curse reveal its regenerating significance.[13] Only through imagination can we see our redemption.

When the curse is first pronounced, the narrator makes it clear to the reader that it is an extension of the romance metaphor that the Son first exploits in the divine council.[14] The narrator's interpretation of the curse as an oracle which would be verified when Jesus

> rising from his Grave
> Spoild Principalities and Powers, triumpht
> In open shew, and with ascension bright
> Captivity led captive through the Aire,
> The Realm it self of Satan long usurpt,
> Whom he shall tread at last under our feet;
> Eeven hee who now foretold his fatal bruise
> (X.185–91)

echoes the Son's description of mankind's deliverance as a chivalric duel:

> But I shall rise Victorious, and subdue
> My vanquisher, spoild of his vanted spoile;
> Death his deaths wound shall then receive, and stoop
> Inglorious, of his mortall sting disarm'd.
> I through the ample Air in Triumph high
> Shall lead Hell Captive maugre Hell, and show
> The powers of darkness bound.
> (III.250–56)

This metaphoric account of man's deliverance enables both the Son and Adam to fulfil their faith: by redescribing fallen man's predica-

13. Cf. Kathleen M. Swaim, "Flower, Fruit, and Seed: A Reading of *Paradise Lost*," *MiltonS* 5 (1973): esp. 172–74.
14. See pp. 162–72.

ment, the metaphor enables the Son to express the spirit of the Father's mercy and rescue mankind from the letter of his logic. Similarly, by revealing the spirit of mercy in the letter of the Law, the metaphor enables Adam to catch a glimpse of things hoped for and so escape from despair. The essence of Adam's imitation of Christ is his imitation of the Son's act of interpretation. In this, Adam's regeneration rehearses the process of the divine council.

In his response to God's judgment, Adam betrays the same fear of the incensed deity, the same bruising of the heart that the Father's opening speech in the divine council is intended to effect. Like Satan on Niphates' top, Adam echoes the remorseless logic of the Father's distributive justice: "God made thee of choice his own, and of his own / To serve him, thy reward was of his grace, / Thy punishment then justly is at his Will" (X.766–68). But without the Father's "grace-note" of mercy (III.131–34), this is the argument of despair. The tragic quality of Adam's soliloquy is emphasized by echoic allusions not only to Satan but to Job and Hamlet. In particular, the mazelike ratiocination which expresses the "troubl'd Sea" (X.718) of Adam's mind is reminiscent of the kind of reasoning with which Hamlet confronts his "sea of troubles" (III.i.59).[15] As in the Father's speech the weak mightiness of man's reasoning can find no resolution:

> O Conscience, into what Abyss of fears
> And horrors hast thou driv'n me; out of which
> I find no way, from deep to deeper plung'd!
> (X.842–44)

With this Adam registers the final hammer-blow in the bruising of his heart, what Perkins describes as "an holy desperation of a man's own power, in the obtaining of eternal life."[16]

Unlike Satan or Hamlet, Adam transcends his role as a tragic hero. His escape from despair is precipitated by Eve's unconscious imitation of the Son's act of intercession in the divine council. Free from the prison-house that discursive reason has now become, Eve is able to do for Adam what Adam cannot do for posterity—sacrifice herself:

> And to the place of judgement [I] will return,
> There with my cries importune Heaven, that all
> The sentence from thy head remov'd may light

15. Cf. Thaler, pp. 158–59.
16. *A Golden Chaine* (*Workes*, I, 78–79).

> On me, sole cause to thee of all this Woe,
> Mee mee onely just object of his ire.
>
> (X.932–36)

Her words echo those of both the Son—"I offer, on mee let thine anger fall; / Account mee man" (III.237–38)—and Adam—

> On mee, mee onely, as the sourse and spring
> Of all corruption, all the blame lights due;
> So might the wrauth.
>
> (X.832–34)

But whereas the offers of Eve and the Son are acts, expressed in the indicative, Adam's offer is only a desire, expressed in the subjunctive. Adam is inhibited by his fallen reason. The "evil Conscience" that now represents "All things with double terror" crushes hope: "Fond wish! couldst thou support / That burden . . . ?" (X.849–50, X.834–35). Eve's act of love appeases Adam's anger and precipitates his forgiveness of her: "As one disarm'd, his anger all he lost, / And thus with peaceful words uprais'd her soon" (X.945–46). In this, Eve imitates the Son's appeasement of the Father's wrath and Adam imitates the Father's release of grace.

Eve's intercession releases grace not only in the sense of moving Adam to forgiveness, but also in the sense of leading him to interpretation. By echoing the words of God's curse on the serpent—

> Between us two let there be peace, both joyning,
> As joyn'd in injuries, one enmitie
> Against a Foe by doom express assign'd us,
> That cruel Serpent
>
> (X.924–27)

—her intercession releases God's grace into his mind. Once Eve's wild thoughts, her misjoined imaginations, her enmity against the actual serpent and desperate plans to free "both our selves and Seed" (X.999), are ordered by Adam's reason, he realizes that the curse is a promise of mankind's eventual triumph over Satan:

> let us seek
> Some safer resolution, which methinks
> I have in view, calling to minde with heed
> Part of our Sentence, that thy Seed shall bruise
> The Serpents head; piteous amends, unless

Be meant, whom I conjecture, our grand Foe
Satan, who in the Serpent hath contriv'd
Against us this deceit: to crush his head
Would be revenge indeed.
(X.1028–35)

Adam does not simply remember the curse [17]—he interprets it: that is, by re-creating it imaginatively ("Some safer resolution, *which methinks / I have in view*" [my emphasis]), by picturing it as a duel ("to crush his head / Would be revenge indeed"), he begins to perceive the secondary signification. And after the prayer of repentance (X.1098–1104), the sentence is transformed in Adam's imagination into a promise, though still inadequately understood, of things hoped for:

> For since I saught
> By Prayer th'offended Deitie to appease,
> Kneel'd and before him humbl'd all my heart,
> Methought I saw him placable and mild,
> Bending his eare; perswasion in me grew
> That I was heard with favour; peace returnd
> Home to my Brest, and to my memorie
> His promise, that thy Seed shall bruise our Foe;
> Which then not minded in dismay, yet now
> Assures me that the bitterness of death
> Is past, and we shall live.
(XI.148–58)

Thus, just as the Son reveals the Father's mercy by interpreting "Th'incensed Deitie" (III.187), so Adam discovers God's mercy by interpreting "th'offended Deitie"—what in the midst of despair sounded like "his dreadful voice" "Thunder in my ears" (X.779, 780). The Son's mediation between God and man, grace, expresses itself in his word: his word is the source of grace. It is for this reason that the curse in the poem reproduces almost to the letter the language of the Authorized Version, the actual word of God. Adam interpreting the curse thus provides a model for the supreme value of the poet

17. In Aristotelian psychology, memory is, in any case, a function of the imagination: "It is obvious, then, that memory belongs to that part of the soul to which imagination belongs; all things which are imaginable are essentially objects of memory, and those which necessarily involve imagination are objects of memory only incidentally" (*On Memory* I [p. 293]). Cf. Hobbes, *Leviathan* I.ii (p. 89): "*Imagination* and *Memory*, are but one thing."

interpreting Scripture, and for the reader interpreting the poem. Like Redcross, Adam escapes from despair by an act of biblical exegesis: just as Una leads Redcross to read the Bible through the eyes of faith—she introduces him to Fidelia and through Fidelia's "sacred Booke . . . That none could read, except she did them teach" he is "agraste" (*FQ* I.x.19, 18)—so Eve's intercession leads Adam to read God's word imaginatively.

That Adam's interpretation is the achievement of "his more attentive minde / Labouring" (X.1011–12) does not exclude Eve from the regenerative process but suggests that Adam's achievement turns on the return of both husband and wife, reason and imagination, to their original garden labor, a labor whose emblem is that of the vine-prop elm (V.215–19).[18] The point here is that without the vine to prop, the elm would be barren: that is, without Eve's misjoined imaginations to inspire it and be ordered by it, Adam's reason could only produce despair. When propped by the elm the vine produces fruit, clusters of grapes; similarly, when ordered by reason imagination perceives revelation. Thus, just as the Son's intercession and interpretation lead to the revelation of the Father's purpose, so Eve's intercession and Adam's interpretation lead to a prayer the response to which is Michael's revelation of God's purpose, a revelation which finally explains the metaphoric significance of the curse. When he comes to identify the curse with Christ's redemptive sacrifice, Michael discards the metaphor: "Dream not of thir fight, / As of a Duel" (XII.386–87). But then in order to emphasize the wondrous nature of mankind's deliverance, echoing the Son's words to the Father and the narrator's to the reader (at X.182–92), he returns to it: Christ's act of faith

> Shall bruise the head of *Satan*, crush his strength
> Defeating Sin and Death . . .
> . . . .
> Then to the Heav'n of Heav'ns he shall ascend
> With victory, triumphing through the aire
> Over his foes and thine; there shall surprise
> The Serpent, Prince of aire, and drag in Chaines
> Through all his Realme.
>   (XII.430–31, 451–55)

The progress of the dragon-slaying metaphor illustrates the operation of prevenient grace. Grace is prevenient because it precedes

18. See pp. 206–8.

both understanding and will, and just as Vaughan's pilgrim first experiences the breath of God, the marvelous words whispered by the Spirit, as the "surly winds" that blast his false spring, so Adam after the Fall first experiences the breath of God, the marvelous words uttered by Michael, as God's curse on the serpent, as "Thunder in my ears." Regeneration comes to mean seeing the one thing in the other, and this act of perception is an act of imagination. This is why Adam and Eve are associated with Deucalion and Pyrrha (XI.8–14): after Deucalion's flood, the classical type of Noah's flood, itself the Old Testament type of baptism, Deucalion and Pyrrha bring about the re-creation of mankind by interpreting the oracle of Themis. Deucalion perceives in the oracle's "Great-Parents bones" (*Met.* I.384) a reference to stones, the bones of our great mother the Earth. And so just as "Prevenient Grace descending . . . remov'd / The stonie" from the hearts of Adam and Eve and "made new flesh / Regenerate grow instead" (XI.2–5), so stones are turned into flesh by the ability of Deucalion and Pyrrha to re-create the oracle imaginatively—in so doing "Both with weake faith rely / On ayding Heaven" (*Met.* I.396–97).[19] This act of imagination is what Augustine means by regeneration when he associates the effect of the Spirit with lifting the eye of the mind above the letter, "above what is corporeal and created, that it may drink in eternal light."[20] This is what Christ means by regeneration when he implicitly identifies the operation of the Spirit with his own figurative mode of discourse: "If I have told you earthly things, and ye believe not, how shall ye believe, if I tell you of heavenly things?" And this is what Milton's contemporary, Thomas Taylor, means by faith when he urges us to

Labour to bring the eye of faith to the word: else shall we be ready to reject holy doctrine (as absurd and impossible) as *Nichodemus* did the doctrine of regeneration. Why else doe most men live no other then a natural life, in the midst of so many supernaturall and divine meanes, but that their reason resists the Spirits perswasions?[21]

Thus, the heavenly grace of faith precedes understanding and will through the persuasive power of the imagination: that is, grace creates the kind of understanding that confirms the will through the

---

19. Sandys cleverly mistranslates the Latin, "adeo caelistibus ambo / diffidunt monitis," to make the sense conform to the Christian idea of regeneration. It is clear that both Ezek. 11 : 19 and Matt. 3 : 9 were in his mind.
20. *Christian Doctrine* III.v (Dods, IX, 86).
21. *Christ Revealed* (London, 1635; rpt. New York: Delmar, 1979), pp. 319–20.

power of the icastic imagination to represent the invisible in terms of the visible, or as Raphael puts it, echoing perhaps the words of Christ to Nicodemus, to measure "things in Heav'n by things on Earth" (VI.893).

Once the process of the divine council has been reenacted in the minds of Adam and Eve, once the regenerating significance of the curse has been released and the divine romance begins to reemerge, so Adam's response to Michael's revelation, like that of the angels to the Son's revelation in the divine council, is one of increasing *admiratio* until "Replete with joy and wonder" he exclaims:

> O goodness infinite, goodness immense!
> That all this good of evil shall produce,
> And evil turn to good; more wonderful
> Then that which by creation first brought forth
> Light out of darkness!
>
> (XII.468–73)

This sense of wonder serves as a register for the operation of the imagination: it is the characteristic effect of both faith and romance. It is a "wonder . . . to heare her [Fidelia's] goodly speech" (*FQ* I.x.19), and we have already noted how Adam's wonderful sense of good coming out of evil close to the end of Michael's revelation is matched by that of Gonzalo at the end of *The Tempest*,[22] and how the angels' response to the Son's revelation resembles the "notable passion of wonder" that fills Leontes and Camillo at the end of *The Winter's Tale*.[23] Just as Milton heightens the wonderful nature of Scripture by emphasizing its own romance quality, so Shakespeare heightens the wonderful nature of romance by echoing the language of Scripture: for instance, life "redeems" Hermione, stone becomes flesh, only after Leontes ceases to be stone—"Does not the stone [statue] rebuke me / For being more stone than it?"—only after he becomes regenerate—"It is required / You do awake your faith" (V.iii.103, 37–38, 94–95). Both romance and Scripture arouse wonder because they deal in marvels, that is, they do what by the rules of everyday experience is "absurd and impossible," they re-create the actual world in the image of human desire. Just as romance, according to the poet Sidney, like all poetry, creates "another nature, in making

22. See p. 29.
23. See pp. 167–68.

things either better than Nature bringeth forth, or, quite anew, forms such as never were in Nature,"[24] so "the wonderful power of saving faith," according to the preacher Perkins, "makes things which are not in nature, to have in some sort a being and subsistence."[25] This re-creation takes place in the imagination: with romance it is an act of invention, with Scripture, the testimony of faith, an act of perception. According to Gianfrancesco Pico, and the elder Brother in the *Mask*, the imagination is not only used but transformed or metamorphosed by the things it perceives:

The Light of Faith, . . . making perspicuous the verities of Holy Writ that are impervious to the light of nature, is of greatest service to either type of imagination [that is, the imagination moved by physical desires or more complex mental ones]. It supports and conducts each by the hand, sweeping each up, so to speak, and elevating it above its own nature.[26]

So things perceived "in cleer dream, and solemn vision" (*Mask* 456) gradually turn the unpolluted mind into soul's essence.

Just as the secret working of grace becomes manifest with Michael's arrival, so the appeal to the imagination implicit in God's curse becomes explicit with Michael's explanation of it—and for the fulfilment of Adam's metamorphosis, the confirmation of his faith, we must finally turn our attention to his mountain vision.

MOUNTAIN VISION

> And he carried me away in the spirit to a great and high mountain, and shewed me that great city, the holy Jerusalem, descending out of heaven from God.
> Revelation 21 : 10

Redcross completes his escape from despair by climbing a hill, which like Vaughan's purgatorial mountain is "both steepe and hy" (*FQ* I.x.46). From its "highest Mount" (I.x.53) he comes to see the City of God and the path leading to it. This sight is revealed to him by Contemplation through the power of Faith: grace in the shape of *Mercie* informs Contemplation that grace in the shape of "wise *Fidelia* . . .

24. *Apology*, p. 100.
25. *A Clowd of Faithfull Witnesses* (*Workes*, III, 9).
26. *On the Imagination*, p. 89.

doth thee require, / To shew it to this knight, according his desire"
(I.x.50). Now the way that Contemplation sees and the place from
which he sees both suggest an affinity, if not identity, with what we
have been calling the icastic imagination.

Contemplation whose earthly eyes are "blunt and bad" sees by
means of his spirit which is "wondrous quick and persant . . . As
Eagles eye, that can behold the Sunne": his internal sight is illuminated by such "Great grace" that "God he often saw from heauens
hight" (I.x.47). That he sees like an eagle and that what he sees is the
New Jerusalem associates his seeing above all with the vision of St.
John the Divine, the supposed author of the Apocalypse.[27] This vision, the culmination of the Bible's process of revelation, is that part
of the Bible most openly thought of as the work of the imagination.
According to Gianfrancesco Pico, for instance,

when we turn the pages of Holy Writ, we find but few things thus divinely
revealed to [the physical eyes of] the prophets in comparison with those dis-
closed to them by imaginative vision. For—to pass over the books of Amos,
Zechariah, and other ancient prophets, all abounding in imaginative visions—the Apocalypse of John is imaginative, including the career of the
whole Church, even to the punishments of the damned and the glory of the
blessed.[28]

And of course Milton, when discussing biblical models for poetry,
considered "the Apocalyps of Saint *John . . .* the majestick image of a
high and stately Tragedy."[29] What he means by tragedy, according to
"the grave autority of *Pareus,*"[30] is, most immediately, "a *Propheticall
Drama,* show, or representation."[31] And it is because the theatrical
metaphor implies the work of imagination (the Greek original of
"theatre," *theasthai,* means to see),[32] that John Smith uses it to explain the psychology of all prophecy (except that of Moses): "*the propheticall scene or stage upon which all apparitions were made to
the prophet, was his imagination.*"[33]

The "highest Mount" from which Contemplation sees the heav-

27. See pp. 141–42. See also Norhnberg, pp. 156–58.
28. *On the Imagination,* p. 57.
29. *Reason of Church-Government* II, Introduction (Yale, I, 815).
30. Ibid.
31. David Pareus, *A Commentary upon the Divine Revelation of the Apostle and
Evangelist John,* trans. Elias Arnold (Amsterdam, 1644), quoted in Barbara K. Lewalski,
"*Samson Agonistes* and the 'Tragedy' of the Apocalypse," *PMLA* 85 (1970): 1051.
32. *OED,* s.v. Theatre.
33. *Of Prophecy* (*Select Discourses,* p. 229).

enly city is carefully associated with Sinai, the Mount of Olives, and Parnassus. This collocation of mountain tops has a very precise significance, a significance emphasized by the stanza organization. On Sinai Moses received the Law and on the Mount of Olives Christ preached the Gospel. The terror of the Law is stressed by imitating the tone of Despair: on Sinai

> writ in stone
> With bloudy letters by the hand of God,
> The bitter doome of death and balefull mone
> He did receiue, whiles flashing fire about him shone.
> (I.x.53)

The graciousness of the Gospel is stressed by carefully associating the Mount of Olives with Parnassus: they share a stanza, looking back across the stanza break at Sinai. The Mount of Olives, the mountain top on which Christ told his stories—the mountain top on which he inspired his disciples by imagining "the Son of man coming in the clouds with great power and glory" (Mark 13:26) and prepared them to give witness by foretelling the descent of grace (Acts 1:8)—has its head "for euer with a flowring girlond crownd" just like the Muses who "play / Their heauenly notes, and make full many a louely lay" (I.x.54) on Parnassus—or perhaps, more important, just like the mysterious fourth grace who "Crownd with a rosie girlond" (VI.x.14) inspires Colin Clout's piping, Spenser's poem, on Mount Acidale. The grace of the Gospel which liberates mankind from the terror of the Law is thus associated with the work most characteristic of the imagination, with poetry. What liberates mankind is the human imagination inspired by God: that is to say, the psychological mechanism which facilitates the descent of grace, the liberation from the Law and revelation, is the imagination. It is this same idea that is at the heart of Vaughan's conviction that the Mount of Olives is the true Parnassus: "Sweete, sacred hill! . . . if Poets mind thee well / They shall find thou art their hill / And fountain too" ("Mount of Olives" 1, 17–19).[34] The opposition between Sinai and the Mount of Olives recurs in the opposition between Sinai and Sion in Vaughan's poem, "The Law, and the Gospel," a poem which indicates the biblical *locus classicus* for this topos as Hebrews 12:18–22. In Milton, as we have seen, the topos recurs in the opposition between Sinai and Sion hill

---

34. For a different view of the significance of Parnassus, see Quilligan, pp. 132–37.

and its flowery brooks in the opening invocations to *Paradise Lost* (I.6–16, III.26–32). The Gospel delights Milton's heavenly muse more (I.11) because it is poetic, poetic in the very precise sense that the Gospel replaces the Law with faith, and faith requires the activity of the imagination. Though Sinai is always necessary to bruise our stony hearts—on Sinai "a firie Law / Pronounc'd with thunder," Vaughan explains, "and thy threats did thaw / Thy Peoples hearts" (2–4)—it is only from the Mount of Olives or Sion hill that we come to see the fullness of God's purpose. It is for this reason that Milton's top of Speculation is most closely related to Spenser's hill of Contemplation.

What Redcross sees, he sees through contemplation; what Adam sees, he sees through Michael. The enlightenment which, as the Father promises in the divine council, will proceed from God in response "To Prayer, repentance, and obedience due" (III.191) finds its means in Michael. In amplifying Adam's interpretation of God's word, Michael, like the Attendant Spirit, gives "*resounding grace to all Heav'ns Harmonies*" (*Mask* 242): he provides the answer and fulfilment of the embryonic faith of Adam and Eve. His purpose, as he explains, is the confirmation of faith—"that thou mayst beleeve, and be confirmd" (XI.355)—and in his method, as a host of allusions suggest, poetry and prophecy become one.

The principal prophetic prototype of Milton's Michael is the Spirit that moves Ezekiel. When Adam led by Michael submits to "the hand of Heav'n" and ascends "In the Visions of God" (XI.372, 377)—visions that culminate in the imagined prospect of the City of God, "New Heav'ns, new Earth" (XII.549)—his experience anticipates that of Ezekiel:

the hand of the Lord was upon me, and brought me thither.
In the visions of God brought he me into the land of Israel, and set me upon a very high mountain, by which was as the frame of a city on the south.

(40:1–2)

Ezekiel is especially important because his epiphany (1:1–28)—according to Northrop Frye, one of the very few direct visualizations of God in Scripture[35]—provides the biblical sanction for Raphael's visualization of the Son mounted on the "Chariot of Paternal Deitie"

35. See Northrop Frye, *The Great Code* (Toronto: Academic Press, 1982), p. 116.

(VI.749–66) right at the center of the poem. The same "four living creatures" (1:5) or "four Cherubic shapes" (VI.753) that bear the throne of God in Ezekiel and convoy the Son's chariot in Raphael now escort Michael himself:

> with him the Cohort bright
> Of watchful Cherubim; four faces each
> Had, like a double *Janus*.
> (XI.127–29)

Because Ezekiel's epiphany is simply meant to explain how "The word of the Lord came expressly unto" him (1:3), because the essential function of the cherubim is to transport the Spirit of God— "Whithersoever the spirit was to go, they went" (1:20)—the four living creatures are traditionally interpreted as types of the four evangelists, mysteriously concealed in the figure of the four beasts who give glory to God as he holds out the Book of Revelation (Rev. 4–5).[36] In detaching the cherubim from the Son's chariot and attaching them to Michael, Milton is imitating the typological evolution of the cherubim from agents of a direct vision to carriers of the Word. In other words, the movement from Raphael's revelation to Michael's, like the progression from seeing to hearing inside Michael's revelation, is meant to direct the reader back to the Bible. Michael's cherubim are Janus-faced because Janus is the keeper of heaven's gate and, rightly understood, Michael's revelation is the Word which will open it for mankind. It is the *eikastike* quality of the Word, as we have seen,[37] that liberates us, that dissolves the *phantastike* illusions of Satan and allows us to see things invisible to mortal sight. Thus, the eyes of the cherubim—

> eyes more numerous then those
> Of *Argus*, and more wakeful then to drouze,
> Charm'd with *Arcadian* Pipe, the Pastoral Reed
> Of *Hermes*, or his opiate Rod
> (XI.130–33)

—are not directed against poetry as such, but only the narcotic songs of Circe, "*Hermes*, or his opiate Rod." The cherubim are able to protect us from the illusions of fancy because the Word they bear

36. Cf. ibid.
37. See pp. 74–79, 122–77.

operates like the Lady's song—it offers such sober certainty of waking bliss.

Michael's poetic prototype is the Attendant Spirit,[38] and through him Ariel and Puck—the latter only when firmly under the control of Oberon. Like these romance characters, Michael achieves his marvelous effects with magic, and just as Puck under the direction of Oberon brings the lovers back to their "faith" by anointing their eyes with magic herbs, so Michael anoints the eyes of Adam and Eve. As he explains to Adam, Michael drenches Eve's eyes so that she may "Here sleep below while thou to foresight wak'st, / As once thou slepst, while Shee to life was formd" (XI.368–69). Just as Adam slept and imagined the creation of Eve, so now she sleeps and imagines the re-creation of mankind. Just as Eve's coming to life was the model creation of Adam's imagination, "the Cell / Of Fancie my internal sight" (VIII.460–61), so now Adam's waking to foresight, the story of the Bible, the story of her seed's triumph, is the perception or procreation of Eve's imagination. What Adam learns on Speculation, she discovers in dream: "Whence thou returnst, and whither wentst, I know; / For God is also in sleep, and Dreams advise" (XII.610–11). Thus, Eve's final words apply as much to the faculty with which she is most associated, the human imagination, as to herself as a historical character:

> though all by mee is lost,
> Such favour I unworthie am voutsaft,
> By mee the Promis'd Seed shall all restore.
>   (XII.622–23)[39]

Michael's treatment of Adam's eyes is more complex. After a film bred by the forbidden fruit is removed, Adam's eyes are purged with herbs and then instilled with three drops of water from the well of life. The herbs purge the "visual Nerve" and then together with the water pierce as far as "the inmost seat of mental sight" (XI.415, 418),

38. There are, of course, others: A. Bartlett Giamatti, "Spenser: From Magic to Miracle," in *Four Essays on Romance*, ed. Herschel Baker (Cambridge, Mass.: Harvard University Press, 1971), pp. 15–31, identifies Michael removing his helmet (XI.245–46) with a long line of romance heroes whose raising their visors or removing their helmets signifies the impulse implicit in chivalric romance "to reveal divinity" (p. 17).

39. For a somewhat different view, see Northrop Frye, "The Revelation to Eve," in *Paradise Lost: A Tercentenary Tribute*, ed. B. Rajan (Toronto: University of Toronto Press, 1969), pp. 18–47.

that is, through the imagination, "the Cell / Of Fancie my internal sight" (VIII.460–61), to the intellect. Both physical and mental sight are treated. The effect is so powerful

> That *Adam* now enforc't to close his eyes,
> Sunk down and all his Spirits became intranst
>   (XI.419–20)

just as he did when he imagined the creation of Eve:

> Dazl'd and spent, [I] sunk down, and sought repair
> Of sleep, which instantly fell on me, call'd
> By Nature as in aide, and clos'd mine eyes.
> Mine eyes he clos'd, but op'n left the Cell
> Of Fancie my internal sight, by which
> Abstract as in a transe methought I saw.
>   (VIII.457–62)

But here on Mount Speculation Adam's eyes are reopened before he begins to witness the re-creation of mankind—to emphasize the point that accurate understanding of the visible, itself dependent on revelation in the form of conscience, must precede true perception of the invisible. Michael's treatment of Adam's eyes symbolizes the subsequent process of revelation, a sequence Milton anticipates in the process of faith we first examined in the *Mask*: first fancy is brought under control and then directed toward the imagination of the good.

Thus, the first stage of Michael's treatment, his treatment of Adam's physical sight, removing the film and purging with herbs, suggests the dissolution of the illusions bred by the sense-bound imagination and the recovery of a true picture of the actual world. The images of external objects shaped in the imagination are now interpreted by conscience, reason informed by revelation, so that appearances no longer delude. Thus, the first half of Michael's prophecy deals with the tragic consequences of mankind's fall, the triumph of Sin and Death, and takes the form of Michael's words checking Adam's understanding of the various images of the triumph of Sin and Death—an understanding initially determined by voluntary appetite or "By pleasure," what to nature seems meet (XI.604). Michael's words do what God's words do when they check Eve's understanding of the image in the pool, an understanding initially determined by her mindless pleasure in the beauty of the image: Michael's words perform the office of conscience. In this, Michael's herbs, euphrasy and rue, are clearly related to the Attendant Spirit's haemony. Both, albeit only eventually in Michael's use of his herbs on Adam, permit the accurate perception of appearances: the effect of haemony—"for by this means / I knew the foul inchanter though disguis'd" (*Mask* 643–44)—is much the same as that of Michael's tempering of Adam's imagination—"Dextrously thou aim'st" (XI.884). Both prevent appearances from creating a truth independent of revelation, and both suggest that true perception depends upon the harmony of the internal senses. In other words, both haemony and Michael's herbs mean temperance: rue means pious sorrow, a consciousness of sin, and euphrasy means cheerfulness, immediately a joy in the "chearful wayes" (III.46) of the visible world, cheerful because they signify the presence of God. But because grace is prevenient and temperance is the effect of grace, because the magic herbs are dispensed by the agent of grace, euphrasy also means revelation. It is eye-bright, the "eye-brightning electuary of knowledge," that "mysterious book of Revelation which the great Evangelist was bid eat"; [40] it is

that *eyesalve* wherewith to anoint our eyes that wee may see, *Revel.* 3.18 . . . the *spirit of illumination*, working sound and saving knowledge in the mind, by which their naturall darknesse is enlightned, as eye-salve sharpens and cleares the dim sight.[41]

The second stage of the treatment, instilling water from the well of life, like Redcross being drenched in "*The well of life*" itself (*FQ* I.xi.29) during his duel with the dragon, refers directly to the descent of the heavenly grace of faith—and its piercing to the inmost seat of mental sight suggests the use grace makes of the educated imagination to present things invisible to mortal sight to the intellect. Thus, the second half of the prophecy deals with the consequences of mankind's faith, the triumph of Eve's seed over Sin and Death, and takes the form of Michael's words on their own; his narrative account of this triumph—a narrative which represents history as a series of types who prefigure some great dragon-slayer, "thy great deliverer, who shall bruise / The Serpents head" (XII.149–50), types like Moses through whom "with ten wounds / The River-dragon tam'd at length submits" (XII.190–91)—appeals directly to the eye of the mind, because its substance is the evidence of things not seen. In its reference to the descent of grace, Michael's water from the well of life is obviously related to the water from "my fountain pure" (*Mask* 911) which Sabrina uses to liberate the Lady.

40. *Reason of Church-Government* II, Introduction (Yale, I, 803).
41. Taylor, *Christ Revealed*, p. 320.

Now the liberation of the Lady signifies the transforming power of grace: Sabrina's own story of transformation exemplifies her effect both on the Lady and on the plot of the *Mask*. The Attendant Spirit's version of her story is thoroughly Ovidian: it re-creates Spenser's version of her story (*FQ* II.x.17–19) in terms of Ovid's version of Daphne's story. Both Daphne and the Attendant Spirit's Sabrina are innocents, chaste and pursued by passion—Daphne by Apollo mad with desire, and Sabrina by "her enraged stepdam *Guendolen*" (*Mask* 829). In order to save themselves, Daphne "cryes unto the Flood" (*Met.* I.542) and Sabrina commends "her fair innocence to the flood" (830). By the power of the flood, Daphne is transformed into an immortal laurel, and Sabrina into an immortal goddess. Whereas Comus interprets Daphne's transformation as imprisonment—"Your nerves are all chain'd up in Alabaster, / And you a statue, or as *Daphne* was / Root-bound, that fled *Apollo*" (659–61)—Sandys interprets it as liberation—"*Daphne* is changed into a never-withering tree, to shew what immortall honour a virgin obtaines by preserving her chastity."[42] Comus's interpretation, though true enough to the letter, is contrary to the spirit of Ovid's story. The Attendant Spirit, however, follows Sandys, so that when he re-creates Sabrina's story in the light of Ovid, the sense of liberation implicit in Daphne's metamorphosis is made explicit. In the Attendant Spirit's interpretation of Ovid, not only does he anticipate the liberation Adam achieves in interpreting the curse, but he calls attention to the relationship between interpretation and metamorphosis. Just as his interpretation of Ovid leads to the metamorphosis of Sabrina's tragic story into something wonderful, so Adam's interpretation of the curse, as Michael's resounding amplification of it reveals, leads to the metamorphosis of human history. Metamorphosis in Ovid is insistently self-reflexive: its very artificiality draws attention to the poet's transforming imagination, the same power that moves interpretation. As interpretation frees us from the miserable slavery of the letter, so metamorphosis frees us from the logic of everyday experience, and as interpretation reveals the activity of grace, so metamorphosis provides an analogy for the effect of grace. Metamorphosis realizes metaphor: for instance, Ezekiel's great metaphor of regeneration—"I will take the stony heart out of their flesh, and will give them an heart of flesh" (11:19)—is realized in the metamorphosis of Deucalion's stones (*Met.* I.313–414) or Pygmalion's statue (*Met.* X.246–300). Thus, metamorphoses, like those of Hermione or

42. Sandys, p. 74.

Eve in Adam's dream (VIII.452–90) are used to express the effect of grace, the realization or fulfilment of the faith, that first articulates itself in metaphor.

What seems especially interesting to the Attendant Spirit is the way Ovid uses metamorphosis to subvert tragedy. It also seems to have interested Shakespeare, and the essence of Ovid's transformation of the tragic into something wonderful is captured in Ariel's account of the "sea-change" that overtakes Alonso:

> Full fathom five thy father lies;
> Of his bones are coral made
> Those are pearls that were his eyes;
> Nothing of him that doth fade
> But doth suffer a sea-change
> Into something rich and strange.
> (*Tmp.* I.ii.396–401)

As Ariel's song transforms Alonso, so the Attendant Spirit's story transforms Sabrina, and in her metamorphosis tragedy is turned into the stuff of romance. It is no accident that in her "quick immortal change" (840), the lazarlike corruption of Hamlet's father, the action that initiates that tragedy—"thy uncle . . . in the porches of my ears did pour / The leperous distilment" (*Hamlet* I.v.61–64)— is reversed: "The water Nymphs . . . through the porch and inlet of each sense / Dropt in Ambrosial Oils" (832–39). Sabrina's "quick immortal change" exemplifies the liberation of the Lady, and both transformations, as we suggested in the opening discussion of the *Mask*,[43] are ways of representing (and enacting) the temple of the mind turning itself to soul's essence through the activity of the icastic imagination, that is, through "oft convers with heav'nly habitants" in "cleer dream, and solemn vision" (452–62). Thus, as the Attendant Spirit's story transforms Sabrina, so Sabrina's water and the perception of the good in the Lady's imagination which Sabrina and her water signify liberate the Lady; in her liberation, the fulfilment of her faith, entrapment is turned into triumph. Similarly, Michael's water and the revelation of God's triumph to Adam's imagination, which Michael himself and his water signify, regenerate Adam—and in his regeneration, the fulfilment of his faith, the tragedy of mankind's fall begins its long metamorphosis into triumph.

As Adam witnesses Noah's flood, he himself sinks drowned in a

43. See pp. 41–42.

flood of tears and sorrow; almost immediately, however, he is raised up by Michael, the agent of grace (XI.754–62). Because Noah's flood is a type of baptism, Adam's response to the flood suggests a "symbolic baptism,"[44] the moment of his spiritual rebirth. This rebirth coincides with the last act of physical seeing before Michael resorts completely to mental seeing; and it is here that the water from the well of life begins its work. Adam rises from Noah's flood like Sabrina from the Severn or the Lady from the water of Sabrina's "fountain pure," like Redcross from the well of life itself. The water from the well of life enables Redcross to grow wings like the regenerate soul in the *Phaedrus* (248–49), to mount up with wings like an eagle (Ps. 103:1–5; Isa. 40:31), and to see with the eagle-sight of Contemplation:

> he vpstarted braue
> Out of the well, wherein he drenched lay;
> As Eagle fresh out of the Ocean waue,
> Where he hath left his plumes all hoary gray,
> And deckt himself with feathers youthly gay,
> Like Eyas hauke vp mounts vnto the skies,
> His newly budded pineons to assay,
> And marueiles at himselfe, still as he flies.
>
> (*FQ* I.xi.34)

Through the revelation of faith, as grace—the water and the words it signifies—does its work, Adam too acquires the eagle-sight of Contemplation.

This is anticipated by the incident that immediately precedes Michael's treatment of Adam's eyes: Adam's initial experience on Mount Speculation, as a prefiguration of Christ overcoming his mountain-top temptation (Matt. 4:8; Luke 4:5), reverses Satan's experience on the sun. In a parody of the eagle-sight of the ascending soul, the descending Satan stares into the meridian sun undazzled, but his sense-bound imagination condemns him to prefer the sun's material wealth, that is, its "Potable Gold" and stones that shine like those "In *Aarons* Brestplate" (III.608, 598), to the spiritual city the wealth signifies.[45] The ascending Adam, however, is associated with Christ as he beholds "all Earths Kingdomes and thir Glory" (XI.384). As Satan "farr and wide his eye commands" (III.614) the material

---

44. Waddington, "The Death of Adam," p. 21.
45. See pp. 137–38. Satan's encounter with Uriel on the sun is a parody of Redcross's encounter with Contemplation.

wealth of the sun, so Adam "His Eye might there command wherever stood" (XI.385) the material wealth of the earth, the golden cities and kingdoms of the world. In as much as "the golden *Chersonese* . . . *Ophir* . . . *El Dorado*" (XI.386–411) comprise the material wealth of the world, they make their appeal to the carnal imagination, and in this appeal they create the kind of delusion or film that covers Adam's fallen eyes. In as much as these kingdoms of the Earth symbolize the heavenly kingdom, in as much as the gold of Ophir ceases to be the negation of wisdom (Job 28:16) and becomes the ornament of Solomon's kingdom (Ps. 45:9), the type of Christ's kingdom,[46] they make their appeal to the icastic imagination, and it is this appeal that Michael's removal of the film is meant to facilitate. As Christ dismisses the earthly kingdoms, so does the narrator. In doing so his language imitates the removal of the film, it imitates what it describes: just as the fanciful account of Mulciber's fate is interrupted—"thus they relate, / Erring" (I.746–47)—so the fanciful sight of the golden cities is cast aside: "but to nobler sights / *Michael* from *Adams* eyes the Filme remov'd" (XI.411–12). This dismissal reenacts Adam's initial act of interpretation and indicates that seeing the spirit in the letter means preferring the heavenly city to its earthly images. As the allusion to Ezekiel suggests, when Adam ascends "In the Visions of God" the city he will eventually see is the same one Redcross sees through the eagle-sight of Contemplation— "New Heav'ns, new Earth" (XII.549).

VICTORY OVER THE DRAGON

> Because thou hast made the Lord, which is my refuge, even the most High, thy habitation. . . .
> Thou shalt tread upon the lion and adder: the young lion and the dragon shalt thou trample under feet.
>
> Psalm 91:9, 13

When Redcross rises from the well of life his eagle-strength enables him to go on and eventually overcome the dragon. When Adam rises from his symbolic baptism his eagle-sight enables him to foresee Christ overcoming the dragon. But, as Michael explains when he discards the dragon-slaying metaphor, the reality of Christ's victory

46. Cf. Carey and Fowler, p. 101n.

over the dragon is Adam's ability to see it, that is, to believe in it. Christ overcomes the dragon "Not by destroying *Satan*, but his works / In thee and in thy Seed" (XII.394–95). Now destroying the works of Satan in man is the achievement first of the faith Christ shows in making his redemptive sacrifice, and second of the faith mankind shows in believing in the efficacy of that sacrifice—that "this God-like act . . . this act / Shall bruise the head of *Satan*" (XII.427, 429–30). In other words, Christ's redemptive sacrifice is imputed to man by faith: "his obedience / Imputed becomes theirs by Faith" (XII.408–9). Christ proclaims "Life to all who shall believe / In his redemption" (XII.407–8), and believing, as we have seen, depends on the persuasive power of the imagination. As Adam's own testimony bears witness, grace presents the invisible to the imagination—"Methought I saw him placable and mild, / Bending his eare" (XI.151–52)—and the effect is faith, the persuasion to believe: "perswasion in me grew / That I was heard with favour" (XI.152–53). What mediates between grace and the imagination is the intensely metaphoric Word, that is, Christ himself, the teacher of parables, or the Bible, Christ's story told in figures and types. Thus, the dragon-slaying metaphor is discarded—"Dream not of thir fight, / As of a Duel" (XII.386–87)—not to demonstrate the need for a mathematical plainness of language, but to prevent Adam from taking the figure literally. When Michael returns to the metaphor Satan's chains reappear: the Son "shall surprise / The Serpent, Prince of aire, and drag in Chaines / Through all his Realme" (XII.453–55). The chains that mysteriously disappeared when evil uncoiled itself at the beginning of the poem through the *phantastike* are now restored through the *eikastike*.

Thus, the victory over the dragon turns out to be Adam's after all, because his heroism, like Abdiel's, consists not in fighting but in believing.

Afterword

Transumption and Typology

In the present study, the basic method of exegesis has been the explication of allusion and echo. In recent criticism, allusion has become a central concern, chiefly because Harold Bloom has made it so. In identifying allusion with the "missing trope we need to restore," that is, the old rhetorical trope of transumption or metalepsis, Bloom has made allusion the principal device by which poets misread and revise their precursors. For Bloom, transumption operates in much the same way as biblical typology: just as "The New Testament purports to 'fulfill' the Old," so, for instance, "Blake came, he sometimes thought, to 'correct' Milton." The poet achieves precedence over his precursors by alluding to them in such a way that their meaning becomes merely a shadowy type of the poet's: his precursors' meaning is revealed in the poet's and the poet's is concealed in his precursors'. Whereas, however, the purpose of biblical typology is divine revelation, the purpose of Bloomian transumption is poetic revision, the revision that constitutes the poet's clearing imaginative space for himself. For Bloom the most powerful example of transumption is Milton: "In Milton . . . the merging of metalepsis with allusion produces the language's most powerful instance of a poet subsuming all his precursors and making of the subsuming process much of the program and meaning of the work." It is through transumptive allusion that Milton masters the anxiety of influence: "only Shakespeare can be judged Milton's rival in allusive triumph over tradition."[1]

As commentators have been quick to point out and as Bloom has implied from the outset, his theory of influence is self-reflexive: according to Frank Lentricchia, the theory is a projection of Bloom's own struggle with his New-Critical precursors, "an attempt to clear

1. Bloom, *Map of Misreading*, pp. 47, 83, 103, 142. As Hollander, pp. 133–34, points out, in patristic Greek metalepsis often *means* typology, to "'refer type of antitype.'"

space for himself in order to create his critical identity out of nothing."[2] But the theory is self-reflexive in another sense. The typological model for transumption encourages it to be seen as a typological interpretation of typology; that is, Bloom's explanation of the way poets transume their precursors by means of allusion implies that biblical typology, the assimilation of the Old Testament into the New by means of allusion, is itself merely a type of transumption. The New Testament only "purports" to fulfil the Old; it does not reveal the divine but merely revises the poetic. It is hard to imagine how the New Testament writers could have seen this revisionary revelation as anything but a catastrophic impoverishment. There would be of course a kind of poetic justice in their discomfiture: in the same way that New Testament allusion to the Old often does violence to the intentions of the Old, so Bloom's implicit transumption of typology does violence to the intentions of the New. Similarly, his explanation of Miltonic allusion as transumptive does violence to some of the more obvious intentions of the poet. His explanation of the allusion to Galileo's telescope as an image of Milton's transumptive vision, for example, is not only a misreading but a weak misreading—weak because it ignores the evidence of the narrator who having escaped from Hell makes it clear that what Galileo sees is merely "imagind" (*PL* V.263),[3] weak because Milton's poem is so much more imaginative than Bloom's attempt to transume it, weak because *Paradise Lost* is an infinitely better poem than *A Map of Misreading*. Confronted by Bloom's account of Miltonic allusion it is difficult not to feel like Fontenelle confronted by the Enlightenment account of the universe: "But pray tell me . . . had you not formerly a more sublime idea of the universe?"

It needs to be emphasized then that the intention of allusion in *Paradise Lost* is not so much transumptive as typological; the poet's concern is not so much poetic revision as divine revelation.[4] Miltonic allusion seeks to reveal all good words as types of the Word, to reveal the informing presence of the Word concealed in a secular chaos of well-seeming verbal forms. In particular, as I have tried to show, allu-

---

2. *After the New Criticism*, p. 326.

3. See pp. 100–1.

4. Another way of looking at the issue is Barbara Lewalski's theory that the angelic narrators in *Paradise Lost* "realize the highest potential of the various genres" they invent, the prototypical genres of literature ("The Genres of *Paradise Lost*," p. 98). The theory transumes transumption by crediting the poem's attempt to gain precedence over its precursors with a divine origin.

sion and echo reveal the autonomous imagination of Shakespeare as a type of the icastic imagination, that is, Shakespearean imagination as the means by which Milton is led to understand the psychological mechanism of faith. For Milton, *The Tempest, A Midsummer Night's Dream, The Winter's Tale* are all imperfect models of the way grace moves the imagination to believe, the way grace moves through the imagination to provide us with an assurance of things hoped for, the evidence of things not seen.

Works Cited
Index

Works Cited

PRIMARY SOURCES

Ariosto, Ludovico. *Sir John Harington's Translation of Orlando Furioso.* Ed. Graham Hough. London: Centaur Press, 1962.

Aristotle. *On the Soul, Parva Naturalia, On Breath.* Trans. W. S. Hett. Rev. ed. Loeb Classical Library. London: Heinemann, 1957.

Augustine. *Introduction to the Philosophy of Saint Augustine: Selected Readings and Commentaries.* Ed. John A. Mourant. University Park: Pennsylvania State University Press, 1964.

Augustine. *The Works of . . . Augustine.* Ed. Marcus Dods. 15 vols. Edinburgh, 1871–76.

Bacon, Francis. *The Works of Francis Bacon.* Ed. James Spedding et al. 5 vols. London, 1858–61; rpt. Stuttgart: Frommann-Holzboog, 1963.

Batman, Stephen. *The Golden Booke of the Leaden Gods.* London, 1577; rpt. The Renaissance and the Gods, No. 13. New York: Garland, 1976.

Boethius. *The Consolation of Philosophy.* Trans. Richard Green. The Library of Liberal Arts. New York: Bobbs-Merrill, 1962.

Browne, Sir Thomas. *Religio Medici and Other Works.* Ed. L. C. Martin. Oxford: Clarendon Press, 1964.

Browne, Sir Thomas. *Selected Writings.* Ed. Sir Geoffrey Keynes. Chicago: University of Chicago Press, 1968.

Burton, Robert. *The Anatomy of Melancholy.* Ed. Floyd Dell and Paul Jordan-Smith. London: Routledge, 1931.

Calvin, John. *Institutes of the Christian Religion.* Trans. Henry Beveridge. 2 vols. Edinburgh, 1875.

Calvin, John. *Institution of the Christian Religion [Basel, 1536].* Trans. Ford Lewis Battles. Atlanta: John Knox Press, 1975.

Cartari, Vincenzo. *The Fountaine of Ancient Fiction.* Trans. Richard Linche. London, 1599; rpt. The English Experience, No. 577. Amsterdam: Da Capo Press, 1973.

Castiglione, Baldassare. *The Book of the Courtier.* Trans. Sir Thomas Hoby. London, 1900; rpt. The Tudor Translations, 23. New York: AMS Press, 1967.

Charron, Peter. *Of Wisdome.* Trans. Samson Lennard. London, n.d. [before 1612]; rpt. The English Experience, No. 315. Amsterdam: Da Capo Press, 1971.

Coleridge, S. T. *Biographia Literaria; or, Biographical Sketches of My Literary Life and Opinions.* Ed. J. Shawcross. 2 vols. 1907; rpt. London: Oxford University Press, 1962.

Coleridge, S. T. *The Complete Poetical Works of Samuel Taylor Coleridge.* Ed. E. H. Coleridge. 2 vols. 1912; rpt. Oxford: Clarendon Press, 1975.

Culverwell, Nathanael. *Spiritual Opticks: Or a Glass Discovering the Weaknesse and Imperfection of a Christians Knowledge in This Life.* London, 1652.

Dante Alighieri. *The Divine Comedy.* Trans. Charles S. Singleton. 3 vols. Bollingen Series LXXX. Princeton: Princeton University Press, 1970–75.

Donne, John. *The Sermons of John Donne.* Ed. Evelyn M. Simpson and George R. Potter. 10 vols. Berkeley: University of California Press, 1962.

Drayton, Michael. *The Works of Michael Drayton.* Ed. J. W. Hebel et al. 5 vols. 1941; rpt. Oxford: Blackwell, 1961.

Du Laurens, André. *A Discourse of the Preservation of Sight: of Melancholike Diseases; of Rheumes, and of Old Age.* Trans. Richard Surphlet. London, 1599.

Erasmus, Desiderius. *The Enchiridion of Erasmus.* Trans. and ed. Raymond Himelick. Bloomington: Indiana University Press, 1963.

Fletcher, Giles, and Phineas Fletcher. *Giles and Phineas Fletcher: Poetical Works.* Ed. Frederick S. Boas. 2 vols. Cambridge: Cambridge University Press, 1908.

Fletcher, John. *The Dramatic Works in the Beaumont and Fletcher Canon.* Gen. ed. Fredson Bowers. 5 vols. Cambridge: Cambridge University Press, 1966–82.

Herbert, George. *The Works of George Herbert.* Ed. F. E. Hutchinson. Oxford: Clarendon Press, 1941.

Hobbes, Thomas. "Answer to Davenant's Preface to *Gondibert* (1650)." In *Critical Essays of the Seventeenth Century.* Ed. J. E. Spingarn. 3 vols. Oxford: Clarendon Press, 1908, II, 54–67.

Hobbes, Thomas. *Leviathan.* Ed. C. B. Macpherson. Harmondsworth: Penguin, 1968.

Homer. *Chapman's Homer: The Iliad, The Odyssey, and The Lesser Homerica.* Ed. Allardyce Nicol. 2d ed. Bollingen Series XLI. 2 vols. Princeton: Princeton University Press, 1967.

Jonson, Ben. *Ben Jonson: The Complete Masques.* Ed. Stephen Orgel. The Yale Ben Jonson. New Haven: Yale University Press, 1969.

Keats, John. *The Letters of John Keats, 1814–21.* Ed. Hyder Edward Rollins. 2 vols. Cambridge, Mass.: Harvard University Press, 1958.

Langland, William. *Piers Plowman: The B Version: Will's Visions of Piers Plowman, Do-Well, Do-Better, and Do-Best.* Ed. George Kane and E. Talbot Donaldson. London: Athlone Press, 1975.

La Primaudaye, Pierre de. *Suite de l'Académie Françoise.* Paris, 1580; rpt. Genève: Slatkine Reprints, 1972.

Literary Criticism: Plato to Dryden. Ed. Allan H. Gilbert. New York: American Book, 1940.

Locke, John. *An Essay Concerning Human Understanding.* Ed. Peter H. Nidditch. Oxford: Clarendon Press, 1979.

Maimonides, Moses. *The Guide of the Perplexed.* Trans. Shlomo Pines. Introd. Leo Strauss. Chicago: University of Chicago Press, 1963.

Marlowe, Christopher. *The Complete Works of Christopher Marlowe.* Ed. Fredson Bowers. 2 vols. Cambridge: Cambridge University Press, 1973.

Milton, John. *Complete Prose Works of John Milton.* Gen. ed. Don M. Wolfe. 8 vols. New Haven: Yale University Press, 1953–82.

Milton, John. *Milton: Poems and Selected Prose.* Ed. Marjorie Hope Nicolson. New York: Bantam, 1969.

Milton, John. *The Works of John Milton.* Gen. ed. Frank Allen Patterson. 18 vols. New York: Columbia University Press, 1931–38.

Montaigne, Michel de. *The Essays.* Trans. John Florio. London, 1603; rpt. Menston, Yorks.: Scolar Press, 1969.

More, Henry. *The Theological Works of . . . Henry More.* London, 1708.

Perkins, William. *The Workes of . . . Mr. W. Perkins.* 3 vols. Cambridge, 1608–37.

Pico della Mirandola, Gianfrancesco. *On the Imagination.* Trans. Harry Caplan. 1930; rpt. Westport, Ct.: Greenwood Press, 1971.

Plato. *The Dialogues of Plato.* Trans. B. Jowett. 4th ed. 4 vols. Oxford: Clarendon Press, 1953.

Pliny. *Natural History.* Trans. H. Rackham et al. 10 vols. Loeb Classical Library. London: Heinemann, 1938–63.

Puttenham, George. *The Arte of English Poesie* (1589). In *Elizabethan Critical Essays.* Ed. G. Gregory Smith. 2 vols. Oxford: Clarendon Press, 1904, II, 1–193.

Reynolds, Edward. *A Treatise of the Passions and Faculties of the Soule of Man.* London, 1640; rpt. History of Psychology Series. Gainesville, Fla.: Scholars' Facsimiles and Reprints, 1971.

Reynolds, Henry. *Mythomystes [1632].* London, n.d.; rpt. Menston, Yorks.: Scolar Press, 1972.

Sandys, George. *Ovid's Metamorphosis: Englished, Mythologized, and Represented in Figures.* Ed. Karl K. Hulley and Stanley V. Vandersall. Lincoln: University of Nebraska Press, 1970.

Scot, Reginald. *The Discoverie of Witchcraft.* Introd. Hugh Ross Williamson. Carbondale: Southern Illinois University Press, 1964.

Shakespeare, William. *William Shakespeare: The Complete Works.* Gen. ed. Alfred Harbage. Rev. ed. The Pelican Shakespeare. London: Penguin, 1969.

Sibbes, Richard. *The Brvised Reede, and Smoaking Flax.* London, 1630; rpt. Menston, Yorks.: Scolar Press, 1973.

Sibbes, Richard. *The Soules Conflict with It Selfe; and Victory over It Selfe by Faith. . . .* London, 1635.

Sidney, Sir Philip. *An Apology for Poetry or The Defence of Poesy.* Ed. Geoffrey Shepherd. London: Nelson, 1965.

Smith, John. *Select Discourses.* Ed. H. G. Williams. 4th ed. Cambridge, 1859.

Spenser, Edmund. *The Poetical Works of Edmund Spenser.* Ed. Ernest de Selincourt and J. C. Smith. 2 vols. 1909–10; rpt. Oxford: Clarendon Press, 1960–61.

Swan, John. *Speculum Mundi; or, A Glasse Representing the Face of the World.* Cambridge, 1635.

Tasso, Torquato. *Discourses on the Heroic Poem.* Trans. Mariella Cavalchini and Irene Samuel. Oxford: Clarendon Press, 1973.

Taylor, Thomas. *Christ Revealed: Or the Old Testament Explained.* London, 1635; rpt. New York: Delmar, 1979.

St. Thomas Aquinas. *Summa Theologiae.* Gen. ed. Thomas Gilby, O.P. 60 vols. New York: Blackfriars, 1964–81.

Vaughan, Henry. *The Works of Henry Vaughan.* Ed. L. C. Martin. 2d ed. Oxford: Clarendon Press, 1957.

Vergil. *The Aeneid.* Trans. W. F. Jackson Knight. Harmondsworth: Penguin, 1964.

Vergil. *P. Vergili Maronis Opera.* Ed. R. A. B. Mynors. Oxford: Clarendon Press, 1969.

Warton, Thomas. *Observations on the Fairy Queen of Spenser.* 2d ed. 2 vols. London, 1762.

Warton, Thomas, ed. *Poems upon Several Occasions . . . by John Milton.* 2d ed. London, 1791.

Wordsworth, William. *The Poetical Works of William Wordsworth.* Ed. E. de Selincourt and H. Darbishire. 2d ed. 5 vols. Oxford: Clarendon Press, 1952.

Wright, Thomas. *The Passions of the Minde.* London, 1601; rpt. Anglistica and Americana, 126. Hildesheim: Georg Olms, 1973.

SECONDARY SOURCES

Babb, Lawrence. *The Elizabethan Malady: A Study of Melancholia in English Literature from 1580 to 1642.* East Lansing: Michigan State College Press, 1951.

Bamborough, J. B. *The Little World of Man.* London: Longmans, 1952.

Barker, Arthur. *"Paradise Lost:* The Relevance of Regeneration." In *Paradise Lost: A Tercentenary Tribute.* Ed. Balachandra Rajan. Toronto: University of Toronto Press, 1969, pp. 48–78.

Berek, Peter. " 'Plain' and 'Ornate' Styles and the Structure of *Paradise Lost.*" *PMLA* 85 (1970): 237–46.

Berry, Boyd M. "Melodramatic Faking in the Narrator's Voice, *Paradise Lost.*" *Milton Quarterly* 10 (1976): 1–5.

Blessington, Francis C. *Paradise Lost and the Classical Epic.* London: Routledge and Kegan Paul, 1979.

Blondel, J. "From *The Tempest* to *Comus.*" *Revue de Littérature Comparée* 49 (1975): 204–16.

Bloom, Harold. *The Anxiety of Influence: A Theory of Poetry.* New York: Oxford University Press, 1973.

Bloom, Harold. *A Map of Misreading.* New York: Oxford University Press, 1975.

Bloomfield, Morton W. *Piers Plowman as Fourteenth-Century Apocalypse.* New Brunswick, N.J.: Rutgers University Press, 1961.

Brisman, Leslie. *Milton's Poetry of Choice and Its Romantic Heirs.* Ithaca: Cornell University Press, 1973.

Broadbent, John. Paradise Lost: *Introduction.* Cambridge: Cambridge University Press, 1972.

Broadbent, John. *Some Graver Subject: An Essay on* Paradise Lost. London: Chatto and Windus, 1960.

Brooks, Harold F., ed. *A Midsummer Night's Dream.* The Arden Shakespeare. London: Methuen, 1979.

Brown, Cedric C. "The Shepherd, the Musician, and the Word in Milton's Masque." *Journal of English and Germanic Philology* 78 (1979): 522–44.

Bundy, Murray W. *The Theory of Imagination in Classical and Medieval Thought.* Urbana: University of Illinois Press, 1927.

Burden, Dennis H. *The Logical Epic: A Study of the Argument of* Paradise Lost. London: Routledge and Kegan Paul, 1967.

Burnett, A. "Milton's 'Paradise Regained,' I.314–19." *Notes and Queries* 25 (1978): 509–10.

Carey, John, and Alastair Fowler, eds. *The Poems of John Milton.* London: Longmans, 1968.

Cassirer, Ernst. *The Platonic Renaissance in England.* Trans. James P. Pettegrove. London: Nelson, 1953.

Charity, A. C. *Events and Their Afterlife: The Dialectics of Christian Typology in the Bible and Dante.* Cambridge: Cambridge University Press, 1966.

Chomsky, Noam. *Cartesian Linguistics: A Chapter in the History of Rationalist Thought.* New York: Harper and Row, 1966.

Christopher, Georgia B. *Milton and the Science of the Saints.* Princeton: Princeton University Press, 1982.

Cohen, Kitty. *The Throne and the Chariot: Studies in Milton's Hebraism.* The Hague: Mouton, 1975.

Collingwood, R. G. *Faith & Reason: Essays in the Philosophy of Reason.* Ed. Lionel Rubinoff. Chicago: Quadrangle Books, 1968.

Cornford, F. M., ed. *The Republic of Plato.* 1941; rpt. Oxford: Clarendon Press, 1966.

Crosman, Robert. *Reading* Paradise Lost. Bloomington: Indiana University Press, 1980.

Cullen, Patrick. *Infernall Triad: The Flesh, the World, and the Devil in Spenser and Milton.* Princeton: Princeton University Press, 1974.

Cumberland, Sharon, and Lynn Veach Sadler. "Phantasia: A Pattern in Milton's Early Poems." *Milton Quarterly* 8 (1974): 50–55.

Daiches, David. *Milton.* London, 1957; rpt. New York: Norton, 1966.

Davidson, Clifford. "The Young Milton, Orpheus, and Poetry." *English Studies* 59 (1978): 27–34.

Demaray, John G. *Milton's Theatrical Epic: The Invention and Design of Paradise Lost.* Cambridge, Mass.: Harvard University Press, 1980.

Empson, William. *Milton's God.* Rev. ed. London: Chatto and Windus, 1965.

Entzminger, Robert L. "Michael's Options and Milton's Poetry: *Paradise Lost* XI and XII." *English Literary Renaissance* 8 (1978): 197–211.

Evans, J. M. Paradise Lost *and the Genesis Tradition.* Oxford: Clarendon Press, 1968.

Ferry, Anne Davidson. *Milton's Epic Voice: The Narrator in* Paradise Lost. Cambridge, Mass.: Harvard University Press, 1963.

Fish, Stanley. *Self-Consuming Artifacts: The Experience of Seventeenth-Century Literature.* Berkeley: University of California Press, 1972.

Fish, Stanley. *Surprised by Sin: The Reader in* Paradise Lost. New York: St. Martin's Press, 1967.

Fletcher, Angus. *The Prophetic Moment: An Essay on Spenser.* Chicago: University of Chicago Press, 1971.

Fletcher, Angus. *The Transcendental Masque: An Essay on Milton's* Comus. Ithaca: Cornell University Press, 1971.

Fowler, Alastair. *Spenser and the Numbers of Time.* London: Routledge and Kegan Paul, 1964.

Frye, Northrop. *Anatomy of Criticism: Four Essays.* Princeton: Princeton University Press, 1957.

Frye, Northrop. *The Great Code: The Bible and Literature.* Toronto: Academic Press, 1982.

Frye, Northrop. "The Revelation to Eve." In Paradise Lost: *A Tercentenary Tribute.* Ed. Balachandra Rajan. Toronto: University of Toronto Press, 1969, pp. 18–47.

Frye, Northrop. *The Return of Eden: Five Essays on Milton's Epics.* Toronto: University of Toronto Press, 1965.

Frye, Roland Mushat. *Milton's Imagery and the Visual Arts: Iconographic Tradition in the Epic Poems.* Princeton: Princeton University Press, 1978.

Galdon, Joseph A. *Typology and Seventeenth-Century Literature.* The Hague: Mouton, 1975.

Garber, Marjorie B. *Dream in Shakespeare: From Metaphor to Metamorphosis.* New Haven: Yale University Press, 1974.

Gardner, Helen. "Milton's 'Satan' and the Theme of Damnation in Elizabethan Tragedy." In *Milton: Modern Essays in Criticism.* Ed. Arthur E. Barker. New York: Oxford University Press, 1965, pp. 205–17.

Giamatti, A. Bartlett. "Spenser: From Magic to Miracle." In *Four Essays on Romance.* Ed. Herschel Baker. Cambridge, Mass.: Harvard University Press, 1971, pp. 15–31.

Grierson, Herbert J. C., and J. C. Smith. *A Critical History of English Poetry.* Rev. ed. London: Chatto and Windus, 1956.

Grose, Christopher. *Milton's Epic Process:* Paradise Lost *and Its Miltonic Background.* New Haven: Yale University Press, 1973.

Guillory, John. *Poetic Authority: Spenser, Milton, and Literary History.* New York: Columbia University Press, 1983.

Hamilton, Gary D. "Milton's Defensive God: A Reappraisal." *Studies in Philology* 69 (1972): 87–100.

Harvey, E. Ruth. *The Inward Wits: Psychological Theory in the Middle Ages and the Renaissance.* London: Warburg Institute, 1975.

Hathaway, Baxter. *The Age of Criticism: The Late Renaissance in Italy.* Ithaca: Cornell University Press, 1962.

Hawkes, Terence. *Structuralism and Semiotics.* London: Methuen, 1977.

Heninger, S. K., Jr. "Sidney and Milton: The Poet as Maker." In *Milton and the Line of Vision.* Ed. Joseph Anthony Wittreich, Jr. Madison: University of Wisconsin Press, 1975, pp. 57–95.

Hick, John. *Faith and Knowledge.* 2d ed. Ithaca: Cornell University Press, 1966.

Hill, John Spencer. *John Milton: Poet, Priest, Prophet.* Totowa, N.J.: Rowman and Littlefield, 1979.

Hollander, John. *The Figure of Echo: A Mode of Allusion in Milton and After.* Berkeley: University of California Press, 1981.

Hoyle, James. " 'If Sion Hill Delight Thee More': The Muse's Choice in *Paradise Lost.*" *English Language Notes* 12 (1974–75): 20–26.

Hughes, Felicity A. "Psychological Allegory in *The Faerie Queene* III. xi–xii." *Review of English Studies,* n.s. 29 (1978): 129–46.

Hughes, Merrit Y. "Milton's Limbo of Vanity." In *Th'Upright Heart and Pure: Essays on John Milton Commemorating the Tercentenary of the Publication of* Paradise Lost. Ed. Amadeus P. Fiore. Pittsburgh: Duquesne University Press, 1967, pp. 7–24.

Hunter, William B., Jr. "Eve's Demonic Dream." *ELH* 13 (1946): 255–65.

Hunter, William B., Jr. "The Liturgical Context of *Comus.*" *English Language Notes* 10 (1972–73): 14–15.

Hunter, William B., Jr. "Prophetic Dreams and Visions in *Paradise Lost.*" *Modern Language Quarterly* 9 (1948): 277–85.

Huntley, John V. "The Images of Poet & Poetry in Milton's *The Reason of Church-Government.*" In *Achievements of the Left Hand: Essays on the Prose of John Milton.* Ed. Michael Leib and John T. Shawcross. Amherst: University of Massachusetts Press, 1974.

Johnston, Arthur. *Enchanted Ground: The Study of Medieval Romance in the Eighteenth Century.* London: Athlone Press, 1964.

Kermode, Frank, ed. *The Tempest.* 6th ed. The Arden Shakespeare. London: Methuen, 1962.

Kerrigan, William. *The Prophetic Milton.* Charlottesville: University Press of Virginia, 1974.

Knight, G. Wilson. *The Burning Oracle: Studies in the Poetry of Action.* London: Oxford University Press, 1939.

Leavis, F. R. *Revaluation: Tradition and Development in English Poetry.* London, 1936; rpt. New York: Norton, 1963.

Leib, Michael. "*Paradise Lost,* Book III: The Dialogue in Heaven Reconsidered." In *Renaissance Papers 1974.* Ed. Dennis G. Donovan and A.

Leigh Deneff. Durham, N.C.: Southeastern Renaissance Conference, 1975, pp. 39–50.

Leib, Michael. *Poetics of the Holy: A Reading of "Paradise Lost."* Chapel Hill: University of North Carolina Press, 1981.

Leishman, J. B. *Milton's Minor Poems.* Pittsburgh: University of Pittsburgh Press, 1969.

Lentricchia, Frank. *After the New Criticism.* Chicago: University of Chicago Press, 1980.

Lewalski, Barbara K. "The Genres of *Paradise Lost*: Literary Genre as a Means of Accommodation." *Milton Studies* 17 (1983): 75–103.

Lewalski, Barbara K. "Innocence and Experience in Milton's Eden." In *New Essays on* Paradise Lost. Ed. Thomas Kranidas. Berkeley: University of California Press, 1969, pp. 86–117.

Lewalski, Barbara K. "Milton: Revaluations of Romance." In *Four Essays on Romance.* Ed. Herschel Baker. Cambridge, Mass.: Harvard University Press, 1971, pp. 56–70.

Lewalski, Barbara K. "*Samson Agonistes* and the 'Tragedy' of the Apocalypse." *PMLA* 85 (1970): 1050–62.

Lewalski, Barbara K. "Structure and the Symbolism of Vision in Michael's Prophecy, *Paradise Lost,* Books XI–XII." *Philological Quarterly* 42 (1963), 25–35.

Lewalski, Barbara K. "Typological Symbolism and 'The Progress of the Soul' in Seventeenth-Century Literature." In *The Literary Uses of Typology: From the Late Middle Ages to the Present.* Ed. Earl Miner. Princeton: Princeton University Press, 1977, pp. 79–114.

Lewis, C. W. *A Preface to* Paradise Lost. 1942; rpt. London: Oxford University Press, 1960.

Low, Anthony. "The Image of the Tower in *Paradise Lost.*" *Studies in English Literature, 1500–1900* 10 (1970): 171–81.

MacCaffrey, Isabel G. *Spenser's Allegory: The Anatomy of Imagination.* Princeton: Princeton University Press, 1975.

MacCaffrey, Isabel G. "The Theme of *Paradise Lost,* Book III." In *New Essays on* Paradise Lost. Ed. Thomas Kranidas. Berkeley: University of California Press, 1969, pp. 58–85.

MacCallum, H. R. "Milton and Figurative Interpretation of the Bible." *University of Toronto Quarterly* 31 (1961–62): 397–415.

Madsen, William G. *From Shadowy Types to Truth: Studies in Milton's Symbolism.* New Haven: Yale University Press, 1968.

Major, John M. "*Comus* and *The Tempest.*" *Shakespeare Quarterly* 10 (1959): 177–83.

Martz, Louis L. *Poet of Exile: A Study of Milton's Poetry.* New Haven: Yale University Press, 1980.

Mendelsohn, I. "Urim and Thummim." In *The Interpreter's Dictionary of the Bible: An Illustrated Encyclopaedia.* Ed. George A. Buttrick et al. 4 vols. New York: Abingdon, 1962, IV, 739–40.

Miller, George. "Archetype and History: Narrative Technique in *Paradise Lost*, Books XI and XII." *Modern Language Studies* 10 (1980): 12–21.

Nohrnberg, James. *The Analogy of* The Faerie Queene. Princeton: Princeton University Press, 1976.

Nuttall, Geoffrey F. *The Holy Spirit in Puritan Faith and Experience.* 2d ed. Oxford: Blackwell, 1947.

O'Brien, Elmer, ed. *Varieties of Mystic Experience.* New York: Holt, Rinehart, and Winston, 1964.

Otten, Charlotte F. "Milton's Haemony." *English Literary Renaissance* 5 (1975): 81–95.

Panofsky, Erwin. *Idea: A Concept in Art Theory.* Trans. Joseph J. S. Peake. Columbia: University of South Carolina Press, 1968.

Parish, John E. "Milton and an Anthropomorphic God." *Studies in Philology* 56 (1959): 619–25.

Parish, John E. "Milton and God's Curse on the Serpent." *Journal of English and Germanic Philology* 58 (1959): 241–47.

Patrides, C. A. "The Godhead in *Paradise Lost*: Dogma or Drama." *Journal of English and Germanic Philology* 64 (1965): 29–34.

Patrides, C. A. *Milton and the Christian Tradition.* Oxford: Clarendon Press, 1966.

Patterson, Annabel M. "*Paradise Regained*: A Last Chance at True Romance." *Milton Studies* 17 (1983): 187–208.

Patterson, Lee W. "'Rapt with Pleasaunce': Vision and Narration in the Epic." *ELH* 48 (1981): 455–75.

Phillips, Norma. "Milton's Limbo of Vanity and Dante's Vestibule." *English Language Notes* 3 (1965–66): 177–82.

Quilligan, Maureen. *Milton's Spenser: The Politics of Reading.* Ithaca: Cornell University Press, 1983.

Qvarnstrom, Gunnar. *The Enchanted Palace: Some Structural Aspects of* Paradise Lost. Stockholm: Almqvist and Wiksell, 1967.

Radzinowicz, Mary Ann. *Towards* Samson Agonistes: *The Growth of Milton's Mind.* Princeton: Princeton University Press, 1978.

Rajan, B. Paradise Lost *& the Seventeenth Century Reader.* London: Chatto and Windus, 1947.

Revard, Stella Purce. "The Dramatic Function of the Son in *Paradise Lost*: A Commentary on Milton's 'Trinitarianism.'" *Journal of English and Germanic Philology* 66 (1967): 45–58.

Revard, Stella Purce. *The War in Heaven:* Paradise Lost *and the Tradition of Satan's Rebellion.* Ithaca: Cornell University Press, 1980.

Samuel, Irene. *Dante and Milton: The* Commedia *and* Paradise Lost. Ithaca: Cornell University Press, 1966.

Samuel, Irene. "The Dialogue in Heaven: A Reconsideration of *Paradise Lost*, III, 1–417." In *Milton: Modern Essays in Criticism.* Ed. Arthur E. Barker. New York: Oxford University Press, 1965, pp. 233–45.

Samuel, Irene. *Plato and Milton.* Ithaca: Cornell University Press, 1947.

Seaton, Ethel. "*Comus* and Shakespeare." *Essays and Studies* 31 (1946): 68–80.

Shawcross, John T. *With Mortal Voice: The Creation of "Paradise Lost."* Lexington: University Press of Kentucky, 1982.

Sims, James H. *The Bible in Milton's Epics.* Gainesville: University of Florida Press, 1962.

Sirluck, Ernest. "Milton Revises *The Faerie Queene.*" *Modern Philology* 48 (1950): 90–96.

Slater, Ann Pasternak. "Variations within a Source: From Isaiah to *The Tempest.*" *Shakespeare Survey* 25 (1972): 125–35.

Smith, R. W. "The Source of Milton's Pandemonium." *Modern Philology* 29 (1931): 187–98.

Stein, Arnold. *Answerable Style: Essays on* Paradise Lost. Minneapolis: University of Minnesota Press, 1953.

Svendsen, Kester. *Milton and Science.* Cambridge, Mass.: Harvard University Press, 1956.

Swaim, Kathleen M. "Flower, Fruit, and Seed: A Reading of *Paradise Lost.*" *Milton Studies* 5 (1973): 155–76.

Taaffe, James G. "Michaelmas, the 'Lawless Hour,' and the Occasion of Milton's *Comus.*" *English Language Notes* 6 (1968–69): 257–62.

Taylor, Gary, ed. *Henry V.* The Oxford Shakespeare. Oxford: Clarendon Press, 1982.

Thaler, Alwin. *Shakespeare and Our World.* Knoxville: University of Tennessee Press, 1966.

Thomas, Keith. *Religion and the Decline of Magic: Studies in Popular Beliefs in Sixteenth and Seventeenth Century England.* London: Weidenfeld and Nicolson, 1971.

Trickett, Rachel. "Shakespeare and Milton." *Essays and Studies,* n.s. 31 (1978): 23–35.

Tuve, Rosemond. *Images & Themes in Five Poems by Milton.* Cambridge, Mass.: Harvard University Press, 1957.

A Variorum Commentary on the Poems of John Milton. Gen. ed. Merrit Y. Hughes. 6 vols. New York: Columbia University Press, 1970–.

Waddington, Raymond B. "The Death of Adam: Vision and Voice in Books XI and XII of *Paradise Lost.*" *Modern Philology* 70 (1972): 9–12.

Waldock, A. J. A. Paradise Lost *and Its Critics.* 1947; rpt. Cambridge: Cambridge University Press, 1964.

Wallace, Ronald S. *Calvin's Doctrine of the Word and the Sacrament.* Edinburgh, 1953; rpt. Grand Rapids, Mich.: Eerdmans, 1957.

Weinberg, Bernard. *A History of Literary Criticism in the Italian Renaissance.* 2 vols. Chicago: University of Chicago Press, 1962.

Weinhouse, Linda. "The Urim and Thummim in *Paradise Lost.*" *Milton Quarterly* 11 (1977): 9–12.

Whaler, James. "Animal Simile in *Paradise Lost.*" *PMLA* 47 (1932): 539–53.

Whiting, George Wesley. *Milton and This Pendant World.* Austin: University of Texas Press, 1958.

Willey, Basil. *The Seventeenth-Century Background.* 1934; rpt. Harmondsworth: Penguin, 1964.

Wind, Edgar. *Pagan Mysteries in the Renaissance.* Rev. ed. New York: Norton, 1968.

Wittreich, Joseph Anthony, Jr., ed. *The Romantics on Milton: Formal Essays and Critical Asides.* Cleveland: Press of Case Western Reserve University, 1970.

Wittreich, Joseph Anthony, Jr. *Visionary Poetics: Milton's Tradition and His Legacy.* San Marino, Calif.: Huntington Library, 1979.

Index

Aaron's breastplate, 137–38, 142–43, 243

Abdiel, 245

Accommodation, 63–64, 68, 73, 157

Achilles' shield, 113

Adam: associated with reason, 186, 208, 217–18; "baptism" of, 242–43; and Eve imitate process of divine council, 226–32; eyes of, treated, 238–43; inhibited by reason, 228; interprets curse, 226–30; love-language of, 196; narcissism of, 188, 216–20; parodies divine council, 219–20; rejects carnal imagination, 243–44; response to Eve's dream, 204–8; responsibility for Fall, 217–18; reunited with Eve, 230; separated from Eve, 210–11; as tragic hero, 227. *See also* Dream(s)

Albo, Joseph, 58

Allusion: biblical, as simulation of Holy Spirit, 90–91, 123–27, 223–25; as consciously intended echo, 7, 122; dissolves Satanic epic, 123–27; fragmentary, 110n; Milton's "transumptive" use of, 246–47; Milton's typological use of, 247–48; penetrates illusion, 17–19, 83–84, 87, 122–27; Satan's transumptive use of, 114–17; Son's typological use of, 157–58, 170–72; subverts denotation, 17–19. *See also* Echo; Transumption

Alta Fantasia. See Imagination

Amaranthus, 175

Amazement, 168, 183

Antimasque: opening books of *PL* as, 87–90

Aquinas, Thomas, St., 52–53, 61–62, 106

Archimago, 11, 92–94, 96, 191, 194n, 197

Ariel, 20–27, 28–31, 34, 39–40, 44–45, 118, 182, 183, 238, 242

Ariosto, Ludovico: *Orlando Furioso*, 132

Aristotle, 50, 52, 186, 189

Attendant Spirit, 19–20, 35–36, 38–45, 66, 109, 124, 128, 168, 236, 238, 241, 242

Augustine, St., 55, 62, 69–70, 101–2, 138, 223, 231

Bacon, Francis, 6, 48, 71–72, 77, 120–21, 133, 164, 177

Barker, Arthur E., 216

Batman, Stephen, 168n

Bazin, Germain, 136

Berek, Peter, 151

Bible: and divine council, 172, 175–76; and Holy Spirit, 73–74; and imagination, 71, 79, 234, 235; medium of faith, 70

Bible, books of: Acts, 71n, 171, 172, 222–23, 225, 235; Colossians, 148, 154; I Corinthians, 26n, 60–61, 73, 89, 171, 206; II Corinthians, 69, 106; Ecclesiastes, 65, 111, 134–35; Ecclesiasticus, 152n; Ephesians, 172, 222; Exodus, 96, 115–17, 125, 138, 150n, 152, 156, 166; Ezekiel, 138, 143, 157–59, 231n, 236–37, 241; Galatians, 176; Genesis, 106, 138, 150n, 151, 152, 155, 156, 209n; Hebrews, 29, 79, 91, 124, 159, 235; Hosea, 165; Isaiah, 28, 56, 64, 114, 116, 124–25, 141, 161, 171, 225, 243; Jeremiah, 63; Job, 38, 63, 141, 152n, 157, 227, 244; John, 79, 148, 154, 174, 223–24, 225–26; Jonah, 28; II Kings, 139; Luke, 123, 139, 243; Mark, 57, 235; Matthew, 127, 166n, 175, 231n, 243; Numbers, 117, 150; Proverbs, 152; Psalms, 28, 63, 79, 152n, 165, 171, 243, 244; Revelation, 63, 90–91, 96–97, 167, 173–74, 233–34, 237, 240; Romans, 33, 103, 174, 216, 222, 224; Song of Solomon, 41n, 50, 63, 195–96;

263

Bible (*continued*)
II Thessalonians, 108*n*; I Timothy, 148;
Wisdom, 161. *See also* Prophecy; Read-
ing; Reason; Shakespeare
Blackmore, Sir William, 15
Blake, William, 176, 246
Blessington, Francis C., 107, 150*n*
Blindness, 74–79, 142
Bloom, Harold, 3, 4*n*, 7–8*n*, 100–101,
246–47
Boethius, 163
Botticelli, Sandro, 168*n*
Brisman, Leslie, 4*n*
Broadbent, John, 97, 102–3, 128*n*, 133–
34, 134–35, 137, 162, 172, 184*n*, 215
Brooks, Harold F., 89, 192*n*, 207*n*
Brown, Cedric C., 39*n*, 40*n*
Browne, Sir Thomas, 12*n*, 83, 141,
158–59
Bundy, Murray W., 31–32
Burden, Dennis, 187, 189, 190*n*, 205,
214*n*
Burke, Edmund, 102
Burton, Robert, 11, 16, 19, 118–19, 133

Calvin, John, 11, 17, 71, 139, 152–53,
160, 169, 174, 177
Cartari, Vincenzo, 118
Cassirer, Ernst, 27–28*n*
Castelvetro, Lodovico, 49
Castiglione, Baldassare, 26*n*
Catholicism, 138
Chapman, George, 113
Charron, Peter, 197
Chastity, 41–43, 182
Chaucer, Geoffrey, 141, 192*n*
Christopher, Georgia B., 30*n*, 151*n*, 221*n*
Circe, 12, 42–43, 96, 105, 118, 120, 127,
144, 197, 237
Civility, 21, 24
Classics: as alternative to revelation,
109, 113, 200–201; as distortion of
Mosaic revelation, 111; Satan's use of,
113, 115; typological interpretation of,
109–10, 112, 113, 129, 201, 231. *See
also* Epic
Coleridge, S. T., 195; *Christabel*, 195*n*
Collingwood, R. G., 69–70
Comanini, Gregorio, 49

Conscience, 24–25, 30, 123, 176, 228,
239
Contemplation, 233–36, 243
Cortona, Pietro da, 136
Creativity: and birth of Eve, 119, 218–
19; independent of God, 110–13,
118–19
Crosman, Robert, 151*n*, 163*n*

Daiches, David, 103*n*
Dante Alighieri, 50–53; *Convivio*, 52;
Inferno, 103, 117, 130–31; *Paradiso*,
51, 130, 141; *Purgatorio*, 51, 74, 78–79,
222
Delight, 78–79, 159, 160, 219
Descartes, René, 196
Despair, 114–15, 163, 222, 227–30, 235
Deucalion and Pyrrha, 231, 241
Donne, John, 62, 222
Dragon-slaying, 226–27, 230–31, 240,
244–45
Drayton, Michael, 61
Dream(s), 27, 32, 83, 188*n*; Adam's, 32,
65–69, 128; Agamemnon's, 107–8;
Bottom's, 84–90; Caliban's 22–23; De-
metrius's, 202–3; Eve's demonic, 14–
15, 106, 131, 134, 189–216; Eve's pro-
phetic, 238; Jacob's, 138–39; opening
books of *PL* as, 87; prophetic, 58, 65–
69; Richard II's, 123; Satan's, 97, 125;
Titiana's, 86–87, 191–92, 203–8
Du Laurens, André, 85, 102

Eagle-sight, 141–42, 234, 243
Echo: degrees of, 7, 122; and grace, 33–
36, 38–39, 124, 154, 215, 227–30, 236.
See also Allusion
Eikastike. See Imagination; Poetry
Eliot, T. S., 59, 103*n*
Empson, William, 97, 101, 176, 199–200
Epic: classical, 113–115, 146–47, 173–
74; divine, 145–47, 164–65, 167; Sa-
tanic, 83, 89–90, 105, 106–21, 122–45
Erasmus, Desiderius, 75
Error, 118, 120–21
Euphrasy, 239–40
Evans, J. M., 184*n*
Eve: associated with imagination, 186,
208, 217–18; bower of, 191–92, 194;

and Christabel, 195*n*; as epitome of life, 217; imitates the Son, 227–28; narcissism of, 186–88, 212, 218; as Pomona, 211; seduction of, 181, 183, 202–16; as Sin, 218–19. *See also* Creativity; Dream(s)

Evil: consolidation of, 38, 91, 144; deconsolidation of, 91–92, 96–103, 109, 124, 197

Eye and ear: symbolism of, 19–20, 32–33, 69–70, 75–79, 139, 222–25

Fable, 111, 113

Faith: and Abraham, 156, 158, 159–60, 219; and Adam's dreams, 68–69; Adam's, destroyed, 219–20; and Jacob's dream, 138–39; justification by, 74, 176; magical, 35–36, 38–45, 72, 238–44; and metamorphosis, 241–42; and metaphor, 164–65, 226–27, 230–31, 240, 244–45; and persuasion, 29, 70–74, 174–75, 231, 245; process of, reversed, 211–16; and romance, 29, 167, 232–33; and sight, 69–70, 71, 76–79, 210–16; and the Son, 154, 157, 159–60, 170–72, 174–77, 216, 219–20, 222; and tree of life, 174–75; and wonder, 29, 165, 167, 232. *See also* Imagination

Fame, 77

Fancy. *See* Imagination

Fealty, 164, 217

Ferry, Anne, 94–96

Ficino, Marsilio, 19

Filia vocis. See Prophecy

Fish, Stanley, 94–96, 107, 151–52, 153, 189*n*, 190, 210, 216

Fletcher, Angus, 4, 34*n*

Fletcher, Giles: *Christ's Victorie on Earth*, 105*n*; *Christ's Victorie in Heaven*, 165–66

Fletcher, John: *The Faith Shepherdess*, 182*n*

Fontenelle, Bernard le Bovier, 247

Fowler, Alistair, 6, 83*n*, 93*n*, 110*n*, 113*n*, 122–23, 128, 130, 134*n*, 140, 155, 160, 184, 185*n*, 207, 209

Frye, Northrop, 87, 110*n*, 150*n*, 152, 163, 169–70*n*, 176, 221, 222*n*, 236, 238*n*

Frye, Roland Mushat, 110*n*, 136–37

Furor poeticus, 127, 128, 131–32

Fury, 23, 40, 128, 131–33

Galileo Galilei, 100–101, 106, 120, 247

Garber, Marjorie B., 85*n*

Gardner, Helen, 113*n*

Gazaeus, Alardus, 144

Giamatti, A. Bartlett, 238*n*

God: fear of, 152–53, 227; four daughters of, 165–66; incomprehensibility of, 148; justice of, 157, 159, 162–66, 176; knowledge of, 52–57, 62, 148; progressive self-revelation of, 158, 175–76; representation of, 68, 151, 176

—the Father: language of, 151–52, 162–66, 172–75, 211, 216; revelation of purpose, 147–50, 172–75, 230; wrath of, 150–62

—the Son: challenges the Father, 156–57; dual role of, 146, 154, 155–56; fulfils biblical and classical types, 157–58, 170–72; image of invisible God, 148, 158–59; intercedes with the Father, 147–48, 154–62; interprets the Father, 149, 154–62; as light of wisdom, 154; as romance hero, 167–72, 227; as the Word, 149, 245. *See also* Faith

—Word of: mediates between grace and imagination, 38, 40, 70, 95–96, 149, 169, 174–75, 222–25, 245; penetrates illusion, 90–91, 123–27, 139, 187, 237; and sacred song, 33; and Urim, 143

Grace: and fear, 153, 227; personifications of, 168–69; prevenient, 30*n*, 33, 169, 230–32; as purpose of divine council, 169; and song, 33–42, 64, 127–28, 148, 154, 204. *See also* Echo; Imagination

Guillory, John, 3–8, 31*n*, 83*n*, 87*n*, 101*n*, 204–5*n*

Gunpowder, 131–32

Haemony, 39–40, 239

Hamilton, Gary D., 151*n*

Harpies, 23–24, 39–40, 132

Harvey, E. Ruth, 188*n*

Hawkes, Terence, 115
Heaven's Gate, 137–41
Hephaestus. *See* Mulciber
Herbert, George, 38
Hermes, 168*n*
Hobbes, Thomas, 21, 224*n*
Hollander, John, 7, 110*n*, 247*n*
Holy Spirit: and breath, 224; and creativity, 161–62; and heavenly muse, 78; and interpretation of the Word, 224–25; and light, 75; and prophecy, 71*n*; and reading, 73–74, 78–79; and wind, 223; and wisdom, 161. *See also* Allusion; Echo; Grace
Homer, 102; *Iliad*, 107–8, 109, 113, 115, 146–47; *Odyssey*, 115, 146–47, 150, 173
Horace, 78
Hughes, Felicity A., 86*n*, 87, 104*n*
Hunter, William B., Jr., 32, 67
Hypocrisy, 11, 93, 126

Idolatry, 106, 112, 217
Images: dependence of understanding on, 52–57; illusory without explanation, 16–17, 139–40; thinking without, 59–60, 68
Imagination: *alta fantasia*, 50–53, 74, 206; carnal, 101–3, 140, 187, 198–99, 201–2, 214, 223, 243–44; delusory, 11–19, 46, 59, 83, 92–94, 181–83; and faith, 5–6, 7, 29–45, 64–79, 157, 159, 160, 164, 174–75, 177, 233, 245, 248; and fancy, 12*n*; and gardening, 184–88; and Holy Spirit, 75; human and animal, 84–85; and invention of the good, 25–27, 30–31, 46; and magic of Attendent Spirit, 19–20, 35–36, 38–45; and magic of Comus, 11–19, 72; and magic of Michael, 238–44; and magic of Prospero, 20–27, 29–31; and magic of Satan, 216–17; and "magic" of the Son, 162; and memory, 229*n*; personified as boy, 86; and prophecy, 57–64; and reason, 5–6 and *passim*; and reflection or mirror of the good, 20, 29, 30–33, 46, 60–62; "renunciation" of, 3–8; separated from reason, 194–202, 209–20; as theatrical stage, 63, 234. *See also* Poetry; Prophecy; Romance

—icastic, 46–79 and *passim*; and grace, 168–69, 204, 206; and Milton's early poetry, 52, 53–57; origins of term, 49–52; poetry of, distinguished from *phantastike*, 46–47; and prophecy, 57–64; and reflection of ideas, 48–49; and the Son, 168; and wisdom, 161
"Imaginations," biblical, 106–7, 123
Imitatio Christi, 222, 227
India, 84, 135–36
Iris, 168*n*

Jonson, Ben: *Vision of Delight*, 87–89

Keats, John, 66–67*n*
Kerrigan, William, 4, 50, 78
Knight, G. Wilson, 3

Langland, William: *Piers Plowman*, 165
Language, 196–97; and serpents, 192–93, 209, 211–16
Law and the Gospel, 79, 163, 166–67, 224, 235–36
Leavis, F. R., 13–17, 102, 111
Leib, Michael, 4*n*, 156*n*, 157, 159
Lentricchia, Frank, 246–47
Lewalski, Barbara K., 109, 184*n*, 185*n*, 247*n*
Lewis, C. S., 110*n*
Linche, Richard, 118
Locke, John, 14–15
Lowes, John Livingston, 122

MacCallum, Hugh, 101*n*
Mad Pranks of Robin Goodfellow, 183
Magic: and creative imagination, 19–27, 167; and faith, 27–45; and icastic or reflective imagination, 27–45, 162; and the imaginary, 11–19, 72, 126, 209; and rhetoric, 13–14, 209; and skepticism, 12*n*, 23. *See also* Imagination
Maimonides, Moses, 57–58
Marlowe, Christopher: *Edward II*, 86; *Faustus*, 113
Martz, Louis, 184*n*, 211*n*
Mathematics, 60*n*
Mazzoni, Jacopo, 49, 50, 62
Memory. *See* Imagination

Metamorphosis, 240–42; and grace, 241; and metaphor, 85*n*, 241
Metaphor. *See* Faith; Metamorphosis
Michael, 103, 152, 158, 159, 168*n*, 224, 230, 232, 233, 236–44; and Attendent Spirit, 238; and Ezekiel, 236–238
Milton, John: *Apology against a Pamphlet*, 12, 162, 165, 169; *Areopagitica*, 91, 95, 114*n*, 134, 135–36, 141–42, 162, 197; *Art of Logic*, 196*n*; "At a Solemn Musick," 20, 53, 57; "At a Vacation Exercise," 53–55, 56, 201; *Christian Doctrine*, 29, 30, 68, 70, 95*n*, 148–49, 150*n*, 151, 157, 158, 161; *Defensio Secunda*, 142; "De Idea Platonica," 54; *Eikonoklastes*, 164; "Il Penseroso," 20, 43–44, 100, 203; "In Quintum Novembris," 99*n*, 132; "L'Allegro," 43, 182, 203; *Likliest Means to Remove Hirelings*, 137; *Lycidas*, 77, 175; *Mask*, 11–45, 66, 68, 72, 73, 77, 87, 90, 91, 92–94, 109, 115, 124, 126–29, 154, 160, 175, 182, 188, 190, 192, 204, 209, 214, 215, 225, 233, 236, 239–43; *Of Education*, 36, 49, 53; *Of Reformation*, 96–97, 140–41, 102, 137, 201; "On *Shakespear* 1630," 29; "On the Morning of Christ's Nativity," 25–26*n*; "On Time," 55; *Paradise Regained*, 24, 109–110, 143, 188, 201; "The Passion," 169; Prolusion IV, 120; Prolusion VII, 77; *Reason of Church-Government*, 5, 21, 53, 56, 57, 63–64, 69, 74, 129, 143, 164, 225, 240; Sonnet XIX, 75–76; "Upon the Circumcision," 176
—*Paradise Lost*, 6–7, 29, 32, 42, 53, 56; divine council in, 145–77; gardening in, 184–88, 206–8, 210; invocations of, 74–79, 127, 161, 170*n*, 235–36; last books of, 221–45; narrator in, 94–96, 97, 111, 123; opening books of, 83, 87, 89–90, 122, 197, 203; psychology of the Fall in, 181–220; regeneration in, 221–45; Romantic interpretation of, 102–3, 108; Book I, 77–79, 83–84, 90–107, 109–16, 119, 122–25, 129, 132, 133, 137, 235–36, 244; Book II, 105–9, 113, 116–17, 121, 127, 131, 136,

144, 183, 218; Book III, 74–79, 91, 117, 126–77, 204, 216, 219–20, 226–30, 235–36, 240, 243; Book IV, 99, 126, 144–45, 160, 184–89, 192, 195, 197–202, 209, 213, 214–15, 218; Book V, 100, 106, 135, 160, 185, 189–91, 194–96, 197–202, 204–8, 213, 230, 247; Book VI, 109, 232, 236–37; Book VII, 161, 213; Book VIII, 65–70, 106, 119, 138, 186, 188, 196, 213, 215, 217–18, 239, 242; Book IX, 123, 160, 170*n*, 181–85, 189, 202, 208–20; Book X, 136–37, 224, 226–30; Book XI, 90, 103, 112, 160, 169, 224, 225, 229, 236–44; Book XII, 108, 152, 158, 160, 172, 222, 224, 230, 231, 236, 238, 244–45
Montaigne, Michel de, 23*n*
More, Alexander, 142
More, Henry, 62, 70
Moses, 96, 116–17, 129, 139, 152, 156, 158, 240
Mulciber, 109–13

Narcissus, 35, 186
Neoplatonism, 27–28*n*
Nohrnberg, James, 78*n*

Opinion, 197, 200, 197–202, 204
Orpheus, 57, 128–29
Orphic song, 40–41, 128–29
Orwell, George, 176
Ovid: *Metamorphoses*, 12, 33, 38, 43, 77, 98, 118, 120, 187*n*, 207, 231, 241

Pandemonium, 103–7, 110–11, 119, 133, 134, 200
Panofsky, Erwin, 49
Paradise of Fools, 132–35, 202
Pareus, David, 234
Parish, John E., 221
Patrides, C. A., 187, 189
Perkins, William, 29, 69, 72, 73, 106, 227
Peter, St., 171–72, 223
Phantastes, 4, 104–5, 107
Phantastike. See Imagination; Poetry
Pico della Mirandola, Gianfrancesco, 69*n*, 233, 234
Pico della Mirandola, Giovanni, 141
Pindar, 64

Plato: *Phaedrus*, 54–56, 102, 140–41, 200–202, 243; *Republic*, 55–56; *Sophist*, 16, 49, 50; *Timaeus*, 31–32, 60–61

Platonism, 20, 30–33, 48, 49–52, 54–57, 60–61, 68, 69–70

Pliny the Elder, 84, 141*n*

Poetry: as breath of God, 225; as diffusion of grace, 35; and faith, 45, 79; and gospel, 79, 235; and mercy, 165–66; Milton's "suspicion" of, 5*n*; as prayer, 205; and prophecy, 48–49, 62–63, 225; superior to prose discourse, 95, 165. *See also* Imagination

—*eikastike*: and admiration, 168, 232; distinguished from *phantastike*, 46–47; opening books of *PL* as, 122, 127

—*phantastike*: opening books of *PL* as, 83–121, 122, 127. *See also* Amazement Primaudaye, Pierre de la, 12*n*

Prophecy, 4, 32; and Adam's dreams, 65–69; degrees of, 58–59; *filia vocis*, 58–59, 123–24, 215; hagiographical grade, 58, 63–64; and imagination, 57–64; psychology of, 57–64, 234; Scripture as, 58. *See also* Dream(s); Holy Spirit; Poetry

Pseudo-Dionysius the Areopagite, 148

Psychology, Aristotelian; 14, 14–15*n*, 52–53, 84–85, 186–87, 188–89, 209–10, 229*n*; and prophecy, 57–64

Puck, 15, 23, 39, 84, 85, 86, 87, 167, 182–83, 185, 191, 192, 205, 238

Puttenham, George, 27–28

Pygmalion, 241

Quilligan, Maureen, 8*n*, 92*n*, 118*n*, 235*n*

Qvarnstrom, Gunnar, 143–44*n*

Radzinowicz, Mary Ann, 4*n*

Raphael, 6–7, 42, 53, 56, 65, 68, 143, 168, 200, 201, 204, 206, 213, 215, 218, 232, 236–37

Reading: active, 95; Classics typologically, 109, 112; errant, 90–103; and the Fall, 211; literal, 101–3, 138; 199; Nature, 65–66; Scripture, 73–74, 78–79, 95, 138, 230; visualization vs.

analysis, 17–19, 101–3, 122, 125–26, 214

Reason: dependence on images, 53; discursive, 55–56, 186; and imagination, 14–19, and *passim*; intuitive, 55–56; and judgment, 14–15; limits of, 65–66, 71, 76–79, 162, 199, 205, 210, 227; and music, 20, 25–26, 77; and Scripture, 57, 95–96; as self-knowledge, 213*n*; subverted by desire through imagination, 16, 106–7, 190–91, 192–94; and vanity, 65; and virtue, 134, 203. *See also* Conscience; Imagination

Redcross, 39, 92–94, 101–2, 103, 157, 163, 190–91, 194*n*, 197, 211, 221–22, 230, 233, 236, 240, 243*n*

Revard, Stella Purce, 217*n*

Reynolds, Edward, 72–73, 117, 145

Reynolds, Henry, 35, 124

Rhetoric. *See* Language; Magic; Wit

Romance, 23, 146, 162–77, 226–27, 232–33, 238; and divine epic, 164–65, 167; and Scripture, 164, 169, 170, 221–22. *See also* Faith

Royal Society, 151

Rue, 239–40

Sabrina, 41–43, 128, 240–43

Samuel, Irene, 54, 133–34*n*

Sandys, George, 33*n*, 42–43, 77, 96, 98, 112, 118, 129, 168*n*, 231*n*, 241

Satan: as Aeneas, 114–15, 117, 122, 130; as Christ, 117; curse on, 224, 226–33; descent of soul, 131–45; as dragon, 91, 97–98, 144–45; fantasies of, dissolved by biblical allusion, 124–128; as King of Tyre, 143; language of, 113, 114, 194–202; literal-mindedness of, 101–3, 140–45, 199–200, 223; as magician, 96; mind of, identified with Hell, 97–101; as Moses, 96, 116–17; narcissism of, 187; as parody of Raphael, 206; "predicament" of, 110*n*; second entry of, into Paradise, 209–10; shield of, 112–13, *see also* Galileo; and Sin, 117–21; and the Son, 199; transumes classical epic, 113–15; transumes Scripture, 115–17, 124; as Typhon, 98, 114, 197

Scholasticism: Bacon's view of, 120–21, 133

Scylla, 118, 120

Shakespeare, William: association with imagination in Milton's mind, 3–8, 15–16, 43–45; and Comus's language, 13–19; imagination of, as type of icastic, 5, 145, 248; Milton's "renunciation" of, 3–8; and use of Bible, 28–29, 232;

—*Hamlet*, 17–18, 227; and subversion of tragedy, 242

—*A Midsummer Night's Dream*: and Eve's dream, 191–94, 204–8, 209; and exorcism of illusion, 85, 133; and fancy-sick transformation, 99–100; love-language in, 191–94, 209, 212; as secular analogy or type of process of faith, 167, 202–8, 238, 248; and ungoverned imagination, 15–16, 20, 22, 23, 66, 135, 182; warning allusion to, 83–90, 122, 191

—*Othello*, 115, 185; rhetoric in, magical, 191, 194

—*The Tempest*, 16; and exorcism of illusion, 22–25, 85, 122, 128, 129, 153–54, 203; imagination in, distinguished from icastic, 30–31, 43–45, 47–49; as secular analogy or type of process of faith, 20–27, 28–31, 70, 167, 232, 238, 242, 248; and ungoverned imagination, 34, 39–40, 97, 118, 131, 182, 183, 202

—*The Winter's Tale*: as secular analogy or type of process of faith, 167, 170, 232, 241, 248

—Other Works: *Comedy of Errors*, 207; I *Henry IV*, 169–70; *Henry V*, 6–7, 145–46; *King Lear*, 155; *Love's Labour's Lost*, 105n; *Macbeth*, 17–18; *Merchant of Venice*, 166; *Richard II*, 122–23, 184n; *Romeo and Juliet*, 15, 17, 34–35; *Venus and Adonis*, 18

Shelley, Percy Bysshe, 108

Sibbes, Richard, 28, 73n, 74, 199, 207n

Sidney, Sir Philip, 46–50, 56, 68–69, 79, 165, 225

Sin, 23–24, 117–21, 133, 157, 183, 187, 218

Smith, John: *Of Prophecy*, 57–64, 66, 215; *Divine Knowledge*, 60n, 61, 181

Smith, R. W., 110n, 136n

Spenser, Edmund, 4, 7, 62n; *Epithalamion*, 183; *The Faerie Queene*: and Eve's dream, 190–91, 197; and regeneration, 221–22, 230, 232, 233–36, 240, 241, 243–45; and ungoverned imagination, 86, 92–94, 120, 211; warning allusion to, 103–6, 122; other references, 95, 98, 118, 132, 141, 157, 163, 206

Stein, Arnold, 151n

Sun, 137–38, 140–45, 243

Swaim, Kathleen M., 226n

Swan, John, 23, 182

Tasso, Torquato, 23, 49–52, 64

Taylor, Thomas, 231, 240

Temperance, 40, 240

Tragedy, 227, 234; subversion of, 242

Transumption, 100–101, 246–48; Satan's, of classical epic, 113–15; Satan's, of Scripture, 115–17, 124

Trinity, 158, 159; demonic parody of, 118

Tubalcain, 112, 118

Tuve, Rosemond, 11, 53n, 93

Typology, 97–98, 246–48; and Classics, 109–10, 112, 113. *See also* Allusion; God the Son

Ulysses, 43

Uriel, 126–27, 141, 142, 243n

Urim and Thummim, 142–43

Vanity, 65, 111, 132–36

Vaughan, Henry: "The Law and the Gospel," 79, 235; "Mount of Olives" I, 235–36; "Regeneration," 222–25, 231, 233; "Upon the Priorie Grove," 207n; *The World Contemned*, 70

Vehemence, 40–41n, 217

Vine-prop Elm, 206–8, 211, 230

Virgil: *Aeneid*, 24, 108, 113, 114–15, 130, 146–47, 173, 175, 195n, 206

Visual arts, 136–37, 139–40

Vulcan. *See* Mulciber

Waddington, Raymond B., 221, 243
Waldock, A. J. A., 128
Warton, Thomas, 3–4
Welsted, Leonard, 102
Whaler, James, 104n
Willey, Basil, 59–60, 89

Will-of-the-wisp, 23, 37, 181–83
Wisdom, 110, 152–54, 161
Wit, 13–14, 120
Wittreich, Joseph Anthony, Jr., 4, 62n
Wordsworth, William, 43–44n

COMPOSED BY G&S TYPESETTERS, AUSTIN, TEXAS
MANUFACTURED BY EDWARDS BROTHERS, INC., ANN ARBOR, MICHIGAN
TEXT AND DISPLAY LINES ARE SET IN TRUMP

Library of Congress Cataloging-in-Publication Data
Stevens, Paul, 1946–
Imagination and the presence of Shakespeare in
Paradise lost.
Bibliography: pp. 251–261.
Includes index.
1. Milton, John, 1608–1674. Paradise lost.
2. Milton, John, 1608–1674—Sources. 3. Shakespeare,
William, 1564–1616—Influence. I. Title.
PR3562.S75   1985   821'.4   85-40378
ISBN 0-299-10420-6